W9-COS-427

FLORIDA STATE
UNIVERSITY LIBRARIES

JUN 1 8 2001

TALLAHASSEE, FLORIDA

SPAIN AND THE RECONSTRUCTION OF WESTERN EUROPE, 1945–57

ST ANTONY'S SERIES
General Editors: Alex Pravda (1993–97), Eugene Rogan (1997–), both
Fellows of St Antony's College, Oxford

Recent titles include:

Mark Brzezinski
THE STRUGGLE FOR CONSTITUTIONALISM IN POLAND

Peter Carey (editor)
BURMA

Stephanie Po-yin Chung
CHINESE BUSINESS GROUPS IN HONG KONG AND POLITICAL
CHANGE IN SOUTH CHINA, 1900–25

Ralf Dahrendorf
AFTER 1989

Alex Danchev
ON SPECIALNESS

Roland Dannreuther
THE SOVIET UNION AND THE PLO

Noreena Hertz
RUSSIAN BUSINESS RELATIONSHIPS IN THE WAKE OF REFORM

Iftikhar H. Malik
STATE AND CIVIL SOCIETY IN PAKISTAN

Steven McGuire
AIRBUS INDUSTRIE

Yossi Shain and Aharon Klieman (editors)
DEMOCRACY

William J. Tompson
KHRUSHCHEV

Marguerite Wells
JAPANESE HUMOUR

St Antony's Series
Series Standing Order ISBN 0–333–71109–2
(outside North America only)

You can receive future titles in this series as they are published by placing a standing order.
Please contact your bookseller or, in case of difficulty, write to us at the address below with
your name and address, the title of the series and the ISBN quoted above.

Customer Services Department, Macmillan Distribution Ltd
Houndmills, Basingstoke, Hampshire RG21 6XS, England

Spain and the Reconstruction of Western Europe, 1945–57

Challenge and Response

Fernando Guirao
Jean Monnet Professor of History
Universitat Pompeu Fabra
Barcelona
Spain

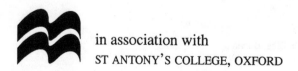

in association with
ST ANTONY'S COLLEGE, OXFORD

HF
1570.5
.E85
G85
1998

First published in Great Britain 1998 by
MACMILLAN PRESS LTD
Houndmills, Basingstoke, Hampshire RG21 6XS and London
Companies and representatives throughout the world

A catalogue record for this book is available from the British Library.

ISBN 0–333–71078–9

First published in the United States of America 1998 by
ST. MARTIN'S PRESS, INC.,
Scholarly and Reference Division,
175 Fifth Avenue, New York, N.Y. 10010

ISBN 0–312–21291–7

Library of Congress Cataloging-in-Publication Data
Guirao, Fernando, 1962–
Spain and the reconstruction of Western Europe, 1945–57 :
challenge and response / Fernando Guirao.
p. cm. — (St. Antony's series)
Includes bibliographical references and index.
ISBN 0–312–21291–7
1. Spain—Foreign economic relations—Europe, Western. 2. Europe,
Western—Foreign economic relations—Spain. 3. Spain—Politics and
government—1939–1975. I. Title. II. Series.
HF1570.5.E85D85 1998
337.4604—dc21   97–32313
                                                   CIP

© Fernando Guirao Piñeyro 1998

All rights reserved. No reproduction, copy or transmission of this publication may be made
without written permission.

No paragraph of this publication may be reproduced, copied or transmitted save with
written permission or in accordance with the provisions of the Copyright, Designs and
Patents Act 1988, or under the terms of any licence permitting limited copying issued by
the Copyright Licensing Agency, 90 Tottenham Court Road, London W1P 9HE.

Any person who does any unauthorised act in relation to this publication may be liable to
criminal prosecution and civil claims for damages.

The author has asserted his right to be identified as the author of this work in accordance
with the Copyright, Designs and Patents Act 1988.

This book is printed on paper suitable for recycling and made from fully managed and
sustained forest sources.

10   9   8   7   6   5   4   3   2   1
07 06 05 04 03 02 01 00 99 98

Printed and bound in Great Britain by
Antony Rowe Ltd, Chippenham, Wiltshire

Stupefatto del mondo mi giunse un'età
che tiravo dei pugni nell'aria e piangevo da solo.
Ascoltare i discorsi di uomini e donne
non sapendo rispondere, è poca allegria.
Ma anche questa è passata: non sono piú solo
e, se non so rispondere, so farne a meno.
Ho trovato compagni trovando me stesso.

Cesare Pavese, Antenati

To A., a bit too late and to P., right on time.

Contents

List of Tables and Figures

Figures

In referring to combination of years, the use of an oblique stroke – 1945/46 – signifies a 12-month period (say, from 1 July 1945 to 30 June 1946). The use of hyphen – 1945–46 – signifies the full period of calendar years covered (say, from 1 January 1945 to 31 December 1946). (..) means not available while (–) means none, negligible or entry not applicable.

For the sake of simplicity, the expression *Spanish monetary area* means the area formed by metropolitan Spain, the Balearic and Canary Islands, Ceuta, and Melilla, although it actually included Spanish Morocco, the territory of Ifni, Rio de Oro and Spanish Guinea also.

Acknowledgements

The best part of doing this book was to run into some of the people I am about to mention. This book needed four years of intense research and one more for writing a first draft in the form of a doctoral dissertation. Three more years elapsed before the manuscript found the right publisher and one more to make the deal. Many are the debts of gratitude I have accumulated during the course of these years.

In the intellectual field, the members of the research group 'The History of European Integration', which was active at the European University Institute of Florence (EUI) between September 1987 and December 1991, deserve the highest praise. They constituted the best group of colleagues I could ever have dreamed of for the launching of this project. In many I continue to find generous encouragement. Albert Carreras, Juan Pablo Fusi, Richard T. Griffiths, Jacob J. Kaplan, Lawrence S. Kaplan, Carles Sudrià, Jesús María Valdaliso, and Manuel Varela made useful comments on various sections of the manuscript. I thank Macmillan referees for helpful suggestions. On numerous occasions, the advice and criticism that I received from Juan J. Linz, Alan S. Milward, and William N. Parker were little short of indispensable. In addition, their example of scholarship is responsible for my not having stepped out of academic business when things turned futureless. Stanley G. Payne and Fernando Rodrigo tried unsuccessfully to get this manuscript published much earlier. Anne Deighton and Charles Powell brought the manuscript to the attention of the general editor of St Antony's Series, Alex Pravda. Joan Ramon Rosés, EUI Publications Officer Brigitte Schwab and David Thomas assisted me in overcoming specific difficulties at the very end of the whole process. To all I express my gratitude, whilst keeping for myself the responsibility for all remaining errors.

The hospitality of the EUI, the Center on West European Studies at Yale University (New Haven), the Department of Economics of Universitat Pompeu Fabra (Barcelona), the Department of Economic History of the London School of Economics and Political Science, and St Antony's College (Oxford) made possible discussing, drafting, and revising the multiple drafts of the present manuscript. To all the institutions mentioned I remain grateful.

Generous financial support is decisive for any book needing intensive transnational archival consultations. Initial support came from Spain's «Ministerio de Asuntos Exteriores» in the form of a two-year doctoral grant at the EUI. The latter's Presidency financed another full year, for which I am grateful to the late M Emile Nöel. The first research steps in British, French, Italian, and Spanish archives were partly financed through the EUI student travel grants and the Erasmus Program of the European Community. The «Ministerio de Educación y Ciencia» and the Fulbright Commission financed a two-year post-doctoral stay at Yale University. As a Fulbrighter I carried on research at the US National Archives and the H.S. Truman Library, Independence (Missouri). The latter helped generously to defray part of the costs. Some visits to the Public Record Office were funded by the Research Commission of the Generalitat de Catalunya (CIRIT grant BE94/Annex 3–232). Again, the «Ministerio de Educación» covered the financial needs involved in the final stage (DGICYT grant PB94–1101). I hope this book does not disappoint these institutions' generous advisers.

I would like to thank those who at the different archives visited found the time and energy for extensive conversations about important documentary aspects. María Luisa Auñón, Dennis Bilger, Rosario Calleja, Maria Isabel Fevereiro, Ken Heger, Ignacio Ruiz Alcaín, Elizabeth Safly, Elisa Carolina de Santos, and Teresa Tortella all deserve special mention. I am aware that some of them were more disappointed than myself for the little or nil results of my research in their respective documentary collections. Notwithstanding this, I acknowledge their always useful suggestions.

Finally, I would like to ask for the forgiveness of my family and friends for having to put up with the drastic consequences of my intense work during the last decade or so. I cannot promise that I will not do it again!

Fernando Guirao, Oxford, 21 May 1997

List of Abbreviations and Acronyms

CEEC	Committee for European Economic Cooperation
ECE	Economic Commission for Europe of the United Nations
EPU	European Payments Union
ERP	European Recovery Program
Eximbank	Export-Import Bank
IEME	Instituto Español de Moneda Extranjera
INI	Instituto Nacional de Industria
NATO	North Atlantic Treaty Organization
OEEC	Organization for European Economic Cooperation
PPS	Policy Planning Staff
RENFE	Red Nacional de Ferrocarriles
UN	United Nations
UNRRA	United Nations Relief and Rehabilitation Administration
US	United States

Key to Archival References

AD	Archives Diplomatiques, Ministère des Relations Extérieures, Paris
DE-CE	Direction Economique/Coopération européenne
Z/E	Series 'Europe 1944–1949, Espagne'
Z/EE	Series 'Europe 1949–1955, Espagne'
AGA	Archivo General de la Administración Civil del Estado, Alcalá de Henares
A	Ministerio de Agricultura
C	Ministerio de Comercio
AHBE	Archivo Histórico del Banco de España, Madrid
IEME	Instituto Español de Moneda Extranjera
C/A	Minutes of the IEME Consejo de Administración
C/P	Minutes of the IEME Comité Permanente
AN	Archives Nationales, Paris
AJ	Commissariat général du Plan de Modernisation
F/10	Ministère de l'Agriculture
APG	Archivo de la Presidencia del Gobierno, Ministerio de Presidencia, Madrid
JE	Jefatura del Estado
ASMAE	Archivio Storico Diplomatico, Ministero degli Affari Esteri, Rome
Amb. b.	Ambasciata, busta
HSTL	The Harry S. Truman Presidential Library, Independence, Missouri. All HSTL records refer to the Truman Papers unless otherwise stated.
IF	Intelligence File, Reports-ORE (Office of Research and Estimates)
NAF	Naval Aide Files
NSC	National Security Council
PSF	President's Secretary's Files
MAE	Archivo Histórico del Ministerio de Asuntos Exteriores, Madrid.
Leg.	Legajo (file)
exp.	expediente (dossier)
carp.	carpeta (folder)

MNE	Arquivo Histórico-Diplomático, Ministério dos Negócios Estrangeiros, Lisbon
SE	Secretaria de Estado
RNP	Repartição dos Negócios Politicos
NARA	National Archives and Records Administration, Washington
RG 59	Record Group 59, General Records of the Department of State
PRO	Public Record Office, Kew (London)
BOT	Board of Trade
CAB	Cabinet Papers
FO	Foreign Office

FOREIGN RELATIONS OF THE UNITED STATES (FRUS)

Documents are referred to by the abbreviation of the archive or document collection, followed by the reference number of the file, author, title and date. Some documents appeared classified without date (n/d) and/or signature (n/s). Probable dates and authors are given where possible. Whenever a document can be found in different archives, one of which being MAE, the reference provided will always be that corresponding to the latter. When a document can be found in a printed source, particularly *FRUS*, the latter will prevail over an archival reference.

British *Parliamentary Debates, House of Commons* will be referred to as HC DEB preceded by a volume number and followed by the corresponding page.

Introduction

Challenge and Response presents the Spanish administration's reactions to the various forms in which economic cooperation took place in Western Europe during the early years following World War II. Despite the fact that, until the late 1950s, Spain was excluded from the most important initiatives for intra-European and Atlantic cooperation as a consequence of the origins and non-democratic nature of the Franco regime, the Spanish authorities were well aware of the negative consequences which resulted from increased isolation. Departing from the simplest concept of interdependence, the hypothesis underlying this book is that the movement toward closer economic cooperation by Western European states imposed costs on the Spanish economy and obliged the Spanish administration, within its limited capacity as an outsider, to articulate a policy response.[1] It is the task of this work to investigate not only the Spanish authorities' assessment of those developments which had a vital bearing on the future shape of Europe but how the most peripheral country of all responded to the challenge.

Following from here, this book aims to shed new light on the fundamental question of how the Franco regime was able to survive in the politically hostile climate which prevailed after 1945. In addition, this book aims to stimulate further discussion on the external factors responsible for Spain's pattern of economic growth after 1945. The reader should know that this book is neither a history of the Franco regime, nor of the Spanish economy, nor of Spain's commercial and foreign relations during the period under scrutiny.[2] Notwithstanding this, I hope that a fresh approach to the European dimension of Spain's foreign political and economic relations in the late 1940s and during the 1950s helps scholars of various fields.

The scholarship dealing with Spain's foreign relations after 1945 concentrates on five principal areas of inquiry:

1. The Spanish question at the United Nations, where the Franco regime was placed under permanent international scrutiny.
2. Efforts to forge relations with the Arab and Latin American countries in order to break out of diplomatic isolation and give Spanish foreign policy a global dimension.
3. Relations with Portugal, which materialized in the form of the Iberian Pact, the real importance of which is still open to discussion.

4. The Concordat with the Vatican, signed in August 1953, which gave the Franco regime an important ideological boost domestically.
5. Bilateral military–economic agreements with the United States, signed in September 1953, portrayed as a significant material and propaganda coup for the regime.

It is possible to accept that Spain's foreign policy was mainly focused on these areas, but only if one also accepts that political policy can be completely divorced from economic reality.

It is a central thesis of this work that foreign policy could, and did, diverge from the public pronouncements of the Franco regime. The actual policy adopted could not, and did not, ignore the simple fact of Spain's heavy reliance on European markets for its economic survival (Table 1). Spain's foreign policy did, therefore, have a strong European dimension. As will be shown, postwar institutional reorganization in Western Europe was at the forefront of the economic and political concerns of the Spanish administration.

TABLE 1   SPAIN'S TRADE WITH MAIN COMMERCIAL PARTNERS,
1935–57 (in percentages)

Year	1935	1947	1948	1949	1950	1951	1952	1953	1954	1955	1956	1957
Imports by Countries of Production in Percentages of Total Imports (TI)												
TI	876	1214	1483	1399	1195	1307	1753	1838	1882	1399	2347	2639
OEEC	46.8	19.8	27.6	32.7	33.1	40.9	46.3	52.5	51.1	69.5	44.7	38.6
Argentina	2.5	21.3	26.8	13.4	2.7	2.5	1.2	1.5	0.6	0.2	0.3	0.2
USA	16.8	8.8	7.0	9.0	13.2	16.0	16.6	5.8	18.4	25.1	26.2	26.1
Exports by Countries of Last Consignment in Percentages of Total Exports (TE)												
TE	570	664	822	886	947	152	1402	1479	1422	1366	1353	1456
OEEC	65.4	51.1	58.8	64.8	51.1	54.5	57.3	55.5	52.5	58.6	55.2	58.1
Argentina	5.6	6.9	3.6	3.0	3.9	0.7	0.3	0.1	0.4	0.2	0.5	0.6
USA	9.5	8.2	9.4	5.7	15.3	13.3	10.6	10.7	10.4	10.5	13.8	9.8

Source: United Nations, *Yearbook(s) of International Trade Statistics*, each year has been listed from the yearbook which incorporated the last updating. Data for 1945 and 1946 is not available. Values in millions of gold pesetas. It includes gold and excludes trade with Canary Islands, Ceuta, Melilla, Spanish Morocco and Guinea.

At this juncture, it should be emphasized that I use the term *administration* in a far broader sense than the strict Spanish legal interpretation of government as being synonymous with the Council of Ministers. For the purposes of this work, I use the term to refer to the body of persons which was responsible for managing foreign policy. All domestic actors shaping foreign economic options are allowed to play their role: top civil servants as well as Cabinet members. Here, attention will be focused primarily on personnel in the foreign affairs and commerce departments.

In the research leading to this book, there was little evidence of Franco's personal role in shaping political and economic guidelines, despite the immense power he wielded over the country. *Generalissimo* Francisco Franco Bahamonde, victor of the Civil War, was Head of State, his own Prime Minister until 1973, Commander-in-Chief of the Armed Forces, and leader of the Falange Party. Between 1936 and 1939, full powers were conferred on him; they remained in force for the rest of his life. He ruled the nation, answerable for his actions to no one but the Almighty.[3] Yet previous studies have been of very little help in elucidating how this power was translated into the daily bread and butter of foreign economic policy-making before 1957.[4]

All we know is that Franco had a special interest in foreign policy, which he oversaw personally until he was sure that the Allies would not intervene to remove him from power. After 1946, he was aware that the main threat to his personal rule did not come from abroad and that international ostracism, if skilfully managed by an efficient propaganda apparatus, actually served to strengthen rather than weaken his regime. Franco's godlike reign over the field of foreign relations declined as his regime's political survival ceased to depend upon actions taken beyond the Pyrenees or across the Atlantic. Even when political isolation was at its zenith, General Franco never delved into the technical detail of foreign economic policy.

Ministers and top civil servants dealing with foreign economic relations thus had a wide discretion in managing affairs. Some of them have attributed a more active role to Franco but often this was more by way of paying tribute to his leadership or else of disclaiming responsibility.[5] The Council of Ministers, meeting once a week, constituted a weak point of reference for day-to-day policy. Franco relied heavily on his ministers to define and implement executive measures, knowing that the important decisions would be made in consultation with him.

The period covered by the present work may be seen as one of economic transition. In the first decade after 1945, the remnants of autarkic philosophy were progressively jettisoned by the organs of state dealing with foreign economic policy in favor of the new philosophy of development. Economic nationalism had been based upon the idea that Spain could stand alone, but the later drive for industrialization effectively increased rather than diminished Spain's reliance on trade. Spanish industry was unable to substitute domestic production for imports and could not do without certain commodities which, at times, paralysed economic activity. In turn, exports provided

Spain the sole earnings of foreign exchange to pay for the necessary imports of foodstuffs, raw materials and capital goods. Foreign trade turned out to be strategic from all points of view: economically, because without imports of a very limited range of products the economy could not function; politically, because scarcity of some basic imports could have accentuated discontent and turmoil; and militarily, because without economic development and political stability there could be no coherent defense policy. The waning star of autarky and the inescapable fact that Western Europe constituted Spain's most dynamic trading area (Table 1) combined to place European economic cooperation events at the forefront of Spanish economic thinking.

After the brief interregnum (1946 to 1949) which saw massive imports from Latin America, the United States, United Kingdom, France and Germany were once again the main suppliers of Spanish imports, accounting for half of total imports. As for Spain's exports from 1947 to 1957, no less than half were directed toward European markets. With no other means to finance imports than exports, exports to Western Europe provided financial fuel to prevent a collapse of the domestic economy.

Franco's propagandists argued that the trade disruptions imposed by World War II and the alleged international boycott in place until 1953 were largely responsible for the slow economic recovery after the Civil War.[6] Spanish historiography after 1975 gives a different version, arguing that the ostracism Spain suffered after 1945 was not as pronounced as had been claimed and that trade relations offered an avenue of escape.[7] Neither version, however, manages to explain with sufficient clarity how, when and why things happened as they did. This work attempts a rigorous examination of the subject along the following lines.

The first section, Trade versus political discrimination, examines Spain's role in early postwar reconstruction efforts. Chapter 1 concentrates on the gap between economic interests and political declarations. It is the story of how fascist oranges became just oranges. Chapters 2 and 3 show the external aspects of discrimination, particularly as adopted by France, the United Kingdom and the United States. Here, the objective will be to determine the extent to which economic performance was affected by the detrimental effects of political ostracism. It was a trying time for Spain, when the attitude of other European countries was that they would buy from Spain and sell to Spain but they would not eat, drink or pray with representatives of the Franco regime.

The second section, *Rara Avis*: Spain and the Marshall Plan, deals with Spain's exclusion from the European Recovery Program (ERP). The Marshall Plan, as the program was more popularly known, was an extraordinary success in political, economic and cultural terms, and continues to enjoy a contemporary resonance. Marshall Plan-type plans have of late been variously suggested to foster economic growth and political stability in post-Communist Eastern Europe, to solve Third World debt problems and to stimulate worldwide employment. The Marshall Plan is considered almost unanimously as the most effective foreign aid program ever carried out. The experience of the only country in Europe not invited to join should therefore be of interest to scholars.

Marshall aid was viewed by the Spanish authorities as an opportunity to overcome the structural deficit of reserves produced by a weak export sector and to end the international isolation of the Franco regime. Once Spain had been excluded from the ERP and Washington had rejected all the alternatives presented by Madrid, the Spanish government responded by offering the United States the use of military bases in exchange for economic assistance on the one hand and by stressing its trade dependence on European countries and the beneficial aspects of bilateral trade on the other.

The significance of the dollar aid in providing major relief to the Spanish economy – and thus to the Franco regime – during the early 1950s has been greatly over-stated. The flow of dollars toward Spain did not amount to any gold rush; perhaps it would be more appropriate to talk of a trickle. Indeed, it was not until 1955 that foreign capital reached a level sufficient to reverse Spain's negative trade balance. Before that year, it was, rather, exports which earned the foreign currency to finance, firstly, the capital goods and raw materials needed for the industrialization effort, and, secondly, the imported foodstuffs necessary to feed an expanding population. Spanish exports to Western Europe were the single major source of foreign currency earnings, whereas imports from Western Europe were an important means for economic development at the time.

The third section of this work, Bilateralism within a Multilateral Context, deals with the mechanisms that impeded the collapse of bilateral trade in a world moving decisively toward multilateralism. Initially, the Organization for European Economic Cooperation (OEEC) was exclusively concerned with distributing aid under the aegis of the Marshall Plan. After 1949, however, OEEC member states themselves embarked on an ambitious program of intra-European trade liberalization which radically changed relations not only between OEEC members but also between themselves and the rest of the world. Prior to the setting up of the European Payments Union (EPU) in 1950, trade expansion with any given country was dependent upon the actual level of exports to it. The multilateral clearing mechanism, the *de facto* convertibility on current account of European currencies and the automatic credits provided for by the EPU removed that constraint for intra-West European trade. Spain, however, continued to be held back by the lack of convertibility of its national currency. Trading partners refused to accept pesetas as payment for exports and provided only limited credits with which to finance temporary trade imbalances. Spain struggled within the strictures of bilateralism due to its exclusion from the two Marshall Plan-based organizations which constituted the most important and effective frameworks of economic cooperation in the second postwar period.

The international settlement of the second postwar period reinforced the political and social consensus reached in many countries of Western Europe with the twofold objective of rising productivity policies with a view to reaping the maximum benefit from the new international order designed at Bretton Woods and of rescuing the Nation-State from general scepticism over its role as a form of organizing social and political life after the war.[8] The awkward position of Franco's Spain during what was the most successful period of economic cooperation in the history of western capitalism constituted the most obvious obstacle to Spanish growth.

Part I
Trade versus Political Discrimination, 1945–7

1 Spain's Contribution to West European Economic Relief and [Early Phase of] Reconstruction

Relief and reconstruction needs during the period immediately after World War II caused West European powers to lay aside their distaste for the Franco regime. The Spanish administration's wide room for manoeuvre in trade relations contrasted with its poor international political position during the first two years after the war. The political discrimination and ostracism that Spain suffered immediately after May 1945 due to the origins and nature of its political regime, were not accompanied by an equal rebuff in economic relations. This was mostly due to the contribution the Spanish economy made to the relief and reconstruction of West European economies in the period of demobilization and abrupt conversion from war to peace-time production. Relief relates to the supply of goods in the form of alternatives to the decline in European production. Reconstruction, however, is neither limited to repairing war dislocations and damage nor to the restoration of capital equipment but implies transforming the European economies through structural economic rationalization and modernization. This chapter will refer to the early phase of reconstruction which took place as a result of separate, often conflicting, national policies. From the summer of 1945 to the spring of 1947 relief and, most especially, reconstruction efforts were so vast that any contribution to ease its path was welcome, despite ideological considerations as to the political regime ruling over countries of supply. This is the sense of the formula *trade versus political discrimination* that introduces the first part of this book.[1]

This chapter will attempt to determine Spain's role in the first efforts for European economic reconstruction. Addressing the so-called *Spanish question*, that is, the political ostracism of the Franco regime, without looking into Spain's role in Western Europe's reconstruction seems senseless. Attempting to understand Spain's attitude toward European multilateral cooperation without being conscious of the lessons learned from the rebuilding of normal trade patterns after the end of World War II seems complete nonsense. Trade experience with Europe's most important economic powers during the months immediately after the war accustomed the administration to a way of dealing with international economic relations which implied little discrimination against Spain. The set of assumptions derived from Spain's effective contribution to Europe's early relief, however, proves inadequate in the subsequent period because attempts to formalize closer cooperation modified the overall pattern of European economic relations.

When in May 1945 the Third Reich capitulated, the Franco regime was not in an easy situation. Spain could certainly expect strong international retaliation after the war due to the origins and nature of its political regime. The Yalta declaration, February 1945, appeared to make any reconciliation with Spain while under Franco virtually impossible. The San Francisco Conference, which took place from April to June that year, adopted a resolution according to which the United Nations Charter could not apply to states whose regimes were established with military assistance from the countries that fought against the United Nations as long as such regimes were in power. In short, the Franco regime was among the problems to be solved in the new postwar international order and Spain's political position in the international arena after 1945 could be labelled as that of a pariah.

The only possible initiative left to Spain was in the domestic arena. The government had no other option, when the three big powers discussed its future at Potsdam, than to adopt some accommodation to the new international circumstances imposed by the victors. The Cortes approved a type of rights charter, the «Fuero de los Españoles» and the «Ley de Bases para el Régimen Local» regulating county elections.[2] On 21 July a new Cabinet was formed where the Falange Party lost some of its traditional ministerial posts. The appointment of Alberto Martín Artajo as Minister of Foreign Affairs was intended to benefit the regime. Artajo's international connections as eminent representative of Catholic organizations and his previous non-political commitment were designed to ease a rapprochement with the Allies. Artajo's task was to end Spain's international political isolation; thus, he was called the *Chancellor of Resistance*.

The internal *democratization* of the regime failed to convince international public opinion. At Potsdam, the Soviet government recommended that the United Nations break off relations with the government of Franco and support the efforts to establish a democratic regime.[3] Prime Minister Winston Churchill resisted the attempts to interfere in Spain's internal affairs, which could not only risk valuable bilateral trade but also create an unpleasant precedent to be followed by the Soviets elsewhere. Finally, the three-Power Berlin Conference agreed not to support the candidacy of Franco Spain to the United Nations.[4] The high echelons of the Franco regime were aware that the exclusion of Spain from the United Nations was agreed upon before

Churchill left Potsdam and that no alteration of the terms of the declaration was made by the new British Labour Prime Minister, Clement R. Attlee, or his Foreign Secretary, Ernest Bevin. They also knew that none of the big powers favored a military intervention to expel Franco or any other measure that might lead to civil strife.[5]

Indeed, Western Europe was in a very delicate position regarding Spain; in particular France and the United Kingdom. Opposition to the Franco regime received sanctuary in both countries and looked to them for ideological guidance and material assistance in the overthrow of Franco as a corollary to the world war. In both countries there existed a hard and vigorous core of Franco-haters, many of whom had fought with the International Brigades in the Spanish Civil War. In both, there was a strong political party ready to cause difficulties if their respective governments decided not to follow a strict policy against Franco. In France, the Communist Party was the most organized political force and in Britain the Labour Party was strongly committed not only to its previous position during the Spanish Civil War when it had bitterly criticized the Conservative policy of non-intervention, but also to the Potsdam Resolution. France and the United Kingdom had endorsed all Allied resolutions on Spain.

The political nature of governments in Western Europe after the first postwar round of free elections was inauspicious for the Franco regime. In Belgium, the Socialist Party formed various coalitions with the Liberals and Communists from 1945 until 1947, when it entered a two-year coalition with the Christian Socials. In the Netherlands, the Labor Party was in power in coalition with the Catholic People's Party. Although in Denmark, after the elections of October 1945, Social Democrats were displaced by a coalition of liberals and radicals, with a shift to the right, Social Democrats and Communists formed a strong opposition. In Sweden and Norway, majority Labor governments were in power and stayed in power until September 1948 and November 1951 respectively. Given this situation, no political compromise with the Franco regime appeared ever to be possible and Spain was to be excluded from all new institutions of a European, as well as world, scope created for the new postwar international order. Public opinion would not easily forget that Franco received assistance from Hitler and Mussolini during the Spanish Civil War. Moreover, the nature of the «Nuevo Estado» and its close association with the aggressor states during the war provided further arguments for isolation. The General Assembly of the United Nations itself, at its opening session in February 1946, confirmed the exclusion of Spain from the new international political order.

Notwithstanding this, most West European countries rapidly resumed trade with Spain. From 1945 Spain negotiated trade and payment agreements with a number of countries, mostly European, which later were to be involved in the Marshall Plan.[6] Portugal had an agreement with Spain after February 1943, revised every six months by a joint committee, to provide timber and colonial produce in exchange of potash, iron, steel and lead. Denmark after August 1941, had annually renewed its commercial arrangement with Spain, and Spanish–Swiss trade was greatly developed during the war. Switzerland, already in June 1943, July 1944 and then in May 1945, exchanged notes relating to the transfer of financial credits and insurance payments, as well as to the exchange of Swiss machinery, electrical equipment and chemicals, in return for a wide variety of products. In July 1945 the exchange of notes was transformed into a bilateral agreement on financial and merchandise traffic regimes, renewed in September 1946 and in December 1947. In December 1945 Italy signed a trade and payments agreement, renewed in August 1947, to export vehicles, chemicals and many types of machinery, and to receive in exchange iron ore, rosin, turpentine, lead, anchovies, tunny and cork. The Netherlands and Sweden exchanged notes with Spain establishing a commercial and payments *modus vivendi* in January 1946. The Netherlands enlarged theirs in April and transformed it into a trade and payments agreement in October which established the most favorable trading clause. The exchange consisted in Spanish agricultural products, iron ore, woollen and rayon goods, and potash for much-needed Dutch petroleum products, seed potatoes, electrical goods, diesel engines and breeding stock, in addition to rubber, copper and tin from the Dutch East Indies. It was renewed in December 1947 and complemented in March 1948. Sweden, although the Social Democrats were in power, renewed its commercial and payments *modus vivendi* with Spain in October 1946 and July 1947. Sweden was to export timber and wood pulp, special steels, marine diesel engines, roller bearings and electrical equipment, and to receive in exchange oranges, potash, cork, grapes and cotton textiles. In practice bilateral trade was conducted on a compensation basis. A proper trade agreement between both countries was signed in July 1948. In February 1946, Spain signed a trade and payments agreement with the Belgium–Luxembourg Economic Union but it was never ratified, perhaps because of the coming to power of a Socialist Prime Minister in Belgium. Nevertheless, the agreement was largely implemented from the beginning of 1947. It provided for an exchange of Belgian sulphate of ammonia, copper sulphate, iron and steel products and a wide variety of machinery against oranges, potash and pyrites. Ireland also signed a trade and payments agreement with Spain in 1946 and renewed it in September 1947, providing primarily for the exchange of seed potatoes for potash. Norway, with an absolute majority Labor government in power after November 1945, signed commercial agreements with compensation. So did

Turkey. Even with the Allied Control Council in Germany an exchange of notes took place in October 1946, renewed in May 1947. When the Federal government took office in September 1949 a formal bilateral trade and payments agreement was finally signed with Spain. Finally, although both the United Kingdom and France were considered by official Spanish propaganda as the leaders of the international political ostracism of Spain, they also competed for a fair share of Spain's products. France signed a very beneficial trade agreement with Spain in September 1945 and, once a short period of diplomatic rupture was over, rushed to obtain a new trading agreement to recover lost trade, signed in May 1948. As for the United Kingdom–Spain relations, the clearing of March 1940 and its secret protocol of November 1940 (signed in April 1941) were still in force after the war, and bilateral trade with or without formal agreements was eagerly promoted. All West European governments, then, tried their best to avoid political questions complicating their economic relations with Spain.

The economic position of the West European countries varied widely. Some had to undertake extensive repairs of war-damaged production capacities, while others emerged from the war with their resources of real capital virtually intact. Most of them, however, faced certain common problems. All governments aimed at quick relief for their populations, and in the shortest possible time the restoration of capital equipment and prewar standards of living through domestic production, trade, interest-free loans or grants. The modernization of economic structures appeared necessary to take full advantage of the new economic international order envisaged at Bretton Woods in July 1944 and eventually embodied in the International Monetary Fund and the International Bank for Reconstruction and Development. This implied a long-term adjustment problem requiring all available resources.

The restoration of a healthy peacetime economy involved heavy imports. Quick relief implied imports of foodstuffs and consumer goods, adding to the import pressures of economic reconstruction. When an immediate increase in exports or gains from invisible earnings was impossible, large import programs were designed for fuel and raw materials, industrial materials like timber, iron and steel, and manufactured goods such as chemicals, machinery and replacement parts necessary for the effective utilization of existing production resources, vehicles and ships. Some of the countries suffering little or no physical damage during the war, with production near or above prewar levels, revealed a ratio of exports to production in 1946/47 only about two-thirds or less of the 1938 relationship, whereas their imports were near or sometimes well above prewar levels in both absolute and relative terms. In most cases, large balance-of-payments deficits were to finance recovery and modernization.

Any significant program of imports imposed a burden on the balance of payments toward the dollar area, which contained the only large surpluses available for world trade. The decline of intra-European trade (Eastern flow toward Western Europe and among West European countries) in foodstuffs and raw materials aggravated dependence on overseas supplies, grains and coal in particular. To reduce the huge deficit in their overseas balances, Europeans had to increase their exports and constrict their imports, especially with the United States. They thus aimed at raising domestic capacity to export while developing those industries that provided substitutes for overseas imports. In manufactured goods, the emphasis rested on heavy industries (iron and steel, chemicals and engineering industries), whose products came almost entirely from the United States. To increase industrial production, Europe raised its imports of raw materials and manufactured goods from overseas above prewar levels. Therefore, agricultural output had to be pushed upwards to save some dollar imports, and in the short term, due to strong deficits in hard currencies, Europe had to force a reduction in food supply from overseas, limiting as much as possible purchases other than grains. It is only under these circumstances that the role to be played by the Spanish economy can be properly understood.

Collaboration with the general effort of European relief and reconstruction was offered by the Minister of Industry and Commerce, Demetrio Carceller Segura, at the beginning of 1945. Spain would supply some important items as well as the financial facilities required to pay for them. It would provide foodstuffs – preserved fish, olive oil, vegetables, citrus fruits and other fruits – for direct relief of the population as well as some basic raw materials, such as pyrites, potash and iron ore, for reconstruction programs; while as exporter of manufactured goods – textiles, footwear and cork – it could not offer any large supply. Spanish assistance was to participate in the United Nations Relief and Rehabilitation Administration (UNRRA), created in November 1943 to supervise short-term relief plans in war-devastated areas once fighting had ceased. In fact, the Spanish government cooperated with Allied arrangements for controlling orderly distribution and procurement of scarce supply items, made shipping available for transport to France of US relief purchases, and showed a willingness to supply liberated areas in negotiations with the Dutch, French, and Belgians. In return, the Spanish administration expected to escape the pressure of blockade, especially concerning the supply of raw materials still controlled by the *navicert system*.[7]

Though weak, Spain's economic potential for postwar economic reconstruction was to be used to establish normal relations with the victorious Allies. For Minister Artajo, economic and trading interests were the 'things that really matter' and which dulled western governments' political sensitivities regarding the nature of the regime.[8] The increasing public dislike of the Franco regime pushed Spanish administrators to use Spain's economic potential to solve political conflicts of a bilateral nature. When only a few Spanish goods were distributed through UNRRA in the first postwar months, due to pricing difficulties and the fear of political repercussions, other means were adopted to channel Spanish goods to Western Europe. There were not many alternatives since much of the continent was in ruins and the traditional pattern of international trade disrupted. Since Spain's participation in Europe's economic reconstruction was considered a technical affair far removed from the political debate, Madrid tried to use commercial diplomacy to bargain for the international acceptance of the Franco regime.

SPAIN'S ROLE AS EXPORTER OF ESSENTIAL FOODSTUFFS

Immediate postwar demand for foodstuff imports, after almost six years of low levels of consumption, was expected to return to prewar levels. The level of liquidity in the countries that had not suffered German occupation was high and long pent-up demands existed from the war years. This, together with the pressure for wage increases that had been blocked during the war, was to result in increased private consumption. Those countries that suffered German occupation were prompt in relaxing the tight control and rationing system installed by the Germans. Consumers in neutral countries had also suffered severely from the Allied blockade. In general, people were less willing to postpone demands and to accept restraints once the war was over and thus the level of consumption could not easily be held down after years of difficulties. An upward trend in agricultural production was programed immediately after the war to feed an increasing and more demanding population and to reduce the import bill of foodstuffs, but a transitional period of several crops, with imports as the only source of supply, was necessary. Although imports were to be kept low by rationing, controls and restrictions to avoid a heavy burden on the balance of payments, it was not desirable to keep imports of essential foodstuffs below wartime levels. This reaction to wartime restrictions was the case throughout Western Europe.

After a few months of direct economic relief, the first element of improvement was diet enrichment with the inclusion, among others, of citrus fruits and nuts. With exports and invisible gains not instantaneously rising to the necessary level, Europeans could not afford a large increase in imports if they were to be paid for in hard currency. In these circumstances the Spanish economy, a traditional foodstuffs exporter, had no foreign constraints on exporting foodstuffs in the immediate postwar period. For the United Kingdom and France, in 1945, foodstuffs amounted to 60 and 57 per cent respectively of total imports from Spain, with preserved fish, fruits and olive oil as the main items. If the population was most concerned, on a daily material basis, about food and if most governments were forced to provide better a livelihood for their people, there were strong reasons not to be deprived of Spanish food supply.

Spain's food supplies to France reduced the pressure of the food shortage, which had become an obsession in France in the months after Liberation. At the end of 1944 a poll revealed that the French population wanted to see the reappearance of bananas, oranges and lemons, as well as other colonial products, such as chocolate, coffee and tea.[9] The French Ministry of Health expressed with insistence the interest in the Spanish supply of citrus fruit and bananas for the feeding of its country's population, especially children and sick people.[10] Current transport difficulties had strongly reduced traditional imports from North Africa into the metropolitan market. The relative importance of the Spanish supply to France can be seen in the following figures: it represented ten per cent of total imports of foodstuffs from continental Europe, provided 76 per cent of foreign supply of olive oil imported from Europe, ranked third in French European imports of preserved fish, and, finally, provided 20 per cent of French imports of fruits from Europe. In France, as in the rest of Western Europe, Spanish foodstuff supplies offered diet variations and enrichment, while preserving hard currency reserves to cope with the bad grain harvest of 1945.

The British Ministry of Food confirmed the importance of Spanish exports for national welfare. The United Kingdom, heavily dependent on food imports, relied on Spain for some of the variations in diet anticipated by the British housewife. Even though Spanish prices were generally high, sweet oranges, bananas and tomatoes were considered essential items and could not be replaced by other sources, as all possible supplies were insufficient to meet the demand. In fact, those West European countries that before the war were large sources of supply showed records of agricultural output in the crop year of 1945/46 appreciably below prewar levels. Oranges alone – both the eatable and the marmalade (bitter) varieties – accounted for 37 per cent of Spain's total exports to the United Kingdom in 1945 and even after the bad orange crop early in 1946, oranges plus bananas and tomatoes represented 38 per cent of British total imports from Spain in 1946. Other large producers of tropical fruits were the American states within the dollar area. Therefore, if the British or anyone else in Western Europe needed tropical fruits, it seemed sensible to obtain all possible non-dollar supplies before importing from the dollar zone.

Failure to import from Spain such items as dried apricots, raisins, nuts and apricot pulp, would give the Ministry of Food considerable concern. Other commodities included in the program of food purchases from Spain had to be sacrificed since they were irreplaceable (notably sherry) or could only be replaced from other sources with varying degrees of difficulty (such as Mediterranean sardines). Though the British did not yet take much canned fish from Spain, they were eager to keep the market open as a bargaining tool to prevent Portugal from establishing a monopoly. To find alternative suppliers to Spanish foodstuffs was probably difficult at the time owing to the dollar situation and the long distances involved in shipments from other countries.[11]

The Spanish economy (and the Franco regime) benefited from world food shortage, the liberation of purchasing power kept low during the war years, strong aspirations to improved standards of living, and worldwide dollar scarcity. The most optimistic agricultural projections for the restoration of prewar levels of output forecast a delay of at least five years from the end of hostilities. Even a full restoration of prewar output still meant a six to eight per cent reduction in output per head compared with 1934–8, owing to the increase in population. It meant that Western Europe had to carry an important burden on its balance of payments with the dollar area. The gap was very difficult to reduce. Overseas imports of foodstuffs consisted partly of products not produced at all in Europe (coffee and tea), of products in which European indigenous production could not be easily expanded (grain), and finally of foodstuffs in which only a minimal contribution could be expected of European production. Opportunities for contraction in imports of these foodstuffs and some industrial materials – such as petroleum, cotton and wool – were extremely limited if a reduction in consumption and production was to be avoided. In these circumstances, Spain's exports constituted a non-dollar supply of foodstuffs, and although highly priced, were presented as dollar-savings and a contribution to solving the balance-of-payments deficits while also being an enrichment of diet. This was the real position of Spain as an exporter of foodstuffs in a world that had declared the Franco regime as the last refuge of fascism.

EXPORTER OF STRATEGIC RAW MATERIALS

Industrial recovery in Western Europe was based on two initially interconnected elements: overcoming the shortage of basic industrial materials and freeing maximum hard currency for the purchase of essentials. The experience of the war and postwar reconstruction heralded a race for resources and a *global struggle* for minerals and fuels.[12] In this scenario, Spain figured as an important source of critical raw materials which constituted its second main export category, amounting to 20 per cent of total exports in 1945–6. A rapid expansion of world industrial production required adequate raw material inputs. In 1946 the rate at which metals and metallic ores were being fed into the production process lagged substantially behind the rate at which finished products were leaving the engineering industries.[13] Apart from being a supplier of foodstuffs to European relief, the Spanish economy also provided raw materials such as pyrites, potash, tungsten, rosin, iron ore and cork.

Pyrites and potash constituted strategic bottlenecks to the recovery of agricultural production. The attempt to reduce overseas food imports paid for in hard currency required the recovery of agricultural production to at least prewar levels. An increase in agricultural production, however, would not be attained as quickly as industrial output. The estimates of the Economic Commission for Europe of the United Nations (ECE) for 23 countries accounting for 90 per cent of the total net value of agricultural production of Europe before the war, showed that in the crop year 1945/46 output was only 63 per cent of the prewar level, while the 1938 level of industrial output was already restored by the last quarter of 1946.[14] In the United Kingdom, agricultural production received special attention in the later stages of war owing to increasing anxiety over the viability of overseas supplies and the ability to finance imports in the transitional period. In France, agricultural machinery and chemical fertilizers were among the basic economic sectors of the *Plan de modernisation et de l'équipement*, the so-called Monnet Plan. An increase in agricultural output was necessary to reduce substantially agricultural imports in order to devote foreign currency resources to long-term economic modernization, thereby increasing the French economy's productivity rates in the open international economy, as promoted in the Bretton Woods Agreements. Thus, food production was an essential element of British and French reconstruction policies, as well as in the rest of Western Europe.

Fertilizer programs were drawn up in most West European countries as an integral part of a strategy to increase agricultural productivity. It was necessitated by labor shortages, the need to divert manpower from agriculture to industry, the cumulative effect of decreased capital investment and use of fertilizers with the consequent impoverishment of the soil and deterioration of agricultural equipment. Loss of livestock, moreover, had reduced the organic materials used to fertilize land, imposing a larger dependency upon inorganic or chemical fertilizers, mainly nitrogen, phosphorus and potassium. In 1945/46 world production of nitrogen was still 69 per cent that of 1938/39, whereas Western Europe only reached 55 per cent.[15] As for phosphorus fertilizers – calcium phosphate from phosphate rock and superphosphate obtained by the treatment of calcium phosphate with sulphuric acid – the situation was critical from 1944 to the end of 1946. French North African production of phosphate was well below prewar levels. The United Kingdom, owing to a shortage of labor and the decline of Belgium's exports, was sending phosphate rock to Spain for processing into superphosphate compound. Supplies arising from this arrangement amounted to about five per cent of British supplies for the season 1945/46. Even with this contribution the British Ministry of Agriculture's target program for superphosphates was about ten per cent short.[16] With the reduced production of nitrogen, to be used as nitrates or ammonium salts, and with limited supplies of phosphorus fertilizers, other chemical compounds, such as potash and pyrites, acquired greater importance in the fertilizer campaign.

Spain constituted the cheapest source of potash and produced approximately five per cent of world potash output in 1944/45.[17] Spain provided approximately two-thirds of total British requirements in 1945/46 and it was maintained at 50 per cent for the following year.[18] No other source of supply appeared possible since French and German production was still far below prewar levels, and the total output from Palestine had already been imported. Dollar considerations overrode the only other source of supply, the United States, which had doubled potash output between 1940 and 1945. Even after securing Spanish supplies the British Ministry of Agriculture's target program for the season envisaged a shortfall of 33 per cent.

Another important component of the fertilizer programs was pyrite, as a source of sulphur in the manufacture of sulphuric acid. Only after the extraction of sulphur were the so-called *spent pyrites* used as low-grade iron ore. Because of the availability of better sources of iron, pyrites were not generally used as an iron ore in the iron and steel industry. Sulphur appeared to be the most important case in which the failure of production to keep pace with consumption had serious consequences. The sulphuric acid extracted from the sulphur had widely varying uses and played some part in the production of nearly all manufactured goods. A major use of sulphuric acid was in the production of fertilizers. In 1944–5 Spain produced roughly 13 per cent of the world's production of pyrites. Discounting extra-European supplies for either financial or transport reasons, Spain represented 40 per cent of the pyrite production of Europe, a vital ingredient in West European fertilizer programs.[19]

With no other sizeable source, the United Kingdom was dependent on Spain for about 90 per cent of its total pyrite supplies for 1945/46. For the year ending 30 June 1947 Spain provided all British imports of pyrites. To obtain current supplies from other European suppliers of pyrites, appeared to require great effort, unnecessary if Spanish supplies were available. An alternative was American sulphur but this would involve a basic alteration of production plants. It was calculated to take six to twelve months to adapt production lines – to be at public expense – so that production of sulphuric acid, sulphate of ammonia and superphosphates would inevitably be curtailed. Apart from that, dollar considerations made it undesirable to buy from American suppliers.

As far as France was concerned, a very limited supply of pyrites could be found in the international market by the end of 1944. France had obtained 100 000 tons from Portugal and Canada when the monthly requirement of the French industry was 40 000 tons.[20] The situation did not change in the following two seasons, resulting in a great shortage in the supply of fertilizer. The planning authorities described the lack of fertilizers as a severe constraint on reaching the planned targets for agricultural output.[21]

The fertilizer bottleneck preventing increased agricultural production was a common feature during the period 1945–7. Before the war, Western Europe accounted for about 50 per cent of the total world consumption of fertilizers, but postwar trade in chemicals and fertilizers was strongly distorted compared with the prewar pattern (1937). In prewar purchasing power, imports from the United States in 1947 were 260 per cent the value reached in 1937, while intra-European trade (excluding the USSR) was only 55 per cent.[22] With world fertilizer supplies substantially below the level needed to meet projected future food programs, Spain was a key supplier at this juncture.

Spain was an important source of other raw materials. The most important ore that Spain exported was iron ore, completely tied to one industry, iron and steel, while the main bottleneck to an expansion of European industry was steel outputs. In this trend, the shortage in scrap and crude steel imposed a larger dependence upon coke and iron ore, the latter being smelted in blast furnaces to produce pig iron. World pig iron, which owing to wartime destruction had plunged by 25 per cent between 1939 and 1945, initiated a long recovery period so that by 1950 it was one-third greater than the 1939 level (with almost half still being produced in the United States). Although Spain produced approximately one per cent of world output of iron ore in 1945, it was the fourth largest European producer, after the United Kingdom, France and Sweden.[23] Even more important was that Spanish iron ore was high grade, that is, of low phosphoric content, which saved on fuel in its processing; this meant less complementary import costs as savings in coal and scrap.

The attempt to enlarge the range of ore suppliers of low phosphoric content was unsuccessful. Considerable difficulties with France over the price of North African ores were frequent at the time. Only a limited quantity of ore of a comparable grade to Spanish Morocco's was obtained from Sweden. Larger amounts had to be made up of Swedish ore of lower grade, demanding more fuel and coal in its metallurgical processing. On currency grounds, this supply constituted an undesirable alternative; since Sweden was unhappy holding sterling and other non-convertible currencies, an increase in purchases of iron ore was believed to entail a cut in the supply of timber and pulp. The only alternative to replacing Spanish ore was an increase in the use of low grade ores that would adversely affect the import bill via an increase in coal requirements.

Spain was also an important producer of mercury, zinc and tin concentrates, and lead and manganese ores, and had exportable surpluses of salt and fluor-spar. It was the world's principal source of mercury, producing 28 per cent of world production in 1944/45; it produced 50 per cent of lead ore, 42 per cent of manganese ore, 28 per cent of Europe's tin concentrates, and 33 per cent of the West European zinc output.[24] Other important items in Spain's foreign trade were rosin and cork. Among the Southern European producers of these raw materials, it was the only one to maintain and even increase its mining activity. In 1946 the Portuguese economy, an important producer to which Western Europe could have diverted its requests if Spain were to be expelled from international markets, suffered the most spectacular drop in output of the group of countries considered.[25] Postwar demand for raw materials, especially non-ferrous minerals, was high for several reasons. First, stocks were low relative to the levels of demand for restoration of war damage and the expansion of industrial activity. Second, basic production was making an extremely slow recovery. In addition to civilian demands, there was also demand for strategic stockpiling purposes. Spain was not to be an exception to gaining access on equal terms to the trade and raw materials of the world called for by the Atlantic Charter of 1941. To the extent that European countries expanded manufacturing production, increased imports of raw or processed non-ferrous metals and chemicals were necessary, especially to support heavy industries. It appeared, therefore, as in the case of foodstuffs, that any net savings in imports was most unlikely and that, conversely, Europe's minimum requirements of imports of raw materials were to expand.

* * *

Since Spain was the only source of supply for some goods and thus saved payments in hard currencies, most West European countries secured their fair share independently of the political circumstances of the debate over the Franco regime. Spain's trading partners took as full advantage as possible of supplies which served both to alleviate overall world scarcity and save dollars. Furthermore, Spain's supplies allowed buyers to increase their bargaining power *vis-à-vis* other European soft currency suppliers in obtaining a larger share of essentials. Spain's contribution to the recovery in production contributed to the capacity of European countries to balance their bilateral trade accounts. For instance, British steel production, to which Spain contributed by providing large quantities of high quality iron ore, permitted Britain to balance with Sweden and Switzerland, whose credit arrangements required gold or dollar settlement. While all over the world economic life had been disrupted by the war, with only the countries in the western hemisphere, especially the dollar area, as large suppliers, any non-dollar supply was to be highly valued. Spain appeared as a scarce but still valid source to be used fully before importing from the dollar area or from countries more awkward on currency grounds. World shortage of foodstuffs and raw materials was the fundamental reason for avoiding economic sanctions or a blockade against Spain, the apparently most logical consequence of the political resentment toward the Franco regime. Spain's potential economic contribution to European recovery was to be channelled, as all other available resources, into productive work in order to achieve fully effective national economies.

2 The Exigencies of French and British Economic Reconstruction

Despite the fact that the Spanish economy was making its contribution to European recovery, there were many problems of a political nature in applying a strict economic or technical approach to the problem of relations with the Franco regime. Indeed, the alternatives to adopting sanctions against Spain were, in an ascending order of severity, the recall of ambassadors and the breaking of diplomatic relations, as demanded by several members of the United Nations, and economic sanctions. The French provisional government of the IV Republic and the British Labour government had to face political reality.

THE FRENCH PROVISIONAL GOVERNMENT OF THE IV REPUBLIC

It is well known that active sectors of French public opinion, across the political spectrum, wanted a rupture of diplomatic relations with Franco Spain. The Foreign Affairs Commission of the Provisional Assembly proposed on different occasions inviting the Allies to ask Franco to resign or, if necessary, to accept the rupture. Despite everything, the government of National Unity-formed in September 1944 and presided over by General Charles de Gaulle-resisted public and parliamentary pressure to sever relations with Spain. The problems posed by the imminent victory over Germany, the restoration of order and authority, the foundations of a new Republic, and economic reconstruction, were such that De Gaulle in complete agreement with Georges Bidault, Minister of Foreign Affairs, was reluctant to create further upheaval. Formal diplomatic relations were broken *de facto*. The Spanish government broke them with the Vichy regime on 24 August 1944 when its ambassador, José Félix de Lequerica, was appointed Minister of Foreign Affairs. Madrid did not appoint a new ambassador although it recognized Jacques Truelle as the official delegate of France. The French provisional government had not appointed an ambassador to Madrid and could perfectly well do without one if unfavourable public opinion continued to persist. On the other hand, the

Presidency and the French Ministry of Foreign Affairs were not ready to do without an ordinary delegate, whose activities were essential to keep the flow of Spanish supply.

Attempts not to worsen the already delicate political situation with the southern neighbor and to reach some trade agreement had been undertaken since the autumn of 1944. Bilateral trade negotiations preceded the official recognition of the provisional government of the French Republic by Madrid, which did not take place until mid-November. This suggests that a commercial agreement with Spain was requested for economic reasons and that, to proceed speedily, a normalization of political relations with Spain was urgent. There were serious incidents in the South of France where the largest concentration of Spanish exilés was placed, some of whom had played an active part in the resistance movement.[1] Following France's liberation in August 1944, Spanish refugees expected the liberation of their homeland. They started by occupying the Spanish diplomatic legations in the Pyrenees with the help of county authorities. The French delegate in Spain strongly supported putting an end to the troubles in the south of France due to 'l'importance des négociations, actuellement engagées... pour l'envoi de vivres et de matières premières en France et le financement de ces opérations'.[2]

While some public pressure favored the cessation of relations, the Spanish government granted a first credit of Pts 200 million in September of 1944. It allowed France to obtain 50 000 tons of blende (sulphide of zinc occurring as natural crystalline mineral) and 20 000 tons of pyrites, apart from other products such as cork, preserved food and citrus fruit, in exchange for North African phosphates and electric energy.[3] The French government was not about to forego this small but effective contribution to the relief of its population and industrial recovery, and which, moreover, brought no pressure to the balance of payments or dollar reserves. Bidault, conscious of France's weak economic situation and of the need to restore order after the period of open political tension following the Liberation, preferred to calm popular pressure in the Pyrenees. The frequent repetition of outbreaks of violence made restablishing trade negotiations even more difficult.[4] Bidault had the President's support. Although Spain was never one of De Gaulle's main concerns, he was aware of the advantages of maintaining relations with Spain: '[L]es moyens économiques de l'Espagne font partie de l'économie du monde. Les pyrites n'ont pas de parti.'[5] The result of this course of action was that by April 1945 the credit offered by the Spanish government increased to Pts 500 million.[6] Although Spanish credits represented only 7.5 per cent of the British credits granted to France in March 1945, the latter required repayment in gold within a year.[7] Spanish credit facilities offered the opportunity to preserve hard currency reserves to purchase raw materials for industrial and agricultural recovery. Therefore, instead of following the recommendations of the parliamentary commissions, the French government accelerated its search for a bilateral trade agreement.

After two months of intense negotiation, a Franco–Spanish trade agreement, the so-called Saint Sebastian Agreement, was signed in mid-September 1945, only four months after the end of the war. The agreement was quite beneficial to the French economy; it guaranteed 400 000 tons of pyrites for the production of superphosphates and sulphuric acid required by agriculture, 50 000 tons of foodstuffs, especially fish and fruit, and finally the supply of textiles to the value of Pts 63 million. The total value of Spanish exports to France was estimated at Pts 552 million while France's exports to Spain were expected to reach Pts 210 million including 200 000 tons of North African phosphates, 70 000 tons of scrap, and three million Kwh electric power per month (after the restoration of the electrical connection between both countries). To cover the trade gap the Spanish negotiators offered a credit of Pts 200 million (to be increased up to 240 million) to be payable in 36 months.[8] This was the result of a foreign policy that followed more closely the needs of peacetime rather than ideological considerations.

The nature of French postwar politics left little room for political ethics. More than in any other case considered in this book, domestic politics became diametrically opposed to foreign policy options. The general elections to the Constituent Assembly of October 1945 put an end to the independent course of action undertaken by Bidault. The Communist Party became the strongest political party with 26 per cent of the electorate vote, claiming a much larger share of power. After the elections, Communists occupied several ministerial posts (Labor and Social Security, Industry and Commerce, Health and Population, Reconstruction and Housing) and demanded one of the three key posts, either Interior, Foreign Affairs or Defense. De Gaulle in November 1945 had refused this, creating a precedent followed by his successors. When, in December 1945, the Foreign Affairs Commission of the Constituent National Assembly repeated the call to break off relations with Spain, the Cabinet opted to adopt a heavy stick policy toward Franco Spain as a political move toward the Communist-dominated Assembly. This concession tried to avoid another confrontation against the Assembly to add to the crisis over the Constitution and the composition of the Cabinet after the elections.

Relations with Franco became a vital question in French foreign policy, even though Spain was relatively unimportant for French politics. Two sets of circumstances might explain this. First, domestic political struggle. The Communists pressed for controversial action in foreign policy so as to embarrass publicly the Mouvement Républicain Populaire. This important coalition partner, as holder of the diplomatic portfolio, was accused of supporting Franco by inaction. Second, France's diminished importance in postwar international politics. The non-Communist French public and parliamentary opinion was convinced that action against Franco would give France the opportunity to take the lead in at least one issue in international politics. In the words of Léon Blum, the Socialist leader who brought about the coalition of the Left in the Popular Front in 1936 and was Premier for little more than a month in 1946–7: 'La question espagnole est une de celles où il appartient légitimement à la France d'orienter la politique internationale, une de celles où, le cas échéant, elle pourrait le plus naturellement manifester son «indépendance».'[9]

Unilateral rupture of relations with Spain appeared expressly cited in the agreement reached in November 1945 for the new government of national unity, which included Communists. De Gaulle felt unwilling to leave the Spanish issue uncontrolled at this sensitive time, governed by an unwillingness to antagonize sectors of government and risk public outbursts over foreign policy already soured over other aspects. He communicated personally to Franco his intention to resist pressure and to maintain diplomatic relations.[10] Spain was not only one question with considerable domestic ramifications but also a factor that intruded upon and further burdened France's already complex agenda of international problems. Hence a solution of the issue, albeit not the most satisfactory, was necessary if the potential for domestic political discontent was not to become permanent.

With no alternative, and lacking any real commitment, the French Minister of Foreign Affairs, on 12 December 1945, called upon the governments of the United States and the United Kingdom for joint action in breaking off relations with the Spanish government to secure the downfall of the Franco regime.[11] Bidault expected that by opposing it the Allies would convince the forces supporting a break with Spain to reconsider their position. As expected, the official British and American replies were negative. As anxious as the French were to see Franco fall from power, the British argued against the proposed joint action in political terms. They expressed their concern that any joint action would not lead to the desired result but to the outbreak of disorder. The bulk of the Spanish people, the army and the important conservative sectors who disliked Franco but traded with the United Kingdom, feared the possibility that the sudden downfall of Franco could lead to another civil war. Resentful of direct foreign intervention in domestic affairs they would tend to reinforce the current situation, leading to a strengthening of Franco's internal position. Following the joint action proposed by the French, the British argued, the three governments would deprive themselves of direct information on what was happening in Spain and the means of exercising a moderating influence on the regime. The State Department was in full agreement with the line of argument set out in the British reply to the French; nothing good could come from a 'premature' rupture of diplomatic relations. Accordingly, the US government would take no action until an informal exchange of views with the British and French governments took place. They certainly had no intention of breaking with Franco and had only agreed to informal consultation without much publicity. The French diplomatic records show that the Anglo-Saxons were preaching to the converted. The Quai d'Orsay and the Presidency of the Republic were aware of the situation described by the Anglo-Saxon Allies. Domestic political circumstances, however, had reduced the room for policy manoeuvre.[12]

The departure of De Gaulle from power on 20 January 1946 left France not only with a solid left-wing influence in the National Assembly but with a majority in Cabinet. In February 1946, Bidault confessed to Bevin that he could do nothing more to restrain those fretful persons who were pushing France to an isolated move which would only strengthen Franco.[13] If western democracies were hesitating over whether to follow strictly the principles for which they had fought the last world war or to forget conflicts and return to more profitable activities, this was not so for some sections of French public and parliamentary opinion. It is certain that the Communist Party was not the only one pressing for the breaking of relations, since antipathy to the Franco regime, considered the last residue of European fascism, was deeply felt by most political parties, but it was the only party strong enough to force the decision upon the Quai d'Orsay.

Bidault had spent the previous 16 weeks trying to placate the anti-Franco campaign and the penultimate week of January declaring to the Constituent Assembly how frustrating a unilateral breaking of relations with Spain was to Allied policy and to French economic recovery. In a new summit with Bevin, Bidault declared further pressure to close the border with Spain.[14] To be fully effective, any action in the direction of breaking relations with Spain would have to be taken jointly by, at least, the British, American and French governments, something he thought highly unlikely. Following unilateral action, France would suffer alone while the rest would benefit from a larger share of whatever the Spanish had to offer. The French population could easily forego Spanish oranges if they wished to but only with difficulty could the French economy forego Spanish raw materials.[15] New calls by the National Assembly on 17 January and 22 February 1946 for unilateral rupture of relations left the Minister of Foreign Affairs without options. Bidault was asked by a majority of ministers to break off diplomatic relations with Spain once the post, telegraph, telecommunications and railways trade unions called for the severance of communications with Spain to hasten the official decision. Even then, it is important to note, Bidault imposed a less drastic measure: the Council of Ministers decided on 26 February 1946 to close down the frontier with Spain from 1 March, but this would not imply a break in diplomatic relations nor affect the Moroccan Empire. The decision would not offer a solution to the Spanish question but it would avoid a crisis in the French government. Public and parliamentary opinion had blocked every other course of action.[16]

THE BRITISH LABOUR GOVERNMENT

In the United Kingdom a different policy toward Spain was followed in which decisive economic factors were not mixed with politics. After the war, the British government was anxious to expand trade relations with Spain. Winston Churchill had stated at Potsdam the arguments that were to be used on many future occasions by his political opponents, the Labour government: the British were not ready to use force but only diplomatic means to speed the departure of Franco; they would do nothing that could risk starting another civil war on Spanish soil; they were against interfering in the internal affairs of any country and they did not want to risk trading losses.[17] With the arrival of the Labour Party to power, the similarities between French and British positions concerning relations with Franco Spain increased.

Labour propaganda during the war agitated for the replacement of Franco. A British Labour government's move in that direction would have represented, presumably, a concrete application of socialist foreign policy. The Chairman of the Labour Party National Executive, Harold Laski, announced that the Labour government was committed to the restoration of democracy in Spain and that it would, if necessary, use economic sanctions to allow a republican coalition to convene free elections.[18] The anti-Franco movement became 'the only subject in foreign affairs on which Left and Right, intellectuals and uneducated trade unionists, rank-and-filers and backbenchers, were able to find themselves in enthusiastic agreement'.[19] The demands ranged from economic blockade, rupture of diplomatic relations and even direct intervention. However, despite the general dislike of Franco felt in both France and the United Kingdom, the Labour government followed a different route to that of its French counterpart, on the basis of a general interdepartmental consensus.

Economic sanctions could take the form of an oil embargo, a traditional weapon in modern economic blockade and warfare. It was frequently suggested that an embargo on oil supply from the United States and British sources in South America would suffice to bring about Franco's downfall.

The Ministry of Fuel and Power denied the effectiveness of oil restrictions given the multiple problems posed in implementation. A policy of enforcing oil sanctions, as with any other economic sanction, would require the reimposition of several wartime controls and procedures such as *navicerts* that would put an appreciable strain on British resources, both in respect of finance and manpower. Britain had ended economic warfare immediately after the German surrender, terminating blacklists and all controls once supply difficulties eased. It was certainly not willing to reimpose these controls for political purposes when their definitive withdrawal was scheduled sometime between May and September 1946.[20]

Previous bans on oil supply to Spain enforced by the United States during the war had not been encouraging. They showed the lack of agreement between Great Britain and the United States on embargo policies and Spain's extraordinary capacity to bring down the rate of consumption. The Spanish government was able to resist for almost five months Allied pressure exerted by denying supplies of petroleum, although stocks on hand at the beginning of such sanctions had been reduced to quantities sufficient to meet consumer needs for less than two months in the case of fuel and for only approximately three months in the case of lubricants. By the time the embargo was lifted, Spain still had sufficient quantities on hand to continue operations at decreased levels for a period of several months. Churchill's disposition to supply oil in 1944 to Spain from Middle Eastern sources despite an American ban to force an end to wolfram exports to Germany made it uncertain whether the Americans would follow the British if they were to apply oil restrictions now. Even assuming the unlikely, that American owned oil companies would be induced to follow British policy, it would probably take about eight months before oil sanctions brought Spain to anything like a standstill. As in the winter of 1943–4, the stocks accumulated provided the Spanish administration time to oppose foreign demands. Stockpiling was possible because, contrary to the US government's intentions of keeping Spanish oil stocks low after the reassumption of oil shipments in April 1944, Britain pressed hard in the opposite direction to get a share of oil trade for British companies. The main reason for opposing an oil embargo was that any unilateral action by British oil companies without the Americans would simply deprive British companies of a market, with probable prejudicial effects both for the future of the companies and for the financing of British purchases in Spain. American business would gain, Spain's oil supply would be little effected and progress toward democracy in the country would be still unclear. Furthermore, it could constitute an awkward precedent if, as the Foreign Office feared, the Americans at some stage wanted the British to join them in sanctions against Argentina.[21]

In addition, it was impossible to control trade across Portugal's frontier, so the Iberian Peninsula had to be treated as a whole. An effective embargo of Spain implied imposing import rationing on Portugal, causing dislocation and confusion for its economy and people; it could also undermine western defense interests in Portugal. This contradicted Britain's cherished goals of not losing the invaluable strategic asset that Portugal constituted for the British Empire while obtaining the maximum commercial advantages. Moreover, the British government was precluded by the wartime Azores agreement from imposing economic sanctions against Portugal. In April/May 1947, the Portuguese government 'stated categorically' that it would not provide assistance to make economic sanctions effective against Spain.[22]

Oil restrictions having been rejected, trade discrimination entered the scene. Yet, any restriction on trade flows with Spain would cause problems for those departments dealing with the supply of foodstuffs and raw materials. The Raw Materials Department of the Ministry of Supply argued that the curtailment or cessation of the supplies of raw materials from Spain would be little short of disastrous. The Ministry of Food thought that it was much easier and safer to stick to Spanish exports of foodstuffs, in spite of political considerations, than desperately to look for other sources of supply. Furthermore, British industry could suffer permanent harm. It was then stated that Spanish supplies were indispensable to meet orders in the iron and steel industries to countries like Switzerland and Sweden.

The financial situation was not any better given Britain's precarious position at the end of the war. This was essentially due to the abrupt termination of Lend–Lease and Mutual Aid after Japan's surrender in August 1945. These financial programs had provided the United Kingdom with essential and less essential supplies during the war.[23] When the Americans proposed to the British the purchase of oranges at $4.5 standard box (all freights included), the British preferred to purchase in sterling at the equivalent of $8 in Spain due to dollar shortages.[24] With extremely limited financial resources and a large external debt, Spain continued to service pre-world war debts. It had been setting aside a proportion of its sterling earnings to meet commercial and financial debts to the United Kingdom already after March 1940, when a clearing agreement was re-established by a trade and payments agreement. These were pre-Civil War debts amounting to about £8 million and a credit of about £4.5 million granted to Spain in 1940. A financial agreement, signed in December 1940, governed those sterling payments not covered by the agreement of March 1940. By the end of the war in Europe, Spain was earmarking ten per cent of the value of exports to the United Kingdom for clearing the arrears of financial debts. British claims still amounted to about £8.5 million. Any break in the continuity of debt transfers would militate against the eventual settlement of these claims. It was certainly not an excessive figure given the conditions that confronted the United Kingdom but the Treasury appreciated Spain's financial efforts at a time of foreign exchange difficulties.

An additional consideration against sanctions was the effect on British control over former German assets in Spain, or *Safehaven*.* It was believed that German capital and scientific personnel had infiltrated into insurance, banking, mining, transport, electrical and optical industries through branches legally established in Spain by complexes such as Krupp, I.G. Farben, AEG, and Telefunken. German investment in Spain was estimated to amount to between $85 and $179 million, whereas it amounted to between $450 and $816 million in Switzerland, $82 million in Sweden and $41 million in Portugal.[25] After a period of dilatory policies, which characterized all neutral countries, the Spanish government was so cooperative with the Joint Trusteeship that the Economic Warfare Department of the British War Office, in early 1946, reported its uncertainty as to whether 'any government which might take the place of the present regime would be equally co-operative'. It was stated that, due to the Spanish government's cooperation, the United Kingdom 'was steadily getting great quantities of German assets in Spain into its hands'.[26] In Austria the Allies ran into considerable problems with the Russians over the definition of German assets. The Swiss were not very happy about letting the Allies inquire into the state of German assets in their country; in fact they remained firm in their refusal to recognize any legal or moral obligation to surrender German assets to the Allies. The Swedish were reluctant not to use German assets for the full recovery of their economy. The special circumstances in which Spain was placed due to its political regime rendered its authorities more cooperative than one would have expected. Spain sought to reverse international political dislike or at least to compensate with a more pragmatic way of dealing with politics and economics. Whatever the reasons, Spanish cooperation would have been lost if a rupture of trade relations had taken place. The French experience was seen as very significant. Closing the border with Spain meant the exclusion of France from the conversations on war reparations between the Spanish government and the three western Allies (a situation that lasted until September 1946).[27]

Moreover, the Treasury argued strongly that Britain could not afford, in its precarious financial position, to deprive itself of the advantages of buying in Spain, which was willing to give credit and to hold sterling. For some goods Spain was the only source of supply and while, in other cases, there might have been alternative sources, it would have involved payment in more difficult currencies. To assess whether the situation was as extreme as British officials put it is difficult to test historically. It is important to stress, however, that this situation was perceived among the British administrative divisions as a threat to the normal development of economic activity. In Cabinet discussions 'there was a general agreement about the importance to our economy of the supplies which we drew from Spain...From the angle of our own economic interests, it was clear that we could ill afford to impose economic sanctions on Spain'.[28] It seemed that, despite the color of its political regime, the Spanish administration was generally cooperative and helpful. After the opinions expressed by the different Cabinet units, there was no option for the Labour government but to avoid further upheaval with Spain, even though Prime Minister Attlee and Foreign Secretary Bevin were known anti-Franco leaders. The British consequently acted by rejecting all the requests presented by both the French after December 1945 and the United States in the spring of 1947.

Instead of cutting off relations with Spain like the French, the British authorities considered devices for developing trade. As early as January 1946, the Treasury and the Board of Trade argued that it was rather more beneficial to negotiate with a view to replacing the 1940 restrictive clearing with Spain with a more liberal type of agreement in accordance with overall British foreign economic policy in Western Europe. Bevin decided that it was 'impolitic' to negotiate since any formal agreement could be presented either in Britain or in Spain 'as giving countenance to the Franco regime'. The material advantages to be derived from affording Spain a more liberal treatment convinced Bevin and it was decided that the Treasury should open informal discussions with the Spaniards, 'making it perfectly clear to them that any publicity which might be twisted for political purposes would inevitably put an end to the discussions'.[29] Bilateral negotiations started with visits to Madrid by Treasury officials and to London by a few Spanish officials who did not occupy any political position. In October 1946 official negotiations began and by the end of February 1947 the essential features of the agreement were decided on, although it could not be signed until certain political problems were overcome.

The payment agreement with Spain was on similar lines to the other agreements concluded by the United Kingdom between October 1944 and May 1946. It provided a more flexible payment mechanism based upon a reciprocal credit margin which permitted as uninterrupted a flow of trade as possible, more in harmony with the exchange obligations undertaken under the Anglo-American Loan Agreement.[30] Both countries agreed to hold up to £2 million (or its equivalent in pesetas) to cover the swing of trade. In addition, although this was never made public, Spain had agreed to hold a further £8 million to cover the expected balance of payments in its favor. In other words, the swing agreed upon allowed the British to obtain credit facilities up to £10 million to finance essential imports of foodstuffs and raw materials.

Once the formal instrument for trade was agreed, the problem was to find the right political occasion to sign it. It was certain that the Spanish government, always eager to signal its return to world affairs, was going to exploit it: despite repeated expressions of hostility, the United Kingdom was prepared to sign a formal agreement with Franco! This could have temporarily given the Spanish government an appearance of increased stability and, on these grounds, political criticism at home and abroad was expected. The Foreign Office decided that, although important, political arguments could not outweigh the practical arguments in favor of making the agreement. It informed the Treasury therefore that in spite of the political disadvantages, the Chancellor of the Exchequer should defend the decision in the House of Commons, Cabinet, or elsewhere. The agreement was presented to Parliament as 'essentially a technical readjustment' with no political implications and a necessity to secure trade with Spain.[31] It would henceforth become the position of other countries, too, to present the potentially controversial confrontation between politics and economics when dealing with Spain as mere technical adjustment. Bilateral agreements were merely the starting point.

Although the British government did not consider the Franco regime as the most appropriate government for Spain, they concluded that there was no alternative administration able to guarantee the supply and the protection of their economic interests. This has important connotations for historical research. First and most importantly, it proves how the commercial and financial behavior of the Spanish government during the first postwar months had a positive effect not only on Britain but on the rest of Western Europe also. Second, the British position reveals the modest impact Spanish opponents to Franco had on western policy-making. Public support of opposition forces served as testimony of goodwill toward democratic Spain but it was not allowed to disturb economic and commercial interests. The Allies disliked the Franco regime but valued highly its stability and supplies. They neither considered supporting the active guerrilla movement nor substituting for the Franco regime democratic institutions from the Republican era, least of all promoting a constitutional Monarchy. Temporary continuance of Franco in power, which posed no threat to any vital British interest, was a far lesser evil than the perceived threat of violence and anarchy which might follow in the wake of his downfall. A few months after the Nazi capitulation, economics had imposed their logic of prudence upon politics.

British policy toward Spain was not isolated from the general paradox of the Labour government's failure to implement a specific Labour approach to foreign affairs. Bevin had taken care to maintain contact with his Conservative predecessor, Anthony Eden, in order to show that Britain had one national foreign policy. In its Spanish policy, the Labour Party followed the same attitude as the War Cabinet. Bevin's first appearance as Foreign Secretary in the House of Commons outlined his policy toward Spain. He refused to embark on a policy of intervention, continuing the Conservative line. It was for the Spanish people, and them alone, to decide whether they would make any change in government. Foreign intervention would have the opposite effect to that desired and would probably strengthen Franco. On the same day, Attlee demanded that Laski, the Labour Party Chairman, 'refrain from issuing further pronouncements on what the government would or would not do in foreign policy'.[32] It was a matter of principle that British foreign policy should be determined not by ideological sympathies or socialist solidarity, but by the national interest.

*   *   *

Including Spain in broader frameworks than those traditionally offered by accounts of bilateral diplomatic relations provide a clearer vision of its international difficulties. Problems of political principle with Spain were not going to be allowed to deflect from efforts aimed at solving the main issues. Demands for economic reconstruction would in practice modify the ideological substance that had committed the French government of National Unity and the British Labour Party to certain principles. Many were the controversial issues on which sections of official, parliamentary, press and public opinion diverged and caused dissatisfaction within cabinets. French and British diplomacy had more important matters to deal with and, as a matter of principle, it was believed that political disturbance should not interfere with a realistic economic policy based on an expansion of trade. This principle applied equally to French and British foreign economic policies. As we shall see in Chapter 3, France reopened its southern border as soon as it was possible to do so and quickly agreed trade deals to recover lost ground in the economic sphere. In effect, the courses of action adopted by the provisional government of the IV Republic and the Labour government were not so different, although the British did manage to overcome pressure from domestic as well as international quarters during 1945 and 1946 to impose economic sanctions on Spain. This was the immediate result of a pragmatic and non-doctrinaire approach to foreign affairs; a stalwart defense of national interests in general.

3 Trade versus Politics: An Instructive Debate

Apart from the French decision to close its southern border, economic sanctions were not deployed against Spain. The idea that political discrimination comprised economic discrimination is however commonplace.[1] Two cases of possible economic discrimination should be analyzed with attention: trade restrictions following the resolution against Franco's regime adopted by the General Assembly of the United Nations (UN) in December 1946; and Spain's exclusion from the financial relief programs carried out by the US government at the end of hostilities in Europe. In both cases, the UN and the US government always showed clear political hostility toward the Franco regime.

THE ECONOMIC EFFECTS OF THE *SPANISH QUESTION* AT THE UNITED NATIONS

At its first meeting of January 1946 the General Assembly endorsed the Potsdam and San Francisco declarations which excluded Spain from the UN agencies and recommended member states to act in accordance with the letter and spirit of these declarations in their future relations with Spain. Henceforth, it was the UN Assembly which dealt with the question of what measures should be adopted in order to secure a change in Spain's political structures, the so-called *Spanish question*. France was the first and only power to take real action against Franco after unsuccessful attempts to enlist the support of Great Britain and the United States. The decision to close the border with Spain was accompanied by the decision to elevate the question of Franco's regime to the Security Council. The reaction of the Anglo-Saxon powers was lukewarm; they preferred the question to stay out of the Security Council where the Soviet Union could interfere.[2] Some argue that the French move reflected Bidault's desire to come closer to the Soviets to obtain their support on the French claims over the Ruhr.[3] In my view, it was no more than a last-ditch attempt to force the Allies into sharing equally the commercial burdens of anti-Franco action. The fact is that the Anglo-Saxon powers hurried to agree upon a common declaration with the French government on 2 March 1946. The tripartite statement of the American, British and French governments advocated the peaceful replacement of Franco by a provisional government that would restore a system of freedoms, although it provided no clear commitment to taking any concrete action against Franco Spain.

After April 1946 the matter was debated within the Security Council until November when it was transferred to the Assembly. In April Oscar Lange, the Polish delegate, described Franco's regime as a threat to world peace. The concentration of troops along the border following its closure by the French, Nazi holdings amounting to between $100 to $200 million, the large German population living in Spain and German scientists working on the production of atomic bombs constituted the charges. The Polish delegate was certainly right concerning the existence of a large Nazi community and a significant accumulation of German assets in Spain, but the Spanish record of cooperation with the Allies in the removal of Germans and the turning over of assets was no worse than that of others. There was no evidence that atomic research was being carried on with or without the assistance of German scientists, despite the existence of uranium deposits in Spain. Although its efficiency was increased by the arrival of a few battalions from Morocco, the Army of the Pyrenees was reduced rather than increased after the closure of the French–Spanish border in an attempt to avoid any action which could then be taken as a provocation. The Spanish army was unable to threaten anyone but the Spaniards themselves due to the inadequacies in its training, equipment, supply, and maintenance. Economically, Spain was incapable of waging an offensive war with any major power: not only did it not produce any up-to-date war material, but it also had to import all crude petroleum. Most of the allegations that Spain was a danger to international peace and security was shown by British and American intelligence services to be very doubtful.[4]

Rejecting the hypothesis of Spain being a 'threat to peace and security' was not just a question of semantics. It was an essential measure to avoid the adoption of drastic action. Art. 41 of the UN Charter authorizes the Security Council to decide measures – short of armed force – to give effect to its decisions and to call upon UN members to apply such measures. These may include complete or partial interruption of economic relations and of all means of communication, and the severance of diplomatic relations. Should these actions be inadequate to maintain international security, the Security Council is authorized by virtue of Art. 42 to adopt measures such as 'blockade, and other operations by air, sea or land forces'. The impossibility of proving that the Spanish regime constituted a danger to world peace was the best argument it had against the adoption of any retaliatory measures.

An opportunity for reaching an agreement regarding economic sanctions against Spain came, after an entire year of fruitless discussions, on 12 December 1946 with the approval of General Assembly resolution 39(I). It condemned the Franco regime as a creation of the Axis powers, called for the withdrawal of ambassadors from Madrid and barred Spain from membership of the United Nations and its specialized agencies as long as the Franco regime remained in power. This resolution was a compromise between the views of those states which urged the removal of Franco regardless of the consequences, and those which felt that there was no case for punitive action by the United Nations. The resolution was still only a verbal attitude, avoiding the imposition of economic sanctions. Application of economic sanctions, it was feared by many, would lead inevitably to political and economic chaos and the resumption of civil strife on a wide scale. Given the unwillingness of a majority to follow the path of economic sanctions, the General Assembly, in turn, emerged with the idea that if, within a reasonable period, the desired democratic change had not come about, the Security Council would have to adopt appropriate measures. All this was very ambiguous.

The political effect of the December resolution could be measured as follows. Thirty UN member states were unaffected by the resolution, simply because they held no diplomatic relations with Spain. Sixteen more had no ambassador or minister accredited in Madrid. The few ambassadors withdrawn were replaced by chargés d'affaires guarding national interests as before. None of the 19 embassies accredited to Madrid were closed. 'The withdrawal of heads of mission', it has been affirmed, 'was symbolic rather than practical in effect.'[5] The very fact that Franco Spain was able to sign trade agreements with all West European countries indicates that the 'anti-Franco ardor' of many of them 'was to be gauged more on the verbiage extended in the United Nations than in the actual conduct of their foreign relations'.[6] All the UN resolutions against Franco amounted to was a mild diplomatic blockade devoid of any economic sanctions.

The UN resolution of December 1946 was broadly similar in scope to the French unilateral action of closing the border with Spain. Both can be qualified as choosing the lesser evil, avoiding the rupture of diplomatic relations. December 1946 might have been the lowest point of formal international recognition for the Spanish regime but the debates in New York confirmed the Spanish authorities' belief that the international community was unwilling to attempt a replacement of the Franco regime or, at the very least, that it was unwilling to implement a *de facto* economic blockade. Political discrimination as a real and direct threat to the Franco regime's survival was then completely overridden, had it not been so much earlier. The immediate short-term effect was favorable to Franco in that the ranks of Civil War victors closed and their hold on the country strengthened. It was, therefore, clearly unfavorable to those working for political change.

That the first retaliatory measures were adopted once Spain had recovered its network of bilateral trade agreements, played in favor of reducing their

impact, contrary to what is still argued.[7] Spain had continued to trade with
France's main competitors after the closing of their common border. Trade
agreements had been signed with the United Kingdom, Switzerland, the
Netherlands and Belgium, and most other European countries had some form
of trade arrangement with Spain in place before March 1946. Spain showed
little difficulty in disposing of its export surpluses, which in fact increased
from 1946 to 1947 (Table 3.1).

**TABLE 3.1   SPAIN'S EXPORT TRADE BY PRINCIPAL COUNTRIES OF
LAST CONSIGNMENT, 1945–7 (fob in millions of gold pesetas)**

	1945	%	1946	%	1947	%
Total Trade	682.9	100	596.0	100	664	100
OEEC countries	413.5	60.5	320.8	53.8	385.1	58
USA	177.6	26	159.7	26.8	77.2	11.5
Rest of the World	91.8	13.5	115.5	19.4	201.7	30.5

Source: 1945 and 1946, *Estadística de Comercio Exterior de España* (Peninsula and
Balearic Islands); 1947, UN, *Yearbook of International Trade Statistics 1950*, p. 140.

The significant fall in exports to the United States was not due to any sort
of discrimination but more likely to the lack of competitiveness in the most
competitive market in the world. In a way, while exports to the rest of the
world partly compensated for the decrease to the United States, the overall
trade increase corresponds almost completely to the increase in exports to the
OEEC countries, which maintained the largest percentage of Spain's exports.
The vacuum left by France was immediately taken up by the rest of Europe.
As soon as France partially recovered the 1935 volume in 1948 and Germany
started to reappear as a consumer market, all West European countries, except Sweden, Norway and the United Kingdom, received less from Spain in
percentage terms of overall exports.

As in exports, Spain's import performance with Western Europe did not
run parallel to the intensity of political dislike against the Franco regime
(Table 3.2). While Spain's overall imports increased 32.6 per cent from 1945
to 1947, the percentage corresponding to the OEEC area was 40.5 per cent. If
Denmark, Norway and Turkey decreased their exports from 1946 to 1947, it
was linked to factors other than discrimination. The demand for foodstuffs
from Turkey (97 per cent of total Turkish exports to Spain in 1946), especially barley and rye, was diverted to Argentina. The latter offered a credit line
while Turkey wanted payments in hard currencies. Trade relations with Norway and Denmark were strongly affected by the scarce exchange stock of

both countries' currencies. Other future members of the OEEC overtook France immediately as Spain's suppliers. On the contrary, imports from the United States decreased 32 per cent. One could argue that this poor performance might be due to the fact that for Spain, as for the rest of the members of the so-called *E Group* (Rumania, Hungary, Bulgaria, Argentina, and a number of possessions and minor colonial areas), all exports were controlled by individual licences issued by the US Department of Commerce after January 1946. Responsibility cannot be attributed to administrative obstacles but to Spain's decreasing capacity to earn enough dollars with which to pay for imports from the United States, in other words, a dollar shortage symptom. This was the main European economic problem at the time: balance-of-payments deficits *vis-à-vis* the United States due to an excess demand for capital goods necessary for a speedy recovery of prewar production levels and the modernization of industrial structures in order to obtain the full benefits of the new international non-discriminatory Bretton Woods system.

TABLE 3.2   **SPAIN'S IMPORTS BY PRINCIPAL OEEC COUNTRIES AND THE UNITED STATES, 1945–7 (cif in gold pesetas)**

Year	1945	1946	1947
Total Trade	743 665 118	773 109 036	986 068 563
Germany	17 235 935	1 617 645	2 064 450
Belgium/Lux.	1 438 895	2 837 240	32 057 049
Denmark	2 497 120	9 582 448	6 555 360
France	12 325 520	4 522 872	987 670
United Kingdom	36 175 754	77 630 334	76 992 110
Netherlands	514 521	4 912 309	27 931 599
Italy	3 036 636	8 806 107	17 870 719
Norway	1 689 454	18 921 370	7 058 559
Portugal	14 294 731	10 932 941	9 265 414
Sweden	18 652 561	24 984 995	25 292 274
Switzerland	62 825 807	52 522 341	29 156 547
Turkey	–	12 882 802	4 649 416
Total OEEC	170 686 934	230 153 404	239 881 167
USA	157 549 412	162 194 961	107 381 800

Source: See Table 3.1.

Trading with Spain was no deviation from the UN obligations. Neither the Assembly resolution of December 1946 nor any other act by the United Nations precluded bilateral arrangements between its individual members and Spain. In fact, most of the countries listed in Table 3.2 showed constant increases in export trade to Spain during the first three postwar years. Germany has disappeared for obvious reasons and France has stepped out as a supplier. The increase in Spanish imports from Switzerland and Sweden in 1945 was due to their special position as neutrals. This increase was most marked in the case of Switzerland, which during the war bought from Spain substantial quantities of fruits and wines, unobtainable elsewhere, and exported in exchange machinery and chemicals. With the resumption of world trade, however, Switzerland turned to cheaper sources of supply. The important decrease in 1947, rather than being due to effective discrimination, was primarily due to the fact that the clearing agreement ceased operations early in that year because of Spanish debts.[8] If one supports the assumption that the decrease in export trade to Spain from 1946 to 1947 was a consequence of the logical extension of political dislike to the economic field, one should also note that other European countries were happy to supply the gap. The total export decrease accounted for by some West European countries toward Spain in 1947 as compared to 1946 equals the increase experienced by the Benelux countries. Apart from Switzerland and France, the only country that went through a constant reduction of its export trade to Spain from 1945 to 1947 was Portugal. It is ironic that this country has been traditionally considered in Spanish historiography as an axis of Franco's foreign policy.

The economic implications of political ostracism did not concern exclusively the question of access to Spanish supplies, whatever the importance of these was. It also involved the problem of filling the Spanish market as a supplier of manufactured goods once German competition had disappeared after the war. Supplies from Spain were mostly relief goods that could soon be replaced by alternative sources, even non-dollar sources, as soon as reconstruction progressed. On the contrary, the substitution of German supplies had long-term consequences; the British and French were decided on profiting from it as much as possible.

Immediately after Liberation, the French delegate in Spain wondered whether there was any other market in Europe or outside Europe offering French industry similar possibilities.[9] In the United Kingdom, from the end of 1944 to the spring of 1947, it was debated whether Spain was a market offering large and long-term prospects for United Kingdom goods.[10] It is unclear what the British thought as to the real benefits to be obtained from the disappearance of the Germans. The trade situation in 1929, the maximum expansion of Spain's import trade in the pre-Civil War decade and only reattained after 1960, provides some clues (Table 3.3). Manufactured goods accounted then for a little more than 48 per cent of Spain's overall imports and four countries alone accounted for 71 per cent of total Spanish imports of these commodities. The disappearance of Germany as a supplier of capital goods and dollar shortages led to a situation from which both the United Kingdom and France hoped to benefit at the expense of the other.

TABLE 3.3   SPAIN'S IMPORTS IN 1929
(imports cif in millions of gold pesetas and in percentages)

Total Imports	2737	100
by Groups of Commodities		
– Foodstuffs	554	20.2
– Manufactured Goods	1323	48.3
– Raw Materials	847	31.0
– Live Animals	13	0.5
Total Imports of Manufactured		
Goods by Countries	1323	100
– United States	249	18.8
– Germany	248	18.7
– France	233	17.6
– United Kingdom	208	15.7
Total	938	70.9

Source: *Estadística General de Comercio Exterior de España* (Peninsula and Balearic Islands).

Spain was one pawn in the general strategy to capture traditional German markets after the war. In applying effective discrimination against Spain, France was to suffer alone. The French Ministry of Foreign Affairs was of a clear-cut position:

> Ce n'est pas au moment où les Américains et les Britanniques, sans se préoccuper de l'attitude passée du Gouvernement du Général Franco, deploient tous leurs efforts pour s'ouvrir en Espagne des débouchés nouveaux et certains approvisionnements, que nous pouvons songer à rompre nos relations consulaires avec l'Espagne qui d'après notre Conseiller Commercial à Madrid, est disposée à expédier vers la France des matières premières nécessaires à la reprise de notre industrie.
>
> Le Départment a toujours été d'avis qu'il n'y avait aucune raison de nous priver des conséquences heureuses résultant de nos relations d'échange avec l'Espagne et de laisser le champ libre à nos concurrents notament la Grande-Bretagne et les Etats-Unis.
>
> La France doit prendre en Espagne une grande part de la place laissée vacante par la défaite de l'Allemagne.[11]

Representatives of French business interests in Spain opposed the political decision to close the border. France had traditionally important economic interests in Spanish companies (automobiles, chemicals, petroleum, phosphates, potash, insurance, banking, iron ore, zinc, and pyrites) and aspired to take part in hydro-electrical projects and the announced modernization of the railroad system. These financial and economic interests could no longer be effectively defended. In terms of capital, French investment, about Ff 10 000 million, represented 50 per cent of total foreign investment in Spain or 60 per cent of France's total foreign investments by the date of the closing the border.[12] A negative economic effect was expected from the diplomatic move and confirmed shortly after the closure:

[L]e bilan d'une initiative qui, du seul point de vue de l'économie française, de notre effort de relèvement et de la reprise de notre expansion, peut être qualifiée de désastreuse... la nature de nos exportations à destination de l'Espagne est telle que la vie économique de la nation voisine ne dépend aucunement de leur maintien ou de leur arrêt. En l'ocurrence, nous sommes les seuls victimes. De même que les seuls bénéficiares seront nos concurrents qui sauront profiter de nos erreurs.

Au moment où la France doit reconstituer son économie et assurer son ravitaillement, faire l'effort pour obtenir à l'étranger matières premières et produits alimentaires... le manque de relations économiques cause à nos affaires un dommage incalculable et permet aux autres nations étrangères de prendre une position prépondérante sur le marché espagnol au détriment du commerce et de l'industrie française.[13]

France was to deprive itself of a primary source of scarce raw materials and foodstuffs when the Monnet Plan was forcing every sinew of the country for an increase in productivity and output. The value of contracts immediately cancelled is a first indicator of the economic effects of closing the Franco-Spanish border. The total value of contracts – either already signed before the date of the closing or ongoing – with Spanish public or private enterprises for French supplies in material or equipment amounted to about Ff 4000 million (Table 3.4).

Half of these contracts related to electrical equipment and transport modernization. In 1945 the Spanish market was perceived as offering French industry immediate and large output targets. Of the five main suppliers of electrical equipment in 1935, Germany had disappeared and the Spaniards were running into payments difficulties with the United States and Switzerland. The Spanish market was thus left to competition between French and British suppliers. The General Director of the National Railroad Company

(RENFE), the Lieutenant-Colonel of Engineers José María Rivero de Aguilar y Otero, informed the French commercial attaché that Spain required electrical equipment and technical assistance for the following decade, although basic production was left to the domestic industry. Paris was informed that Spain was willing to sign contracts to the value Ff 1000 million; these were all lost in February 1946.[14]

TABLE 3.4   FINANCIAL LOSSES FOR FRENCH INDUSTRY, 1946
(in millions of French francs)

	Contracts signed before 1 March 1946	Percentage lost	Deal orders	Percentage
Items				
Electrical equipment	275	12.5	600	34.5
Equipment for public works and fire brigades	8	0.4	220	12.6
Lorries and vehicles automobiles	740	33.5		
Peugot tools	20	0.9		
Optical apparatus			100	5.7
Material for Naval building			63	3.6
Mining equipment	700	31.7	557	32
Scrap	180	8.2		
Dyes	6	0.3		
Textile Industry Material	250	11.3	150	8.6
Equipment for distilling	28	1.3	50	2.9
Totals	2207	100	1740	100

General Total (contracts + deals) = 3947

Source: AD, Z/E vol. 67: 'Pertes que la fermature de la frontière causé à l'industrie française', n/d, n/s; and Z/E vol. 84: 'Préjudice causé à notre industrie sidérurgique par la fermeture de la frontière', Hardion's despatch, 12 March 1946.

Neither France nor Spain gained anything. On the one hand, even if most countries were willing to trade once the French had decided to step out of the Spanish market, Spain was not able to trade with most of them on a large scale due to payments problems, in particular concerning equipment supplies. On the other hand, forcing Spain to obtain supplies from the United States, Great Britain or any other western competitor, made it difficult for France to regain its share of the lost Spanish market once the political decision could be withdrawn.[15] From a historical perspective, one can always argue that the modernization of the Spanish economy certainly did not take place in the 1940s. Notwithstanding this, the French carefully noted the intended modernization efforts of the Spanish administration, presented in Chapter 4, and saw themselves as being an important beneficiary.

In contrast to France, the Anglo-Spanish payments agreement of March 1947 provided the tool for bilateral trade expansion, plus the guarantee of avoiding economic retaliation linked to political quarrels. The program of trade agreed upon provided for the export to the United Kingdom of its minimum requirements of potash and iron ore and also its needs as regards pyrites, cork, rosin and other raw materials. Provision was made for substantial exports of numerous desirable, but less essential, Spanish products, all traditional exports to the United Kingdom, chiefly oranges, tomatoes, bananas, onions, fruit pulp, nuts, olive oil and sherry. In the first year of implementation, the agreement permitted the first big increase in British post-world war imports from Spain (about £6.7 million). The increase in foodstuffs (£7.7 million) covered the bad performance in manufactured goods (£1 million fall). On the other hand, British export trade to Spain held level and prepared the conditions for a further increase in the following years. The important decrease in British exports of raw materials to Spain in 1947 corresponded to the fuel crisis in February and March which led to the suspension of exports of hard coal previously available from this source. In the United Kingdom, it was generally agreed that a break in commercial relations would be unfortunate coming just at a time when Spain was beginning to resume normal purchases.

Avoiding economic sanctions meant maintaining British exports to Spain as well as British imports from Spain, which could be further increased in the immediate postwar period (although, certainly, on a very limited scale given the scarce increase in output in Spain). It was not claimed that excluding Spain temporarily would seriously interfere with the development of British production and export trade since Spain was a small and highly protected market and world demand for British goods still greatly exceeded the possible supply. However, a prolonged break in commercial relations was undesirable. The British would not have voluntarily excluded themselves from a market perceived as having considerable potential for the British industry in machine tools and other manufactured goods, at the time when German competition had disappeared and the French were willing to abandon it. On the contrary, any such action would probably increase Spain's tendency to economic protectionism and nationalism and thereby magnify obstacles to the full development of trade. The British, read from the minutes of an interdepartmental meeting held at the Foreign Office on 28 February 1946, 'have always tried to take the long view in the hope that sooner or later we should return to normal conditions and reap some benefit'.[16] In fact, the only constant feature in trade relations between Spain and Britain during the period 1945–7 was the increase in exports of British manufactures (Table 3.5) due to the disappearance of German and French competition.

TABLE 3.5   BRITISH IMPORTS FROM AND EXPORTS TO SPAIN, 1945–7
(value in sterling)

	1945	%	1946	%	1947	%
TOTAL IMPORTS	19 978 167	100	18 727 101	100	25 571 008	100
Class I	13 598 898	68	10 656 665	57	18 316 060	72
Class II	4 242 957	21	5 005 593	27	5 042 270	20
Class III	2 135 525	11	3 060 518	16	2 212 417	8
TOTAL EXPORTS	3 142 531	100	7 250 319	100	7 387 669	100
Class I	185 423	6	325 456	5	153 882	2
Class II	559 706	18	1 081 966	15	691 574	9
Class III	2 373 497	76	5 806 508	80	6 497 652	89

Source: *Annual Statement of the Trade of the United Kingdom with Commonwealth countries and Foreign Countries*, imp. cif, exports fob; including Canary Islands and excluding Spanish ports in North Africa, except for raw materials. Value of total imports, not of articles retained in the United Kingdom. Class I, food, drink and tobacco; Class II, raw materials, minerals, fuels and lubricants; Class III, manufactured goods.

A final question is whether some governments discouraged private credits to and investment in Spain. The reduction of foreign private investment is a general postwar phenomenon. In the case of Spain, it was intensified due to domestic legislation, the lack of attractive investment targets, and the inability to provide any credit guarantees. Spanish legislation limited foreign investment by restricting foreign capital in enterprises to a maximum of 25 per cent on the basis of the Regulation and Defense of Domestic Industry Act of 24 November 1939.[17] The difficulties involved in *Safehaven* negotiations reduced the use of Spain's gold resources to back any credit operation, either public or private. The Spanish Foreign Exchange Institute (IEME) made several attempts to sell gold in the United States to provide for dollar purchases, which the US Treasury rejected. Madrid argued that the gold offered was always that purchased from the Bank of Portugal, the Swiss National Bank, and, particularly, the Bank of England as payment for wolfram and other purchases. This might be true, but it was also true that the IEME held former Axis gold and nazi-looted gold, on which the Spaniards were not willing to submit complete information. Until an agreed settlement was reached on looted gold, the capacity of the authorities to provide a credible collateral for the few credit attempts then formulated was nil. There was, for instance, the attempt of the Chase National Bank of New York to advance dollars to finance cotton purchases against the guarantee of Spanish gold. The State Department had no objections on political grounds but warned that accepting Spanish gold as collateral was 'bad risk'.[18] The Chase National Bank called back the operation fearing that the gold offered as collateral could be German-looted gold.

THE UNITED STATES FINANCIAL AND RELIEF PROGRAMS

Once reasonable doubt has been cast upon the idea that the UN resolutions provoked a retraction of trade flows with and private investment in Spain, it is necessary to tackle the second argument proposed at the beginning of this chapter, that political dislike of the Franco regime resulted in the US administration's unwillingness to provide official aid to Spain. This argument is based on statements made by President Franklin D. Roosevelt and Acting Secretary of State Dean Acheson, in 1945–7.[19] Roosevelt explained that taking measures in economic and other fields to demonstrate Spanish–American friendship was 'out of the question' at the time when American sentiment was 'so profoundly opposed' to the Franco regime. Two years later Acheson declared that as long as Franco continued in power '[we] will continue to be blocked from providing the effective assistance which would make possible the economic reconstruction of that country'. Notwithstanding this, to accept that Spain was excluded from US relief programs implies accepting the hypothesis that American aid could have been programed for Spain. No real support can be given to this hypothesis. It was the specific nature of American financial relief in the immediate postwar period, very significant for some countries (Table 3.6), which deprived the Spanish economy of its benefits and not the nature of the Franco regime.

Initial postwar American economic assistance was planned as short-term relief for countries that had participated in the war. American participation in programs such as UNRRA or GARIOA (Government and Relief in Occupied Areas), civilian supplies, dollar credits to purchase American property and government loans were not intended to be turned into medium-term reconstruction aid, used for the modernization of national economies. They were *ad hoc* measures pending fuller action from the International Monetary Fund and the International Bank for Reconstruction and Development, whose conventions were approved at the Monetary and Financial Conference of Bretton Woods, New Hampshire, July 1944.

American relief made accessible through UNRRA (73 per cent of UNRRA's $2700 million subscriptions) was intended for immediate rehabilitation to be completed by July 1946. Rehabilitation, Congress made clear, was not to be considered the beginning of reconstruction with medium-term commitments, it was 'coterminous with relief'.[20] As the preamble of the UNRRA agreement stated, relief was immediate aid to the victims of war to diminish their suffering by providing food, clothing and shelter, aid in prevention of pestilence and in the recovery of the health of the people, assistance in the resumption of urgently needed agriculture and industrial production, and the restoration of essential services.[21] Once export trade had recovered in the participating countries, the UNRRA Council refused to recommend new contributions arguing that additional foreign exchange was to be obtained through the reestablishment of bilateral deals between countries.[22] The Spanish government could never have benefited from relief in the form of UNRRA, which accounted for almost 44 per cent of American postwar relief aid, because it had not participated in the world war. The UNRRA program by definition was limited to liberated areas. Spain needed financial aid for reconstruction and modernization six years after its Civil War but UNRRA explicitly excluded such purposes from its scope. It is therefore highly improbable that Spain could have benefited from UNRRA even if it had been ruled by a democratic regime.

TABLE 3.6   US EUROPEAN ECONOMIC AND MILITARY ASSISTANCE IN THE POSTWAR PERIOD OF RELIEF, 1946–8* (in millions of dollars)

Countries	US FY 1946–8	%
United Kingdom	3836.9	38
France	1909.1	19
Federal Republic	1344.4	13
Italy	1271.3	13
Total Four	8361.7	84
Greece	723.5	7
Yugoslavia	298.1	3
Netherlands	238.2	3
Belgium/Luxembourg	163.4	2
Turkey	113.3	1
Norway	75	1
Denmark	21	–
Total US AID	9994.2	100

Source: *US Overseas Loans and Grants and Assistance from International Organizations. Obligations and Loans Authorizations July 1, 1945 – September 30, 1982.* (*) It also includes Eximbank loans, which were not included in reports of official economic and military assistance.

Another important source of American financial relief, loans granted to governments, came directly from the settlement of wartime lend-leases, which did not apply to Spain. Furthermore, US government loans, accounting in the case of the four main recipients for 50.5 per cent of total US postwar financial aid, were not a straightforward phenomenon of generosity but granted on an *ad hoc* country-by-country basis for the promotion of long-term American politico-economic goals for the new international order. As we shall immediately see, Spain had nothing to do with the reasons that impelled the Truman administration to provide this type of help to Western Europe.

The United Kingdom received special treatment. Apart from its unique efforts against Nazi forces, it was one of the largest trading nations in the world by virtue of the Sterling bloc. The latter was a large network of commercial arrangements based on the *imperial preference*, which enabled trade among its members on terms more favorable than those offered to other countries. However, only after openly declaring its wish to be associated with the United States in setting up a system of multilateral trade and payments, could Britain obtain transitional financial assistance from the United States. Even then, it took from December 1945 to July 1946 to get the Loan-Agreement definitively approved by the US Congress and signed by President Truman, ten months after lend-lease had been suspended. To obtain a loan of $3750 million and a further credit of $650 million to settle debts under previous lend-lease, the United Kingdom had to declare its acceptance of American proposals, including the principle of unconditional most-favored-nation treatment, the reduction of quantitative restrictions and tariffs, and the removal of foreign exchange restrictions with the objective of making the pound sterling convertible on current transactions in July 1947.

When the French lend-lease settlement was negotiated in May 1946, providing 72 per cent of the total financial assistance granted by the United States to France, a declaration similar to that made by the United Kingdom was necessary. Moreover, in this case, as in the Italian, with Communist parties sharing government responsibility, financial relief was seen as necessary for a successful economic recovery. Acceptance of the American model for the international economic system was the price that had to be paid. The Soviet occupation of East Germany imposed quick and decisive assistance to improve the economic performance in the bizone in order to serve as the political basis for resistance to Communism. In West Germany, financial aid was the most potent political advertisement that could be made in the campaign to win over German hearts and minds for the west. Finally, President Harry S. Truman's call for economic and military assistance to Greece and Turkey in March 1947 was directed against a perceived Communist threat. In Greece terrorist activities of several thousand armed men, led by Communists, threatened the stability of the country and thus, according to the domino theory, the entire area. The Benelux countries, Norway and Denmark, by contrast, deserved only limited attention because war damage and Communist threat was perceived to be negligible.

No actual relief was pertinent in the case of Spain. It had been a neutral country – with all its different nuances – and as such, as in the cases of Sweden, Switzerland, Ireland and Portugal, it did not deserve one single American cent. Only Turkey, among the neutral countries, received American aid due to security reasons which did not concur in the case of Spain, which was far from being endangered by Communism. The Communist guerrilla forces crossing the Pyrenees and attacking installations in Northern Spain were successfully smashed by the armed forces of a government which declared itself a crusader against Communism. Certainly, the Spanish economy was still recovering from Civil War disruption. This was, however, not a valid argument as far as the Truman administration was concerned, particularly when it was perceived that the Spanish economy was not on the edge of economic collapse: it was up to Spaniards to reconstruct their economy by joining the trend toward freer trade.[23]

Despite unfavorable political attitudes toward the Franco regime, the Spanish administration saw opportunity in the immediate postwar period. The competitive purchasing of certain war materials by the belligerents had enabled Spain to keep its balance of payments in a good position and to build up some modest reserves of foreign exchange during the war. After the war this fortuitous support disappeared but European reconstruction favored the development of traditional exports. The years 1944 and 1945 produced a positive balance of payments and reserves of foreign currencies increased by 19 per cent (Table 3.7).

West European demand had favored a trauma-free reconversion of Spain's pattern of trade between 1944 and 1945. This was so despite the decrease of £12 million in earnings of foreign currency due mainly to the elimination of wolfram exports. Commercial authorities ordained that wolfram exports had to cease once hostilities were over, which provoked an immediate drop in earnings of £16 million. Their main concern was traditional exports, which in turn gave a satisfactory result. Wolfram aside, exports were able to earn in 1945 a little more than £4 million over their level in 1944 (partly due to price increase). The main export commodities were oranges, wine, iron ore, olives and olive oil, nuts, cork, potash, and mercury, which in 1945 earned 58 per cent of total foreign currency earnings. The decrease in some traditional export commodities, in particular sherry, was expected to be only temporary. Any artificial promotion of exports was excluded by the Minister of Industry and Commerce because of the dangers of subsidy: 'Once the door opens, it is very difficult to limit the sectors of application.' Although a system of premiums was studied after November 1945 for several products, it was announced at the end of May 1946 only with the idea of compensating for lower Portuguese prices (the Iberian Peninsula had almost a world monopoly of cork production); wines, brandy and textiles would soon follow.[24]

TABLE 3.7   SPAIN'S FOREIGN CURRENCY RESERVES IN 1944–6
(position on 31 December, in pesetas)

Year	1944	1945	1946
Currency	Holdings	Holdings	Holdings
Dollar	269 258 720	188 758 181	21 435 437
Argentine peso	86 418 662	49 524 521	−149 491 019
Swiss franc	37 142 070	63 031 169	−45 338 571
Sterling	24 664 472	103 037 179	138 711 618
Escudo	13 845 727	38 051 108	16 507 986
Lira	6 509 658	−28 654 183	−38 834 703
Belgian franc	3 098 640	2 875 010	26 638 489
Swedish kroner	715 993	36 935 705	49 874 779
Dutch guilder	24 429	−57 398	4 480 495
Uruguayan peso	3422	3443	3773
Norweg. kroner	−50 126	1 571 019	−5 049 846
Chilean peso	−183 949	504 603	1 153 720
Danish kroner	−9 843 701	547 704	1 043 832
French franc*	−11 783 448	−169 431	−4 136 807
Reichsmarks	−41 658 617	−67 283	63 850
Total	378 161 954	449 788 631	109 316 425
		Total – Argentine peso	258 807 444

Source: AHBE, IEME, box 7: IEME's annual reports for 1944, 1945 and 1946. (*) Including Moroccan francs.

The path from a war to peace economy also meant that war material (which in 1944 accounted for 18 per cent of the total purchases in foreign currency) disappeared from the import list. Raw cotton and textile fibers, machinery, aircraft and their parts, electrical material, chemicals, and tobacco were the main import commodities.* The low import levels were also considered transitional due to the relief demand in Western Europe, the disappearance of Germany, and the closing of many markets after the war. It was also due to the effort made to pay off arrears, some previous financial credits and commercial debts, and to increase gold reserves. The intention behind this financial move was twofold: to present the Spanish economy as a good commercial dealer, ready to benefit from an open economy, and to eliminate future obstacles in trade negotiations. A further reduction of imports was, however, imposed by the policy of cashing bonds in foreign hands. All these non-commercial operations involved a heavy drain on resources, accounting for 34 per cent of the foreign currency expenditure in 1945.[25] The IEME authorities considered this period as transitional to a future expansion of trade following economic recovery in Western Europe. An efficient use of economic resources (once debts had been paid) and the network of bilateral agreements negotiated or being negotiated in the second half of 1945 would open prosperous perspectives for the future.[26]

In fact, Spain's economic policy makers looked anxiously at the transforming world economy. A report on the IMF presented for consideration to the Council of the Bank of Spain in July 1944, before the Bretton Woods Conference ended, was laudatory concerning the Bretton Woods system and considered it inevitable that all neutrals would join it.[27] In December 1945, the IEME Chairman explained at the IEME Council the benefits to be derived if currency convertibility were established. The dominant position of the dollar and the sterling (65 per cent of the country's foreign reserves) and the dollar decrease having been offset by an increase in most European currencies, particularly sterling, could explain this favorable attitude. In January the Minister of Industry and Commerce set up a commission to study, from a specifically Spanish perspective, the Bretton Woods agreements. The favorable attitude shown by top economic officials toward the Bretton Woods system would have been senseless if they had not been convinced that the Spanish economy could benefit from freer trade.

The Minister recognized that the scarcity of hard currencies and the recourse to bilateralism did not promote purchases based on relative qualities and prices, which was to the disadvantage of everyone involved. The IEME Chairman also explained that there was no fixed criterion to maintain the value of the peseta invariable. For its modification it was necessary, however, to consider the measures undertaken by other countries. As long as European sales stayed high there seemed no point in devaluing, for it would merely decrease the price of exports, put up the price of imports and possibly worsen the trade deficits. On the export side, the ability of the Spanish economy was likely to remain low due to output levels and the fact that world demand had still not recovered prewar levels concerning traditional agricultural exports, such as wine, fruits and vegetables. On the import side, any expansion was difficult given world levels of production and trade. The acute shortage of some products in Europe allowed export commodities to coexist with what seemed an over-valued exchange rate and high prices.

The Ministry of Industry and the IEME had assumed an increase of reserves in 1945 and a somewhat large deficit in the balance of payments in

1946, with an immediate fall in gold and foreign exchange reserves. Reparations, once some normality had returned to international trade, and various
international payments due from the Spanish State were to be responsible for
the expected fall in reserves. That import licenses were to follow closely the
path of foreign currency reserves, was considered a transitory measure.[28] The
real problem came in 1947 when the deficit in the balance of payments,
which was expected to diminish, increased.

*   *   *

Spain suffered political discrimination in international politics but not economic discrimination. This was especially true of the period when Spain
was an important source of supply for an extremely limited European productive capacity. Europe's national reconstruction policies aimed at continuous high levels of output and employment and high rates of growth,
demanding an uninterrupted import trend. Furthermore, the population of
Western Europe wanted a higher standard of living with a better and more
highly diversified supply of foodstuffs. The Spanish supply made its contribution to the more effective use of tight dollar reserves, allowed them to be
dedicated to the purchase of capital goods and raw materials, and contributed to a diversification of diet. This role was not based upon the potential of
the Spanish economy but upon the short-term needs of relief. Therefore, the
important point is not the low level of Spanish exports but that West European governments did not need a large economic contribution from Spain to
calm their democratic thrust. Anything that could hamper national reconstruction policies was immediately rejected. In other words, Spain's limited
supply had a strategic value in the circumstances of the immediate postwar
period.

The study of postwar commercial behavior proves that politics and economics followed somewhat opposite directions. The common denominator
for the United Kingdom and France was that despite their opposite courses of
action, policy makers understood the distinction between political ostracism
and economic sanctions. Reconstruction policies and political stability, on
the one hand, and the elimination of Germany, leaving a potential market to
be filled up, on the other, helped to draw a clear line between both. The
records consulted provide no reference suggesting foreign economic discrimination against Spain.

International hostility favored Franco in domestic affairs. The image of a
foreign front against Spain, the so-called *policy of siege* («*cerco*»), was a propaganda device to promote domestic support for General Franco. It served to
legitimate repression and the reinforcement of Franco's leadership. International political ostracism allowed Franco to transform an office ostensibly

designed for national emergency into a source of permanent personal power. After the world war, Franco and his ministers had to demonstrate that the menace of foreign intervention was ever-present in order to maintain military control of the country. Political ostracism, first, and the Communist threat, later on, served the purpose. 'The more we are misunderstood, the more the foreign world fights us, the more they discuss our gestures,' Franco himself declared, 'the more we will be forced to affirm our revolution.'[29]

A useful path for Spain to break political isolation was bilateral trade agreements. Although nowadays they are considered the origin of great inconveniences and ill-fated effects, in the period after 1945, they fulfilled essential economic as well as purely political functions. The role that Spain played in European economic reconstruction, set against the background of an inefficient and frustrating diplomatic policy, made the Spanish government more conscious than ever before of the strategic importance of commercial relations. This was a potential element in pressing for the solution of political disputes of a bilateral nature. Spanish historiography has assumed that Franco did not have a foreign policy in the strict sense but a form of management of technical agreements with the foreign world. Whether or not this assessment is accepted is of no interest here; what really matters is that political gains were made through technical deals. Trade relations proved useful means for international recognition and could be used to put pressure upon European governments to avoid direct action against Franco Spain.

Finally, a clear understanding of Spain's post-1945 economic relations provides the necessary background for understanding the circumstances in which the Spanish position toward the first form of European multilateral economic cooperation emerged. The official attitude toward the Marshall Plan was a reflection of a substantial mirage. Spanish contribution to the immediate postwar European reconstruction efforts, limited as it might have been, created a distorted crystal through which future relations with Spain's western partners were perceived. Future forms of reconstruction, however, no longer based on completely independent national policies but on multilateral cooperation, were to become qualitatively different from those of the first postwar period and Spain would not have a place within them.

The problem in the attempt to cast light on the implications of foreign action in domestic strategies for growth lies in making a clear distinction between the economic effects stemming from political ostracism and the direct effect of the domestic policies adopted by the Spanish authorities themselves. The chapters listed in this section under Trade versus Political Discrimination have basically foregone an analysis of the performance of the Spanish economy in order to concentrate on the external elements conditioning the formation of the country's foreign economic policy. To confront the action described here with the poor domestic performance of the Spanish economy will be one of the tasks of the following chapters. So far this book strongly questions the proposition that political ostracism had any real effect on Spain's economic performance.

Part II
Rara Avis: Spain and the Marshall Plan, 1947–8

4 Import Requirements for National Reconstruction and Modernization

The origins of European multilateral economic cooperation have traditionally been placed in the speech by the US Secretary of State, General George C. Marshall, on 5 June 1947, which proposed a coordinated program for European economic as well as social and political reconstruction. That Spain was excluded from the Marshall Plan, given the origins and nature of Franco's regime, does not represent anything new.[1] It might be that Franco, personally, was ultimately responsible for Spain's exclusion because he stayed in power and maintained unaltered the undemocratic institutional character of his regime. The relation of Spain to the Marshall Plan cannot, however, be viewed solely within such narrow terms. Although Spain did not participate, its authorities had great expectations of Marshall aid and responded to exclusion. This second set of chapters attempts to take Spain out of the footnotes and contributes to a better understanding of the origins of West European cooperation by presenting the position, goals and response of the only country in Western Europe not invited to join.[2]

THE ORIGINS OF THE MARSHALL PLAN AND SPAIN

Whether or not Marshall's offer of assistance to the whole of Europe was sincere is open to debate, though it is usually explored only in connection with the possible participation of the Soviet Union.[3] The truth is that Marshall did not explicitly exclude Spain; it was, however, likely that he intended to do so. The Spanish administration believed then, as do many scholars today, that Marshall offered unconditional assistance to the whole of Europe, directed against no one country or doctrine but against hunger, poverty, despair and chaos. The Chargé d'Affaires in Washington explained to the Minister of Foreign Affairs that Marshall's reference to 'governments... which seek to perpetuate human mistery in order to profit therefrom politically or otherwise' only concerned the Soviet Union.[4] Notwithstanding this, the prevailing State Department attitude precluded any financial aid to Spain prior to the Franco regime adopting far-reaching political changes, which included General

Franco leaving power. In fact, the attitude adopted toward Spain arose from the State Department's search for a new policy toward Western Europe after President Truman's special address on aid to Greece and Turkey. When the new policy was finally found, initially articulated in the most famous of Marshall's speeches, the exclusion of Spain was a condition for its success.

The State Department was at pains to figure out how it could by-pass the negative implications of what was shortly to become the Truman doctrine. Truman's speech of 12 March 1947 was not identified as a call for a crusade to restore democracy all over the world; despite its anti-totalitarian wording, it was perceived as the official announcement of a break with the Soviets and as a strictly anti-Communist statement.[5] The Franco regime provided the State Department with an initial chance to distance itself from the Truman doctrine. Truman's statement was widely publicized in Spain as a blow to the United Nations and full recognition of Franco's past and future role in the inevitable fight against Communism. Probably instructed from Moscow by Marshall who was at the Council of Foreign Ministers, early in April 1947, Acting Secretary of State and future Secretary (1949–53) Dean Acheson consulted the British upon a joint plan of action to eliminate Franco and replace his regime with a democratic one. Only Franco's departure would allow an extension of American assistance to Spain. All interested Spaniards should know that *gains* would accrue to Spain from a change in regime. International public opinion should also come to know that America's national interest was not limited to the military aspects of the Truman doctrine. The message was not necessarily addressed to the British and Spanish exclusively, but to the entire international community: American assistance was not meant to be extended to just anyone who claimed to be anti-Communist.[6]

The Foreign Office stopped the State Department from taking any effective step toward the plan to eliminate Franco, which had appeared to them unconvincing from the outset: 'The matter was too dangerous to take up.'[7] The same arguments used against the French proposals after December 1945, served now to stop Washington. The American proposal was based on the assumption that the economic situation of Spain was critical and that an alternative government could be formed. Published records show, however, that the State Department was perfectly aware that the Spanish economy was not on the edge of collapse and that there was no stable alternative government in the wings. The State Department was perfectly informed about the special circumstances of this case and opted to obviate them as nonexistent. This would support the hypothesis that Acheson's initiative was a sort of propaganda device addressed to the international community. The British did not support it.

No secure alternative to Francoism appeared feasible to the British. They saw no guarantee that the alternative to the fall of Franco would necessarily be an ordered democratic process. They feared anarchy. Between Franco and democracy there seemed to be, for the British, civil strife, chaos and misery. On the economic side, there was little reason to suppose that the Spanish economy would collapse unless sanctions were applied. Marshall and Bevin agreed that the economic situation was improving. There was no need to foster unstable conditions in Spain. Any such action would have meant intervention in the internal affairs of another country, providing a dangerous precedent. It ran counter to previous Allied recommendations which left it to the Spaniards to solve their own political problems. It would only have strengthened the position of those who asked for more extreme forms of intervention at the UN Security Council. The Allies, the British firmly believed, should not risk finding themselves progressively forced down the path of intervention which might in the end lead to armed force. The Soviet Union had already derived considerable benefit from the status quo reached with Franco by placing the western powers as defenders of fascism. However, action such as that proposed by Acheson would have involved, in British eyes, playing Moscow's game of spreading instability. For London, temporary continuance of Franco in power, which did not threaten any British or American interest, was the preferable alternative at hand.[8]

It is difficult to believe that the Department of State could ever have considered Spain joining the Marshall Plan when its initiative to remove Franco from power was being discussed with the British until the end of July 1947. It was only on 26 July that Bevin conveyed the final rejection of the State Department's initiative. For the Foreign Office, the inclusion of Spain would have fed Soviet propaganda about America's intentions and distorted the plan's ideological integrity. To trade openly with Spain was completely different from inviting Franco to join an initiative whose declared intention was to build European Unity.

By demanding mutual coordination of Europeans, Madrid was automatically excluded, since many participating countries could never have joined in a common effort with Franco, while Marshall avoided any responsibility. Like the Russians, some top Spanish civil servants were unwilling to accept the proposed conditions and recommended not joining the initiative in order to preserve national sovereignty. Marshall's preconditions seemed to imply the surrender of part of all governments' absolute right to economic planning to the United States or to a multilateral planning body which would set priorities, supply quotas and allocate resources. Spain's aim was to make an inventory of its economic needs and to avoid inquiry into its resources. This attitude was based on the deeply held conviction that the United States would help Spain in any case. Some officials at the Spanish Embassy in Paris feared that the British and French, agreeing before consulting anyone else on the fundamentals of the European response, would place Spain exclusively as a supplier to the French economy.[9] It is obvious that Spain's diplomatic personnel was not gifted with a keen perception of reality. It was not difficult to see that France had no place for Spain within any common European reconstruction plan.

The exclusion of Spain was not the consequence of the American commitment to democracy, liberty and justice (while ensuring the restoration of the economic health and vigor of Europe). It was the result of the vast amount of emotion invested in debate on Spain, making any move toward closer relations with the Franco regime unpalatable to public opinion. Spain did not present any of the circumstances which favored other non-democratic governments invited to join. Greece and Turkey could not be left outside if the Marshall Plan wanted to replace the multiplicity of piecemeal, *ad hoc* and emergency economic and military programs with a comprehensive and consistent plan. There was some cogency in the argument that Portugal also belonged to the club of dictatorships and there was no question as to the arbitrary and undemocratic character of the country's political institutions. Notwithstanding this, Portugal's experience was less turbulent and the origins of its dictatorship were somehow lost in the past, while the Spanish Civil War, with the intervention of Hitler and Mussolini, was fresh in people's minds.

Portugal, it was argued, behaved more neutrally than Spain during World War II and, in a way, Dr António de Oliveira Salazar had rejected the fascist and military covering which characterized the earlier years of the Franco regime. If, following the formal liberalization of political and parliamentary systems adopted after 1945, Portugal was seen as more democratic that Spain, it was exclusively because the Allies preferred to see things that way. If the authoritarian Portuguese regime deserved different treatment by the Allies, it was certainly neither for its contribution to constructing a new democratic Europe nor for its commitment to European unity. It is indisputable that after 1945 Salazar continued to hold an iron rule over Portugal as Franco did over Spain. But international public opinion had made the Franco regime a moral question. Enduring political passions amongst the peoples of Western Europe and elsewhere precluded the use of any analogy between the Franco and Salazar regimes as a conclusive argument in favor of Spain.[10]

The exclusion of Spain added some guarantee of collaboration in Western Europe and diminished the opposition on Capitol Hill. The inclusion of Portugal could be diluted in a package of 16 nations. According to Italy's Embassy in London, British and American viewpoints agreed on the issue of Spain not joining the conference.[11] The expected French hostility made it unnecessary to make publicly explicit the possible implications of any Spanish participation in the joint venture. With the border closed and having denounced the Franco regime as a potential danger to international peace, the French government dared not consider Spain's inclusion in any common initiative. Bidault was perfectly aware that the internal difficulties that the Communist Party was ready to cause concerning French ERP participation could become practically insurmountable if Spain were invited to join. Therefore, Bidault's opening address to the Three Power Conference of 27 June 1947, and the French proposal for Marshall Plan membership presented the following day, envisaged the participation of all European countries with the temporary exception of Spain. After the Soviets had abandoned the conference, the joint Anglo-French note of 3 July explicitly excluded Spain, which was not invited to the European Conference for Economic Cooperation convened to determine the resources and needs of Europe.[12]

IMPORT REQUIREMENTS FOR NATIONAL RECONSTRUCTION AND MODERNIZATION

In addition to a general diplomatic mobilization, at home the Ministry of Industry and Commerce studied the country's economic needs and drafted an estimate of imports necessary to complete national reconstruction, the «Cuadros resúmenes de las importaciones necesarias para la reconstrucción nacional», henceforth referred to as Import Program (Table 4.1). The Import Program was drafted with the intention of presenting it in the eventuality of Spain joining the negotiations for European economic cooperation. Some of the many ambiguous points contained in the Import Program can be clarified by the documentation which, based on its calculations, was subsequently drafted by the Ministry of Foreign Affairs to provide its personnel with arguments to promote Spain's ERP participation.[13] No official request for membership was ever presented.

The Import Program called for the foreign capital (expressed in dollars) necessary to finance a package of imports over an indeterminate period. The total value of the imports required to complete reconstruction amounted to $676 million. It seems reasonable to consider that if Spain had joined the negotiations, the Import Program would have been cut by a fixed percentage on the total, as happened with each ERP country's aid program in the first weeks of September 1947. Some comparative figures might help to assess the Spanish program properly. It doubled the value of foreign currency expenditure (Spain's basic balance of payments) in 1946 and it was 68 per cent above what it was in 1947.[14] It was 2.3 times the value of total imports in 1946. It should be borne in mind that the Import Program was restricted to a few sectors and

62

TABLE 4.1   NECESSARY IMPORTS FOR SPAIN'S ECONOMIC RECONSTRUCTION, FIRST AND SECOND DRAFTS, SUMMER 1947 (henceforth referred to as Import Program)

(a) Concept Industrial Settings for the production of	(b) Required Period to Complete the industrial plans in (a)	(c) Planned Output Either Annual Targets (AT) or Increase of Existing Output (IO)	(d) Unit Price of Required Imports in $ ($)	(e) (c)×(d) Total Value of Required Imports in $ million	(f) Percentage of (e) in General Total	(g) Annual Savings that (c) would produce in future imports in $ millions	(h) (e)/(g) Redemption Period in Years
GENERAL TOTAL	5 years (4.7 years)			675.912 (451.181)	100 (100)	134.25 (108.25)	5 (4)
AGRICULTURAL PRODUCTION							
1. Nitrogen Fertilizers	5 years (=)	AT 100 000 T. of N_2 (=)	400	40 (=)	5.9 (8.9)	27 (=)	1.5 (=)
2. Tractors	4 years (=)	AT 2000 Units (=)	5000	10 (=)	1.5 (2.2)	8 (=)	1.25 (=)
TOTAL AGRICULTURAL SECTOR	4.5 years (=)			50 (50)	7.4 (11.1)	35 (=)	1.43 (=)
BASIC PRODUCTIONS							
ENERGY							
3. Coal	4 years (=)						
3.1. Modernization		6 million T. (=)	1.5	9 (=)	1.3 (2)	6(t) (=)	1.5 (=)
3.2. New Mines		IO 3 million T. (=)	3	9 (=)	1.3 (2)	(#)	–
4. Electric Energy	5 years (=)	AT 2 million Kw(=)	50	100 (=)	14.8 (22.2)	(#)	–
5. Petroleum Products	6 years (=)	AT 335 000 T. (235 000)	183 (&)	61.5 (36)	9.1 (8)	13.5 (1) (9.5)	4.5 (3.8)
6. Oil Refineries	6 years (=)	AT 1 million T.(500 000)	10.5	10.5 (5.25)	1.5 (1.2)	7.5 (5)	1.5 (1)
TOTAL ENERGY SECTOR	5.2 years (=)			190 (159.25)	28.1 (35.3)	–	–

7. Iron and Steel							
7.1. Modernization	750 000 T. (=)	3 years (=)	8	6 (=)	0.9 (1.3)	4.5 (=)	1.3 (=)
7.2. New Settings	IO 500 000 T. (250 000)	6 years (=)	40	20 (10)	3 (2.2)	(#)	–
8. Aluminum	AT 2500 T. (=)	3 years (=)	100	0.25 (=)	./. (0.1)	0.75 (=)	0.3 (=)
9. Synthetic fiber	AT 10 000 T. (=)	2 years (=)	650	6.5 (=)	1 (1.4)	5 (=)	1.3 (=)
10. Cellulose	AT 50 000 T. (=)	4 years (=)	150	7.5 (=)	1.1 (1.7)	9 (=)	0.75 (=)
TOTAL BASIC NON-ENERGY SECTOR		3.6 years (=)		40.25 (**30.25**)	6 (**6.7**)	–	–
TOTAL BASIC PRODUCTIONS		4.6 years (=)		230.25 (**189.5**)	34.1 (**42**)	46.25 (**39.75**)	5 (**4.75**)
RAILWAY TRANSPORT							
11. Track Reconstruction	Complete Network (*)	3 years (**2 years**)	–	45.09 (**22.545**)	6.7 (**5**)	(#)	–
12. New Rolling Stock	(*)	2 years (=)	–	45.422 (**22.711**)	6.7 (**5**)	(#)	–
13. Rolling Stock Reparation	(*)	2 years (=)	–	47.6 (**23.8**)	7 (**5.3**)	(#)	–
14. Telephone Communications	Complete Network (*)	5 years (**3 years**)	–	1.25 (**0.625**)	0.2 (**0.1**)	(#)	–
15. Signposting	Complete Network (*)	6 years (**3 years**)	–	8.8 (**4.4**)	1.3 (**1.0**)	(#)	–
16. Electrification	4500 Km. (*)	12 years (**6 years**)	–	45 (**22.5**)	6.7 (**5.0**)	(#)	–
TOTAL RAILWAY TRANSPORT SECTOR		5 years (**3.5 years**)		193.162 (**96.581**)	28.6 (**21.4**)	(#)	–

TABLE 4.1 (contd.)

(a) Concept Industrial Settings for the production of	(b) Required Period to Complete the industrial plans in (a)	(c) Planned Output Either Annual Targets (AT) or Increase of Existing Output (IO)	(d) Unit Price of Required Imports in $ ($)	(e) (c)×(d) Total Value of Required Imports in $ million	(f) Percentage of (e) in General Total	(g) Annual Savings that (c) would produce in future imports in $ millions	(h) (e)/(g) Redemption Period in Years
TRANSPORT OTHER THAN RAILWAYS							
17. Diesel Trucks Production	4 years (=)	AT 1500 of 7/8 T. (=)	5000	7.5 (=)	1.1 (**1.7**)	6 (=)	1.2 (=)
18. Passenger Cars	5 years (=)	AT 16 000 Units (**8000**)	1550	24.8 (**12.4**)	3.7 (**2.7**)	24 (**12**)	1 (=)
19. Aircraft	1 year (=)						
19.1. State's IBERIA		AT 5 Transatlantic (=) 50% of Existing Parking (=)		11.2 (=)	1.7 (**2.5**)	5.5 (=)	2 (=)
19.1.1. New Airplanes							
19.1.2. Repairs							
19.2. Other Companies		(**)	–	5 (=)	0.7 (**1.1**)	2.5 (=)	2 (=)
19.3. General Infrastructure		(**)	–	4 (=)	0.6 (**0.9**)	(#)	–
20. Ship Equipment	13 years (=)	(*)	–	20 (**10**)	3 (**2.2**)	10 (**5**)	2 (=)
TOTAL TRANSPORT OTHER THAN RAILWAY	5.7 years (=)			72.5 (**50.1**)	10.7 (**11.1**)	48 (**31**)	1.5 (**1.6**)
TOTAL TRANSPORT SECTOR	5.4 years (**4.6 years**)			265.662 (**146.681**)	39.3 (**32.5**)	(#)	–

MACHINERY AND TOOLS INDUSTRY

21. Machinery and Tools	5 years (=)	25 000 T. (**12 500**)	4000	100 (**50**)	14.8 (**7.4**)	(#)	–
22. Textile Sector	5 years (=)	–	–	20 (**10**)	3 (**2.2**)	5 (**2.5**)	4 (=)
23. Food-Processing Sector	4 years (=)	(*)	–	10 (**5**)	1.5 (**1.1**)	(#)	–
TOTAL MACH. AND TOOLS SECTOR	4.7 years (=)			130 (**65**)	19.2 (**14.4**)	(#)	–
GENERAL TOTAL	5 years (**4.7 years**)			675.912 (**451.181**)	100 (**100**)	134.25 (**108.25**)	5 (**4**)

Source: MAE, Leg. 5281, exp. 13: Ministry of Industry and Commerce: 'Cuadro resúmenes de las importaciones necesarias para la reconstrucción nacional (1ª y 2ª solución)'. For the entire period covered by this chapter the peseta was officially exchanged (for imports) at Pt 10.95 to $1. (–) Data not given (./.) Negligible (**) Not processed (*) See explanation in text (§) The entire program was drafted with fixed prices at the period without considering the change in relative prices of imports and exports (&) Average unit cost of ton produced at major industrial complexes ($255.3) and of fuel ton produced by distilling agricultural by-products (‡) Freights not included (#) Not computed due to complexity in calculi although assumed important indirect savings (¶) Not considering indirect savings (=) No variation **Figures in bold** correspond to the second draft to the first draft.

excluded, in particular, agricultural commodities which accounted, in 1946, for 23.3 per cent of total imports. The Import Program's dollar requirement represented 5.4 times the accumulated commercial deficit registered in 1946 and 1947 and 3.2 times the value of the accumulated deficit during the ERP period, 1948 to 1952. Finally, the generation of $676 million worth of resources, without foreign credits and allowing for some duplication with current imports, required Spain's exports to grow by 161 per cent. The Program's first draft was thus an import shopping list of goods the Ministry of Industry and Commerce would have wanted to purchase had it had the resources.

Feeling the amount of dollars initially requested was too high, a more economical version of the same program was drafted. The second draft amounted to $451.2 million. It included cuts worth $225 million, 43 per cent of which were at the expense of the transport sector, 39 per cent of industries producing semi-manufactured goods and 18 per cent of basic production. All transport items were cut by half, as well as the production of cars, the supply of parts to the shipbuilding industry, the investment of the textile and food-processing industries, tools and machinery. Output targets for fuel and lubricants were reduced by 100 000 tons, and the iron and steel as well as the refining capacity were reduced by half. Consequently, this second draft can be considered the Ministry of Industry's true minimal import requirements for reconstruction.[15]

The Import Program selected (by order of importance) transportation, energy, equipment and tools for the machinery and tools industry, agricultural machinery, fertilizers, and iron and steel, as priority sectors. These were considered basic, that is, able to act as multipliers for the entire national economy following vigorous public intervention. The first selection criterion was the importance of output to eliminating bottlenecks for industrial rehabilitation. Factories required power, the transport system had to permit the movement of goods and agriculture had to free some exchange resources to import raw materials and equipment. The second criterion was to continue earlier public intervention and, thus, this Program was an estimate of the essential needs of the public sector. It was firmly believed that the aims of efficiency and the channelling of all available resources into productive work could only be effectively induced by the public sector. Those economic sectors where public firms existed – not necessarily in monopoly terms – provided (in principle) a better guarantee of control over imports and the implementation of planned targets. That most of the industrial plants mentioned here related to the public sector, to the National Institute for Industry (INI) in particular, is not surprising. The INI was designed for the industrial recovery of the country in priority sectors and its president was, in perfect symbiosis, the Minister of Industry.[16] Action from the public sector also eased the technical problems involved in the drafting.

The Import Program summed up, arithmetically, previous individual piecemeal plans in the different public sectors. The Ministry of Industry argued that the Program should comprise exclusively those industrial projects at the final stage of construction. The Ministry explained that cases were frequent of industrial plants having completed capital formation, obtained the necessary quotas for raw materials, built housing, arranged transport and other auxiliary services – such as energy and water equipment – but still requiring equipment to complete construction and the supply of raw materials to initiate production. This argument was far-fetched. Although work had been started on a number of ambitious schemes for industrial production, in many cases government-sponsored, only a few schemes, as we will see, were nearing completion and some were scarcely beyond the drawing-board stage. The vast majority of requirements were for investment plans which were considerably less advanced. In fact the Import Program shows clearly the lack of success of previous State initiatives in the basic sectors of the economy. It was now expected that Marshall aid would provide effective and adequate assistance for the development and modernization of a small group of industrial sectors which would produce a feed-back effect bringing about general economic recovery and expansion.

The Import Program was complementary to the country's normal pattern of trade. The Ministry of Industry and Commerce relied on imports from the United States, which yielded savings in the cost of commodities, delivery and technological adjustment for Spanish industrial plants. If supply or financial difficulties appeared, at least between one-third and one-half of the total requested would still come from the United States. The rest could be obtained through normal trade channels with traditional suppliers, such as the United Kingdom, Switzerland, Belgium, Sweden, Italy and eventually, France. Imports coming through bilateral channels would continue to help achieve the recovery of pre-Civil War levels of output and, in particular, provide consumer goods and foodstuffs. The Import Program concentrated resources where trade channels appeared insufficient to finance ambitious plans, most particularly concerning the immediate short-term goal of breaking bottlenecks. The Ministry of Industry and Commerce was conscious that removing specific obstacles to the full utilization of existing capacity was not enough and that new industrial capacity and structural modernization based on decisive action from the public sector was necessary. Although the Americans had clearly argued that long-term investment and expansion could not take precedence over immediate rehabilitation of existing productive capacities, most Western Europeans, including Spain, disregarded that argument. Power installations, oil refineries, railroad equipment and steel plants attempted everywhere to expand industrial capacity beyond short-term needs. The Import Program's shopping list was a mirror-image of the country's economic requirements and it provides a useful instrument for studying the results of economic policy during the period.

The Program's highest attention went to the energy sector (heading 3 to 6) since primary energy supply is basic to industrial development. Top priority thus went to expanding the production of coal, electricity, and oil. In both drafts, they were allocated an average of 32 per cent of total planned investment. Since the energy sector was a State priority immediately after 1939, it is not surprising it received particular attention. Fuel and power shortage characterized post-world-war economic life in Spain. The country had scarce refining capacity and there were periodical petrol shortages. The disappearance of the bulk of rich British coal could not be compensated by an increased use of poorer indigenous substitutes. Low electricity prices stimulated industrial demand for electricity – which could not be met – while depressing private investment. This was the main result of subjecting electricity to political prices. Furthermore, being primarily dependent on hydro-electric power, an occasional drought, as in 1944–5, could temporarily cripple the Spanish economy. Despite the lack of significant increases in capacity, a marked increase in output nevertheless took place. This rise in output, however, meant that the existing plant was over-worked and required replacement, making the supply of equipment the sector's main problem.[17]

The Import Program aimed at increasing capacity and output. Previous INI and private programs aimed at bringing plants into service by 1953 to increase total capacity by 800 000 Kw. The 1944–5 crisis gave an added impetus to many schemes to step up the output of electricity. The various private companies producing electricity, mainly grouped, since 1944, in «Unidad Eléctrica SA», aimed to bring into service an increase in capacity of 200 000 Kw. For its part, the INI hoped, by 1953, to put into service power plants with a total capacity of 400 000 Kw, most of it through the «Empresa Nacional Hidroeléctrica de Ribagorzana», set up in December 1946. The INI's firm «Empresa Nacional de Electricidad, SA», set up in 1944, implemented some long-term plans for a further increase of 200 000 Kw.[18] It was to create power stations consuming low-grade coal produced at the INI's industrial complexes which were unsuitable for other purposes. The INI considered that its own demands for electricity would not be attained without a parallel increase in electricity output by the same INI plants. The construction program increased Spain's total electricity capacity, which had been 1.9 million Kw in 1939, by 454 200 Kw at the end of 1947. The Ministry of Industry's new targets were for a new potential capacity of two million Kw with a production of 7000 million Kwh, hydro-electric and thermic (heading 4).

Doubling the country's electricity capacity could be possible only through the sector's modernization. The Ministry required imports up to a value of

$100 million, or 14.8 per cent of the total investment program. It was the highest single heading of the whole program. There had been an equal amount for imports of machinery and tools, but it was cut by one-half in the second draft. Since the reduced draft had not modified the amount corresponding to energy, its share of the overall rose to 22.2 per cent. Overcoming the electricity supply problem was therefore priority number one of the economic authorities.

Imports of $100 million constituted a sum which the authorities found extremely difficult to provide in view of their heavy foreign exchange commitments for scarce foodstuffs and basic raw materials. The largest orders for heavy electrical equipment in 1945–6 went to Switzerland and the United States. When drafting the Import Program, exchange difficulties had almost completely stopped imports from both hard currency countries. The closing of the border with France prevented any diversion of part of the demand to the French electrical industry, while British exports of electrical goods, which had expanded almost tenfold from 1945 to 1946, could no longer meet the demand, largely because of the immense power generation reequipment program underway in the United Kingdom. British exports of electrical machinery, apparatus and goods to Spain dropped from £1.4 to £0.5 million from 1946 to 1947. In the spring of 1947 the French Embassy informed Paris that the offer of Ff 1000 million for electrical supply, suspended in February 1946, was still valid since contracts could not be signed elsewhere.[19] Marshall aid was thus expected to increase the capacity of the local electrical engineering industry by providing sufficient supply of equipment and raw materials.

Petroleum products were the second major category within the energy sector (heading 5), particularly because the country was entirely dependent upon foreign supply. As in the previous case, the sector inherited ineffective public action. In May 1944, the Cortes approved a national plan to obtain petroleum products, including motor spirit and lubricants, with a total budget of $183.6 million. The INI was charged to carry it out through its largest subsidiary enterprise, «Empresa Nacional Calvo Sotelo de combustibles líquidos y lubrificantes», created in January 1942. The 1944 Plan included the setting up of three integrated industrial complexes – Puertollano (Ciudad Real), Escatrón (Sagarossa) and Puentes de García Rodríguez (La Coruña) – and an oil refinery at Escombreras (Cartagena).[20] Puertollano's industrial plant aimed to obtain petroleum products from distillation of bituminous shales, to produce nitrogenous fertilizers and to construct coal-fired power stations. Estimates were of an annual output of 132 000 tons of petroleum products to be obtained from the distillation of 1 200 000 tons of shales. The industrial complex on the Ebro river, near Sagarossa, included plants for lignite mining and their industrial treatment to obtain petroleum products (annual planned output of 100 000 tons), production plants for nitrogenous fertilizers and coal-fired power stations. Puentes included another coal-fired power station, installations for lignite distillation and fertilizer production and other mining installations. Lignite mining was to produce annually 450 000 tons, treating part of which would produce an annual output of 15 000 tons of refined oil products. The 1944 Plan's target was an output production of 335 000 metric tons of petroleum products per year from the distillation of shale, lignite and agricultural by-products (in particular olive oil). The treatment of imported petroleum and primary petroleum products at Cartagena, whose oil refinery could not be completed until 1949/50, was to produce 450 000 tons more. Having failed to achieve previous planning targets, the Ministry of Industry included the 1944 Oil Plan within the scope of the Import Program.

The four complexes of the 1944 Plan were to be the sole beneficiaries of Marshall aid. The target was identical, production of 335 000 tons of petroleum products, although now it was considered to represent only 20 per cent of the country's requirements. The Import Program's target was distributed as follows: Puertollano 120 000 tons, Escatrón 100 000 tons and Puentes de García Rodríguez 15 000 tons; distillation of agricultural by-products would represent an additional 100 000 tons. As for oil refining, recent experience favored the doubling of the 1944 output target to an annual output of one million tons (heading 6). Motor spirit, diesel oil and lubricants, which had been strictly rationed throughout World War II and placed on free sale in August/September 1946, were rationed again in October 1947. The petroleum sector shows better than any other, that the Import Program reflected the frustration of previous State intervention in those sectors considered strategic for the entire national economy. It was impossible to end dependence on foreign supply of petroleum products but an expansion of domestic output was to act as a very important future exchange-saver.

American assistance would, in addition, alleviate the heavy burden which the import of high technology involved and by-pass worldwide delivery delays. Given Spain's foreign exchange reserves, requests of this kind placed with foreign enterprises could only be financed at a very slow rate. American assistance was also designed to redress the technological dependence which the plan originally had on Germany. Most of the new industrial plants referred to in the Program were originally dependent upon German exports of machinery and technological support. After 1945, with Germany unable to deliver, great difficulty was experienced in obtaining technical aid and equipment from other countries. Some of the firms concerned contracted for the supply of machinery from Italy, Switzerland, Sweden, and the United Kingdom, but Spain's shortage of foreign exchange impeded these plants in approaching full production as planned.

Coal production – as elsewhere in Europe – constituted probably the most crippling economic bottleneck. The inadequacy of domestic coal supply blocked any increase in iron and steel supplies and prevented any relief of the acute transport problem by seriously hampering the working of railways. Although coal production had increased considerably, chronic shortages occurred, and each winter the delays in transport became especially serious. The expansion of output was achieved by extracting lower grades of coal, bringing on unmined anthracite deposits and developing lignite deposits in the north. No real improvement could be expected without a further increase in domestic production and imports of high-grade coal.

The Import Program aimed at modernizing existing mines with an estimated output of some six million tons (heading 3.1). The incorporation of mining machinery, which foreign exchange shortages and difficulties in world supply had previously made impossible, would raise productivity (kg/day/miner) by ten per cent after three years. This could be considered a modest productivity increase. However, without the planned investment, the productivity in the coal sector dropped from 81.2 in 1947 (as compared to 1933 = 100) to 77.9 by 1952, while in the most of the ERP countries it increased at the end of the ERP period.[21]

New mines would further increase output by three million tons of coal, anthracite and lignite (heading 3.2). The authorities also considered imports of high quality coal. Before the war, Spain imported 1.7 million tons of coal and over one million tons of high-grade coal a year, in particular from the United Kingdom. The decrease in world trade after 1945, the low quantities of coal which the British authorities allowed for trading, and Spain's currency problems, had reduced imports to a minimum. Total coal imports from 1940 to 1947 were less than the imports of 1935 alone and represented one per cent of the country's total consumption (against 20 per cent in 1935). The country's mines produced ten million tons of hard coal against a requirement of 12 million tons for heavy industries and transport. The deficit to be covered by imports was 1.5 to 2 million tons (formerly imported from the United Kingdom) plus 60 000 tons of coal tar. In sum, Marshall aid would have decisively helped to push up imports, to increase output and to raise the productivity level of the sector.

Contrary to the energy sector and, despite the shortage of iron and steel which created a spiral of frustration throughout industry, the iron and steel industry was not a high priority for the government. Only 3.9 per cent of the Program's imports were reserved for the sector and it was further reduced to 3.5 per cent in the second draft (heading 7). The priority given by the State to unblocking bottlenecks for industrial development meant that, in the years before 1951, domestic steel production was not perceived as a key element for the development of other industries. In fact, the INI's investment in the mining and steel industry was only 5.5 per cent of its total investments from 1942 to 1951, while it was 49.3 per cent in the energy sector.[22]

Shortages of scrap, coal and iron ore prevented Spain's iron and steel industry from working at full capacity. In 1947, output of iron and steel ingots was 87 and 79 per cent respectively of the 1940 levels of output, which were in turn almost 30 per cent below the levels of 1929, the maximum historical level of output. The scrap problem proved intractable. The country's shortage of foreign exchange and world scarcity had pushed down scrap import figures to an almost insignificant level. The shortage of scrap aggravated the outlook for an industry already characterized by the gradual exhaustion of the more easily worked high-grade ore deposits in Vizcaya and coal shortages. A further diversion of Spanish Moroccan ores of high mineral content to local industry would have reduced the country's capacity to earn foreign exchange, which was by far the most important problem facing the Spanish economy. Finally, although the iron and steel industry was receiving more coal than before the war, much of it was poor quality and demanded greater allocations for the same caloric content. Any increase in coal consumption required a decrease in the railways' quota, since economies in consumption were not easily obtainable from other sources. In fact, the pattern of coal consumption shows that only the lowering of the railways' share allowed the iron and steel industry's coal consumption to be increased, at least until mid-1950. There was no prospect of early relief while bottlenecks of all kinds remained and until a way to finance the large equipment purchases could be found.

A lower dependence on coal supply necessarily implied the modernization of the existing productive capacity, which was hampered by the shortage of foreign exchange. A total amount of $6 million was requested to modernize existing iron and steel mills with a total productive capacity of 750 000 tons (heading 7.1). The installation of electric furnaces and a shift from the Siemens-Martin process (still producing 65 per cent of total steel output by 1947) to the Thomas process, together with a larger supply of ferro-alloys would raise productivity by six per cent. Another investment of $20 million was intended for the installation of new plants to increase annual output by 500 000 tons after three years. The only hope for developing output at low cost appeared to be establishing a new steel works in Asturias using low-grade ores and the coal available close by, and speeding up the electrification of the railway network.

The state of transport, railways in particular, had always been perceived as a handicap to economic recovery after the Civil War. In 1941, all the broad-gauge railway companies which could not cope with the reconstruction of their individual network, were *rescued* (expropriated) by the State and grouped together as one system under RENFE, which also operated some of the narrow lines. To complete the recovery of this sector was essential to the program of industrial expansion which the government hoped to be able to carry out. In this sense, the Ministry of Industry assigned a high priority to transport in both drafts, 36 per cent on average. RENFE received the lion's share, 25 per cent (on average) of the total figure of imports and 70 per cent of the sector. As previously, the Import Program combined the more pressing features of earlier investment plans.

In January 1946, Madrid decided to replace rolling stock and locomotives and to undertake the electrification and modernization of the signalling of the whole railway network. A first Five-Year Plan (1946–50) for reconstruction and modernization of RENFE, and the General Plan of Railway Electrification, covered urgent work to 4500 kilometers of track with limited budgets of $137 million and $27.5 million respectively. The funds authorized under earlier plans had, in part, been swallowed by the mounting costs of labor and the rising price of both imported and local materials, notably coal and steel. In the first two post-world war years progress was slow because of three major problems: inadequate supply of high-grade coal, insufficient rolling stock and the state of the track. Again, these three elements could only be satisfactorily solved within a general program of economic modernization.[23]

To overcome the most serious problems of the railways, the Import Program initially planned an investment of $193 million. Proof that the Ministry of Industry was not daydreaming in the drafting of the figures comes from the fact that this figure, reduced in the second draft to $97 million, was far from RENFE's original petition, which amounted to $395.[24] The first draft envisaged $45 million of railway equipment to assist the replacement and rehabilitation of the entire state-owned and operated track network (heading 11). With a time limit of three years, this section of the program was the logical implementation of the first five-year plan approved in 1946. The modernization of the network deserved $10 million. An up-to-date telecommunications system and adequate signalling equipment would be installed on the lines to be electrified and on the existing steam lines, over five and six years respectively (headings 14 and 15). The section concerning the electrification of the network maintained the period of implementation (12 years) and the track affected (4500 kilometers of normal gauge), as announced in previous governmental planning (heading 16). Marshall aid would have allowed investment into the scheme to rise from $27 to $45 million and made State guarantee for RENFE bonds no longer necessary. The rolling stock provisions show how the Program was not aimed at completing Civil War recovery but was an ambitious attempt at modernization.

The second major problem of the railway system, insufficient and inappropriate rolling stock, resulted in a planned investment of $93 million, divided equally between new rolling stock and repairs (headings 12 and 13). The initial planned investment was to allow domestic industry, after two years, to reach the following targets: 20 electric locomotives, 200 metallic passenger carriages, 12 autorails and 10 freight cars, 100 ballast wagons for truck-repair works and 100 000 goods wagons. The construction of electric locomotives bore no relation to the 1930s (Table 4.2). It was the logical consequence of modernization.

TABLE 4.2   BROAD GAUGE ROLLING STOCK, 1936–47

Year	1936	1939	1945	1946	1947	OoS
Steam Locomotives	2800	1837	2705	2712	2689	529
Electric Locomotives	–	–	78	80	79	30
Carriages	4383	1740	2797	2719	2868	539
Goods Wagons	69 222	41 700	72 526*	70 042*	71 085*	5927

Source: *Anuario Estadístico de España* (1948) 734. Situation as recorded on 31 December, except 1 April 1939. Units out of service (OoS) recorded by the British Commercial Counsellor in Madrid, C.G. Pelham, *Economic and Commercial Conditions in Spain* (London, 1951) 155. (*) Including freight cars.

The electrification of a major sector of the network, the increase of electric locomotives and the plans to improve the supply of fuel, were the first signs of the official attempt to reduce dependency upon an inadequate local coal supply. Although the railways obtained 50 per cent more fuel than before the Civil War, this increase was largely counterbalanced by the low-caloric content of domestic coal and the wastefulness of obsolescent and inefficient locomotives. Any contraction of hydraulic power supplies, due to a drought, would divert part of the coal production to coal-fired power stations, strongly limiting the coal quotas for railways. Without the possibility of resuming large-scale imports of high quality coal, in particular British coal which the railways had consumed before 1936, no real relief for the railways could be expected before the electrification of the system.

Two hundred metal passenger carriages were certainly not designed to restore the pre-Civil War figure of output. Post-1939 repairs and new construction resulted in 1947 in a deficit of 1515 passenger cars over 1936. Planned targets alone could alleviate the unpopular situation of overcrowded trains. In 1947 there were 51 million more passengers than in 1935 in 1515 less carriages.[25] Marshall aid was destined to expand those sectors considered top priority, which was not the case for passenger cars. Further recovery would have to be reached by repairing out of service units. The Import Program reserved a high amount of investment to accelerate repairs of existing rolling stock (heading 13); most of it was over-run, with the consequence that repairs constantly increased from 1944 to 1947. The only fundamental solution was the renewal and modernization of a large part of the equipment in addition to an adequate level of normal maintenance. Marshall aid would complement Spain's exchange reserves to import the material required to proceed adequately with the normal renovation of rolling stock and to effect repairs against a background of scarce key materials and shortages of electric power and liquid fuels. In this regard, it should be noticed that deficiencies were not attributable to lack of mechanical ability; Spanish cleverness in maintaining obsolete equipment was high, as was evidenced by the fact that the trains ran at all!

Marshall aid was not aimed at returning to prewar levels but at modernizing basic structures and creating a railway system which could serve the Ministry of Industry's industrialization plans. The target of 100 ballast wagons was in direct relation to the building of new lines, particularly destined to improve access to the coal mines in the north of Spain and to the laying of a double track on many lines. The figure of 100 000 units of goods wagons certainly did not attempt simply to restore the number of broad-gauge goods wagons in service in 1936. The railways had made a rapid recovery from the losses of goods wagons which they had suffered during the Civil War, repairs of which were given an absolute priority over passengers' carriages (Table 4.2). The spectacular increase the industrialization schemes expected to generate in local traffic of goods explains the target set for goods wagons. It is really significant that the forecast figure could not be reached in Spain until 1974. The size of the task compared to the limited resources allowed only slow progress and bequeathed the miserable state of the sector to future generations. Marshall aid, the Ministry of Industry had expected, would have helped it solve the most important deficiencies in the railroad system. It would have ended the unremitting efforts to expedite its rehabilitation and modernization.

Alternative transport means were considered, such as road, air and sea. Road transport was limited to diesel truck and private car production (headings 17 and 18). The poor condition of the road system received no attention. When the Import Program was drafted, the roads suitable for motor transport were, by and large, the same as in 1935, although in worse condition due to shortage of bitumen, again the result of foreign exchange difficulties. The priority went to increasing the number of vehicles in circulation and improving their poor condition. Supplies valued at $24.8 million would allow the domestic industry to produce (after five years, and once shortages of petrol, tires and other parts had been overcome) an annual output target of 16 000 cars. Diesel trucks were to be built, after four years, at an annual rate of 1500 units with an initial investment of $7.5 million. The annual savings which the planned targets would produce in the future were estimated at $30 million, second only to agriculture.

Promotion of local manufacture of vehicles was not expected to result in immediate import savings but to reduce the heavy burden on the balance of payments in the future. Few cars and lorries could be imported during the nine years following the outbreak of the Civil War. In 1946 only 1400 vehicles were imported as compared with the 22 000 units imported in 1935. The 1300 units (mostly passenger vehicles) imported in the first six months of 1947 from the United States entered the country without foreign currency expenditure. This was because an administrative measure adopted in August 1946 allowed the granting of import licenses without any foreign exchange provision (the so-called «sin divisas» licenses). Their purpose was to mobilize any foreign exchange held by Spaniards living either in Spain or abroad. The great bulk of these licenses, freely granted during 1947, their issue being suspended at the beginning of 1948, was for the import of motor vehicles; other goods authorized for imports in this way were essential products, such as foodstuffs, raw materials and certain types of machinery.[26] Moreover, the protection of local manufacture, after its incipient development during the war years, and the country's shortage of foreign exchange, resulted in a marked restriction of imports of motor spares and accessories. Imports related to the automobile sector fell from a prewar figure of 1500 tons a year to a postwar figure of 100 tons. Distributors were no longer allowed to import a full range of spares with the vehicles they brought into the country except where they could not be produced locally in any quantities. The Ministry of Industry faced a situation where imports of motor vehicles, ranked as a comparative luxury, were clearly inadequate compared to requirements. The Import Program revealed the official intention to cover a minimal percentage of what actual demand was thought to be, provided the basic car population was kept reasonably efficient and sufficient foreign exchange made available. Difficult to estimate precisely, the Ministry of Industry placed the initial annual production target at 16 000 passenger cars, which was the number of cars imported in 1935.[27]

The Import Program also wanted to improve civil aviation. It aimed at renewing half of the existing non-transatlantic capacity, obtaining one year's supply of repair parts, and purchasing five transatlantic aircraft. The heavier types of long-range aircraft were capable of earning foreign exchange in voyages to Central and South America and were expected to show a return on the initial investment in two years. An investment of $11.2 million (heading 19) went to the State-owned airlines, «Iberia Líneas Aéreas», founded in 1943, which held the monopoly of regular civil air lines. A further investment of $5 million went to private companies and $4 million to airport equipment, airfield construction, radar, radio, and other items of modern communication equipment. Imports in 1945 and 1946 of aircraft and air transport accessories consisted almost entirely of US passenger aircraft and aircraft parts available to Iberia. Until the fall of 1945, Iberia equipment consisted of 12 obsolete aircraft. In 1946, this equipment was somewhat modernized with the purchase of 15 late-model US planes and four DC-3s, but the need to obtain 100-octane gasoline and repair parts represented a major difficulty in operating the new type of aircraft.[28] Difficulties in obtaining aircraft, fuel, and necessary spare parts, hampered IBERIA's development. In 1947, Spain's dollar shortage had diverted most of the licenses to the United Kingdom, mainly for freight planes or the small touring aircraft required by newly formed charter companies. The existing ban on the sale of military aircraft and equipment of any kind to the Spanish Air Force also affected non-military production. The objective was to restore the United States as principal supplier and Iberia as the leading air company.

Finally, the transport sector required naval equipment for the merchant fleet. Production of ships in Spanish yards had been exceedingly low since the war years. New orders went to the para-state organization «Empresa Nacional Elcano», a subsidiary of the INI, with planned yards at Seville and Barcelona. While the official aspirations of the shipping authorities were to possess a merchant fleet of at least 1.5 million tons gross, at the end of 1946 the fleet consisted of 1193 vessels and of 1 099 807 tons register (excluding ships of under 100 tons), while at the outbreak of the Civil War it consisted of 955 ships of 1 177 357 tons gross register.[29] Efforts to increase output from shipyards had little result, the difficulty in the supply of raw and auxiliary materials being apparently insurmountable. There was a great scarcity of every kind of shipbuilding material, while the situation regarding auxiliaries – pumps, winches and electrical equipment – was particularly difficult. Some of these items could not be produced locally and Spain lacked the foreign exchange to acquire them abroad, while supply difficulties abroad also impeded acquisitions even when exchange was available. An import package of $20 million was foreseen to reduce the construction time of the State plans aiming to expand shipbuilding capacity, which was imposed – as everywhere in Wester Europe – due to the shortage of foreign exchange and the high dollar cost of using American ships. As in the case of military aircraft, the navy could not be considered within the scope of assistance. The Import Program did not include the «Empresa Nacional Bazán, SA», which was also controlled by INI and which became responsible in 1947 for the building of all navy warships.

The Import Program concentrated its resources on the reconstruction and modernization of heavy industry, leaving agriculture outside its basic goals. However, if Spain was to stand on its own two feet in the future it was necessary to increase agricultural production. In 1947 agricultural output was at 94 per cent of the 1935 level.[30] This inadequate recovery is most relevant since agriculture was Spain's most important economic activity, directly employing about 55 per cent of the working population and accounting for one-third of the country's GDP. While, before the Civil War, Spain was entirely self-supporting in all essential foodstuffs, having only to import some wheat when the harvest was extremely poor, it had become a heavy importer due to the stationary level of output after 1939. In 1944–7 Spain produced one million tons less wheat than the average in 1931–5. Taking the extremes of both periods, in 1945 it produced 2.8 million tons less wheat than in 1934.[31]

Foodstuffs (particularly wheat) now weighed heavily on the import bill and the low level of agricultural output affected foreign currency earnings negatively through a fall in exports. Agricultural produce had accounted, on average, for 67 per cent of Spain's exports in 1931–5. It decreased to 53 per cent in 1944–7. Conversely, the percentage of foodstuffs in total imports increased from 17 per cent to 23 per cent. The import bill for agricultural commodities during those same years amounted to an average value of $284.5 million. Imports of foodstuffs, beverages and tobacco increased from $50 million in 1945 to $111 million in 1947.[32] This amount represented three times the figure of annual import savings that the planned output in nitrogenous fertilizers and tractors was to produce. Imports of foodstuffs did not increase further due to restrictions in consumption. Ration books were issued in May 1939 and not abolished until 1952, in particular, for bread and other essential foodstuffs. Black markets satisfied an important part of domestic consumption not covered by imports or officially recorded domestic output. Although production diverted to black markets was not statistically considered, the black market was even larger than the official market. In 1946/48 clandestine wheat accounted for 44 per cent of total wheat sales.[33]

At the time of drafting the Import Program, an expansion of agricultural output was necessary due to an increasing population (0.7 per cent annual growth rate from 1940 to 1950) and for economic stability. The reader should consider that between June and September 1947 bread rations were much reduced due to the small harvests of wheat and other cereal crops and the very slender prospects of adequate imports of cereals. In June first class rations were reduced to 100 grams daily, second class to 150 grams, and third class to 250 grams. Less than two months later, the third class ration, which included the majority of workers except miners who continued to receive 450 grams, was reduced to 150 grams.[34] Even with the reduced rations, imports on about the same scale as in previous campaigns continued to be needed. A bad harvest, such as that of 1945, could brutally aggravate the national economic situation and force a large share of foreign exchange (already reduced by the fall in exports) to be used to buy essential foodstuffs rather than capital goods and raw materials. In other words, the Spanish economy was in a state of permanent instability owing to the poor performance of agriculture. This was incompatible with the modernization efforts of the Ministry of Industry's Import Program.

Agriculture also received attention for import-savings reasons. Eliminating (or at least substantially reducing) imports of agricultural commodities would automatically free foreign exchange to import raw materials and capital goods to continue the industrial effort. It was estimated that the production of chemical fertilizers and tractors would produce 26 per cent of the annual savings which the Program was to achieve after five years (raised to 32 per cent in the second draft). Savings stemming from increased agricultural output were not estimated and agricultural exports, as financiers of economic growth through foreign currency earnings, were of no concern to the Import Program. However, decreased imports and increased exports were important elements in the strategy to generate resources for industrial development.

Agriculture benefited neither from imports nor from investment, despite the official agrarian idealism where peasant farmers embodied national values as against the urban and industrial population.[35] Investment in agriculture was extremely limited until 1952/53. The Ministry of Agriculture's appropriations within the national budget represented 0.8 per cent of the total budget – an insignificant share considering that Spain was basically an agricultural country. On the other hand, 3.8 per cent of total private and public investment reached the countryside between 1942 and 1947. The orientation of the nation's importing capacity toward essentials left no room for imports of capital goods for agriculture. These accounted for 0.8 per cent on average of total imports from 1939 to 1946; in 1947 the percentage increased to 1.09 per cent. It was not possible to substitute tractors for animals as imports since the outbreak of the Civil War had been negligible.

The inaccessability of adequate supplies of chemical fertilizers was considered the main cause for the slow recovery in agricultural output, the fall in productivity levels, and increased dependence upon foreign sources of supplies for certain agricultural products in which Spain had formerly been self-sufficient. Import trade had traditionally satisfied domestic consumption of nitrogenous fertilizers. During the five pre-Civil War years agriculture received imports of 513 000 tons of nitrogenous fertilizers on average per year.

These imports decreased, on average, by 95 000 tons in 1941–5 and by 122 000 tons in the following five years. Local production of superphosphates decreased. With an output capacity of two million tons per year, real output in 1948 was 50 per cent of pre-Civil War levels. Spain previously imported North African phosphates bought from France, as its own production was very small. The interruption of trade relations with France after March 1946 had obliged the use of domestic phosphates of a poorer quality and the importation of phosphates and potash from the United States. Quite apart from constituting a severe strain on Spain's dollar holdings, the substitution of North African phosphates by American potash caused problems in production lines. National production of nitrogen was also very limited and foreign allocations to Spain allowed no relief. The International Emergency Food Council (IEFC) allocated 31 632 tons of N_2 to Spain for the crop year 1947–8, but this, plus domestic production of 3600 tons, still left a deficit of 74 768 tons to cover minimal import requirements in the field.[*] In 1947, some 200 000 tons of phosphate rock imported from Sudan, somewhat larger shipments of Chilean nitrate, which increased to a figure similar to the 1935 level and an exchange of potash for Belgian ammonium sulphate, slightly reduced the deficiency, but there was such shortage that a large and unsatisfied demand for fertilizers remained. Difficulties in supply would continue as long as the world shortage and Spain's purchasing capacity continued unchanged.

Without adequate capital infrastructure Spanish agriculture was heavily dependent upon climatological factors. Rainfall in the second half of the 1940s was not so much lower than in previous years, but given the profile of capital infrastructure, any reduction in waterfall produced an important drop in output levels. Domestic agriculture suffered, furthermore, from intense State intervention which held back the transformation of the countryside. The first Franco government set up the National Wheat Office to control the sale and distribution of wheat and its main by-products. The General Commissariat of Supply and Transport was responsible for marketing many other essential foodstuffs. They were to guarantee prices and buy entire harvests at State regulated prices (initially lower than expected market prices) with the intention of keeping down the price of wheat, expanding output and reducing dependence on foreign supply to a minimum. Peasant resistance to compulsory purchasing of cereals at low prices discouraged production. It favored local consumption and diverted a substantial proportion of production to the more profitable black market. Furthermore, it provoked a shift from the production of cereals and pulses to uncontrolled products which fetched higher prices, such as cotton, tobacco, grass, fruit and vegetables, meat, and eggs.

The Import Program was certainly not designed to change agrarian policy; it limited itself to pointing out the need to improve productivity. From the

Ministry of Industry's viewpoint, modernizing agriculture passed necessarily through increased mechanization, extended use of chemical fertilizers, and the development of the food-processing industry. The institutional effort to boost production of farm machinery and nitrogen fertilizers had taken place since February 1940 when both sectors were declared of national interest according to the Act for Protection and Promotion of New Industries of National Interest of October 1939. Such a declaration however did not provide the firms concerned any special priority in the allocation of foreign exchange for imports.[36] For chemical fertilizers, the National Nitrogen Plan of February 1940 forecast an annual output capacity of 121 355 tons of N_2.[37] Thirty per cent was to be produced at the previously-mentioned four industrial settings of Calvo Sotelo and a further 7.4 per cent by «Sociedad Ibérica de Nitrógeno», with INI participation. During the summer of 1947 the desirability of setting up fertilizer manufacturing industries for currency conservation through import substitution was reaffirmed, which indicates that previous State initiatives had no effect whatever.[38] None of the forecast installations initiated production before the drafting of the Import Program (in fact, not before 1950).

On the other hand, although production of farm equipment is not intensive in high technology and the domestic industry was technically capable of undertaking production on a large scale, output levels were extremely low. The INI firms «Empresa Nacional de Autocamiones SA» and «SA de Construcciones Agrícolas» had plans for the production of 1000 tractors a year by 1951. Such output was more a legal fiction than a real economic target. Actually Spain's production of tractors did not reach a thousand units until 1957.[39] The problem was that the regular supply of raw materials to the sector proved too heavy a burden on the balance of payments, especially when foreign exchange was necessary to import raw materials for heavy industry. Consequently, Spanish agriculture remained hardly mechanized at all since annual imports of tractors were limited to a few hundred units, the consequence of a combination of foreign exchange shortage and world supply difficulties. Reaching none of the targets set previously in the sectors concerned, the Import Program made the commitment to end the traditional backwardness of the country's agriculture.

Activities with a direct contribution to agricultural production (including food processing) received an investment of $50 million, that is nine per cent of the total (headings 1, 2 and 23). In the food processing sector, Spain, it was argued, needed 30 000 tons per year of tin plate for its canned goods industries (fish and vegetable industries), a commodity whose scarcity had imposed limits on the sector. As for nitrogen, the output target was set at 100 000 tons, similar to the target of the 1940 National Plan for Nitrogen. It was estimated, some time later, that 100 kilograms of nitrogenous fertilizers would bring an increase of between 120 to 160 kilograms of wheat per acre.[40] The target was to be reached once the initial industrial installations had received equipment during the following five years. It was calculated to be only 60 per cent of the country's overall needs, set at 166 000 tons per year, capable of producing approximately 775 000 tons per year of by-products. With tractors, the Import Program doubled the 1940 target. Even then, 2000 units were considered to cover only half of the production needed. Annual output targets for the production of nitrogenous fertilizers and farm tractors were to be reached in 1952. The subsequent savings of $35 million would allow the redemption of the credit in one-and-a-half years. The reduced version of the Program did not modify the investment figure (except for food processing), representing thus essential imports for the sector.

The Import Program aimed at modernization, not Civil War recovery, when dealing with agriculture. The output targets set had nothing to do with previous production. The maximum output level of nitrogeneous fertilizers reached in the 20th century was 5100 tons in 1929 and Spain had little productive tradition in farm tractors. Prewar Spanish agriculture was, on the whole, backwards, employing a total of 4000 tractors (or only about one tractor per 5000 hectares of cultivated land), many of which were destroyed during the fighting or had since deteriorated. Increased use of fertilizers and farm machinery were part of public consciousness toward improving farming methods.

The Spanish administration did not request any imports of foodstuffs despite the country's urgent needs. It can be argued that it did not because it expected to boost output and because Argentina was to provide the necessary minimal supply in the interin. In any case, imports of foodstuffs were not to be allowed to sacrifice the possibilities for industrialization and equipment which Marshall aid offered. The various bilateral trade and payments agreements with Argentina guaranteed a certain level of foodstuffs imports on credit during 1948: 300 000 tons of wheat, 110 000 tons of maize plus 40 000 tons remaining from the 120 000 tons of the 1947 quota; 38 000 tons of barley, 20 000 tons of frozen meat, 10 000 tons of bacon and fats, 500 tons of industrial grease, 1000 tons of powdered milk, and beans, salt meat, wool, cotton, fresh eggs, and vegetables.[41] Consequently, the only food commodity requested by the Ministry of Foreign Affairs' Memorandum of 15 November 1947 consisted of 80 000 tons of sugar (apart from the $50 million of goods directed to farm machinery and fertilizer production).

Imports from Argentina were far from covering the needs of the domestic market, but allowed Spanish officials to concentrate eventual American assistance on fostering industrial production. Argentine credits solved food problems for some time, but they did not solve the basic problem of the Spanish economy, technological equipment and capital goods. Trade with Argentina, supposedly the bridgehead of «Hispanidad» was not a substitute for other, more ambitious targets. Commercial relations with Argentina were clearly of a transitory nature: Argentina could be neither a market for Spanish exports nor a supplier of capital goods; it supplied wheat at twice the price of corn and wheat sold to other European countries, taking advantages of Spain's lack of access to low-priced cereals from North America and the favorable purchasing conditions of the International Wheat Agreement.[42] On its side, Argentina received high cost and slow delivery of Spanish manufactured goods. This clearly unbalanced commercial relation was useful in providing temporary economic relief but certainly did not help Spanish industrial modernization. In other words, the Franco-Perón dealings could not be taken as substitutes for Marshall aid.

In the case of the textile industry, where deconcentration was at a maximum, the Ministry of Industry and Commerce, as in the case of agriculture, did not risk direct involvement and the Import Program did not set any precise output targets. It limited itself to setting an import figure for raw materials and equipment to renew the looms. On the one hand, without foreign assistance, it was difficult to give priority to imports of textile machinery, in view of the large quantities of foreign exchange required for imports of hydro-electric machinery and other top-priority needs. On the other hand, the sector's annual cotton requirements (discounting domestic production) were placed at 110 000 tons, against imports of 57 200 tons in 1947. Since the end of the Civil War imports had, on average, only amounted to some 80 per cent of the target import figure. The rise in the cotton price could partially explain Spain's low import capacity: the export value of American cotton rose by 354 per cent between 1938 and January 1947.[43] Local production, in spite of strong public encouragement, was unable to bridge the gap, and was more expensive than imported cotton.

The textile industry was considered one of the few manufacturing industries able to export. The government made strenuous efforts to encourage the export of textiles, using the allocation of raw cotton to force out a given percentage of output. The value of exports of textiles in 1946 tripled their 1945 level, while their foreign currency earnings in 1947 (an increase of £8.3 million over 1946) completely covered the loss involved in traditional export items.[44] It seemed necessary to boost these exports following the recovery of West European purchasing power, when it was perceived that traditional exports had difficulties in expanding due to prices and to a change in international demand. Serious competition on the world market would only take place if Spanish industry could overcome its raw material difficulties with foreign supply. Otherwise, Spanish textile prices would remain high and with the revival of competition in a number of markets, orders would be more difficult to obtain.

Synthetic textile fiber and cellulose accounted for 2.1 per cent of the overall import figure (headings 9 and 10). Previous State intervention in these sectors had little success. The «Sociedad Nacional de Industrias y Aplicaciones de la Celulosa Española» was created in 1941 to produce staple fiber yarn using eucalyptus wood as a raw material, as was «Fabricación Española de Fibras Artificiales SA» – based on the use of straw. Both plants could not start manufacturing cellulose and synthetic fiber until after 1950 when the first supplies and foreign technical cooperation had arrived.[45] The Import Program included $14 million aimed at producing 50 000 tons of cellulose and 10 000 tons of synthetic textile fiber. The important feature of both sectors (and aluminum) was that in one year on average the import savings would cover the value of the initial import bill.

Finally, the Import Program requested $100 million to supply the necessary machine tools and spare parts to produce 25 000 tons of tools and machinery by local manufacturing industry over five years. This constituted a serious obstacle to Spanish economic development. While Germany, Spain's largest prewar supplier, remained unable to deliver, imports came mainly from Switzerland, the United Kingdom, and the United States. After supplying the bulk of the trade in 1945, Switzerland lost much ground during 1947, owing to exchange difficulties and for the same reason imports from the United States also fell away. Consequently, the United Kingdom's share of the trade actually increased. There had also been some imports on a smaller scale from Sweden and Italy. Supplies from all sources, however, did not satisfy more than a small fraction of the potential demand. With the help of Marshall aid, imports would have worked for the modernization of the obsolete industrial equipment. Foreign firms were invited to submit preliminary offers based on the production of all equipment in Spain under license.

*   *   *

The reader's first reaction might be to think of the Import Program exclusively in terms of reducing dependence on foreign supply and increasing self-sufficiency. However, the two main incentives behind the Program, foreign exchange difficulties and economic modernization, were outside any ideological commitment toward autarchy. This Program estimated that future foreign exchange savings, if domestic production reached the planned targets, were to be $134.25 million ($108.25 million in the second draft), which would have covered in five years the cost of the initial investment (Table 4.1, g and h). Reducing the need for imports, which was anticipated to remain far in excess of Spain's capacity to earn foreign exchange, implied making full use of foreign exchange reserves to increase imports aimed at breaking bottlenecks to allow sustained growth. It was to be a spill-over process departing from strategic sectors to future economic development. The full productive capacity of existing plant could not be used due to shortages of raw materials, especially those of foreign origin, and the shortage of spare parts kept machinery idle. There could be no relief for the engineering industry as a whole without technological modernization. Imports could be arranged through bilateral dealings but the volume, which was limited by reduced availability in the international market as well as by Spain's scarcity of foreign exchange, proved insufficient to prevent further decline in operating efficiency. Only limited modernization was possible. There could be no recovery in agricultural or industrial production without the large expansion in imports of essential materials and equipment which was vital for raising productivity. Overcoming bottlenecks as well as increasing output could not be conceived outside modernization.

5 Spain's Limited Financial Resources

When Secretary of State Marshall offered American economic assistance for the reconstruction of Europe, the Spanish economic authorities encountered the utmost difficulty in financing their planned program of imports. The country's reserves were declining, especially rapidly in 1947. The deficit in current account, which was expected to diminish in 1947, increased with a direct negative impact on foreign currency reserves. The postwar export boom, if there had ever been one to speak of, slowed its pace during 1946 and died along the first half of 1947. The Minister of Industry and Commerce described the lack of foreign currency reserves to pay for imports as Spain's 'main problem' in July 1947.[1] The Minister declared the need to increase existing resources threefold so as to enable the reconstruction and modernization of the national economy.

The financial situation in the autumn of 1947 was viewed sceptically by leading officials. It was a situation completely different from a normal seasonal fluctuation. Not taking into account the debt with Argentina, which constituted a credit, Spain's reserves of its main trading currencies had decreased by 96.6 per cent during 1947.[2] By September, and for the first time since 1945, they could not cover authorizations. The corresponding departments suspended import licenses and credit authorizations (except for a limited number of licenses with deferred payment). The IEME had wrongly expected larger earnings of foreign exchange and had granted authorizations at a faster rate than foreign exchange earnings actually permitted. In September, foreign exchange reserves remained at 29 per cent of the value of authorizations and at 16 per cent of total demand (authorizations plus pending requests). Fifteen days later, IEME's exchange stock covered only 11 per cent of the potential import demand to be paid off in the main trading currencies. Spain's reserves of foreign currency had to be multiplied 4.4 times to cover authorizations, 9 times to satisfy demand completely and, splitting the Import Program into four years, 7.4 times to finance the annual import quota of the Ministry of Industry's second draft of minimal import requirements.

The main obstacle to financing the reconstruction program was the dollar shortage. Dollar holdings passed from the position of being the largest reserve at the end of 1944 and 1945, although further reduced, to that of the largest deficit after Swiss francs (compare Tables 3.7 and 5.1). A credit of

TABLE 5.1 SPAIN'S RESERVES OF MAIN TRADING CURRENCIES, AUTUMN 1947

	30 September 1947			Currency		15 October 1947				
Holdings Nat. Curr.	Pesetas	Authorized Credits	Pending Requests		Holdings Nat. Curr.	Pesetas (a)	Authorized Credits (b)	Pending Requests (c)	(a) % (b)	(a) % (b)+(c)
−1 113 890	−12 197 095	70 754 257	139 413 581	Dollar	−2 339 217	−25 614 426	61 791 857	155 498 815	(**)	(**)
3 632 523	159 831 012	271 885 988	100 981 716	Sterling	3 406 927	149 904 788	265 014 860	145 627 944	57	36
3 666 205	11 145 263	34 205 493	34 398 335	Swedish kr.	3 560 204	10 823 020	32 552 763	37 921 397	33	15
−9 469 198	−4 119 101	13 747 847	5 982 156	Escudo	−4 464 730	−1 942 157	14 574 664	13 233 701	51	37
5 344 042	31 048 884	40 123 994	15 979 612	Guilder	5 051 581	29 349 685	57 147 889	21 711 171	36	26
−24 187 826	−61 195 199	11 936 990	62 369 835	Swiss franc*f*	−23 267 239	−58 866 114	11 479 902	67 000 904	(**)	(**)
−23 695 113	−5 923 778	(*)	18 929 065	Belg. franc	−36 306 363	−9 076 591	(*)	24 147 059	–	–
2 211 842	4 895 912	(*)	..	Danish kr.	2 237 198	4 952 038	(*)	..	..	..
123 485 898		442 654 569	359 125 235	Total Europe + $	90 972 865		442 561 935	465 140 991	23	11
..		..	..	Arg. Pesos	−173 528 039	−451 172 901			..	..
128 754 143		442 654 569	378 054 300	Total General	−360 200 036		442 561 935	465 140 991	..	..

Sources: AHBE, IEME, box 3: C/P; 3 and 16 October 1947, respectively. (**) See explanation in text; (*f*) the Swiss francs recorded in September were composed of 7 985 341 free francs and 16 202 485 corresponding to the clearing, while those registered in October corresponded to 7 581 191 and 15 686 048 to both categories, respectively; (*) no authorization of credit without the immediate release of the corresponding amounts was allowed in trade relations with Denmark and Belgium. The Spanish import licensing formalities required that when a license had been granted, an application had to be made through a local bank for authority to open the corresponding credit in the country concerned. Importers of Spanish goods were well advised not to consider an order as firm until the necessary credit had been opened in their respective countries. French francs are not mentioned because they were of no use to import trade.

$3.5 million granted in the summer of 1947 by the Société de Banque Suisse, Geneva, allowed for the deficit. By then, the IEME's dollar reserves amounted to $1.4 million, that is, seven per cent of the credit authorizations granted plus the pending requests to import from the dollar area. Dividing the Import Program's second draft into four years, dollar reserves by October 1947 could only finance 1.2 per cent of the annual rate.[3]

The government of Spain had important non-commercial dollar commitments which further reduced the use of dollar reserves for commodity trade. These related, in particular, to the nationalization of the national telephone company. Although it followed ideological commitments, it was an immediate consequence of the overestimation of future dollar earnings. The positive results of 1941–5 created a small gold stock with which to cancel some commercial and political debts, provide some credits, and allow the nationalization of the telephone company.[4] Unexpected circumstances turned this decision, adopted during more prosperous times, into a heavy burden for all dollar payments. But once the decision to *rescue* the telephone company had been adopted, its payment could not be a matter of discussion: it would have destroyed the Spanish administration's financial reputation.

The unfortunate 1945 harvest and the sudden decision adopted by Argentina to reduce supply made it clear that Madrid had misjudged the burden of the ITT debt. The 1945 wheat harvest – 1.5 million tons less than in 1944 – increased the already high domestic demand for cereals. The reduction of Argentina's supply imposed an increase in dollar imports. Official estimates placed essential wheat imports from North America at 160 000 tons in October and November 1945, at a total cost of $12 million. The need for cash on the nail pushed wheat purchases down to 50 000 tons. On the other hand, ITT received $6.7 million before the end of the year and $2 million of the loan the Spanish government had floated was paid off. If the dollar situation in 1945 was still not perceived as pressing (the annual ITT redemption was much higher than necessary and paid two months in advance), it changed in 1946 so that ITT payment became a serious strain placed on the country's limited dollar resources. The cancellation of some contracts for Spanish manufactured goods to be paid for in dollars after the summer of 1945 reduced dollar earnings while ITT payments ($6.3 million plus $4 million of the loan floated) subsisted. The result was the collapse of the IEME's dollar holdings by the end of 1946 to eight per cent of the 1944 level (Table 3.7). The government had expected the renegotiation of the ITT bond indebtedness to take place before mid-1947 and on favorable terms, which was not the case. By the end of September 1947, the IEME's dollar reserves were already below the annual ITT debt repayment due before the end of the year; the IEME's dollar reserves amounted to $2.1 million while ITT payments amounted to

$2.6 million. Under these circumstances, dollars for trading purposes were reduced to zero and all dollar imports suspended, leaving this currency supporting the largest pent-up demand. Consequently, the IEME Assistant General Director presented the dollar situation as 'disastrous'.[5]

Without special credits of one type or another, imports from the dollar area were to be balanced on virtually a week-to-week basis with exports to the dollar area. Exports to the United States were unpromising (Table 5.2). They dropped after 1945, losing in two years the level gained after the war. In 1947 the effort to maintain a high import level (an increase of 16 per cent of the 1943 values) at a time of rising inflation in the United States resulted in a dollar shortage since exports financed only 70 per cent of imports. In Spain, as in the rest of Europe the deterioration of the terms of trade was partially created by American inflation.[6] The United Nations' Economic Commission for Europe estimated that, in January 1947, American export prices had increased by 243 per cent as regards the 1938 level and by 301 per cent in January 1948, wheat and cotton being above both levels.[7] There was open concern among Spanish authorities about the rise in prices of most import commodities which drastically reduced the import volumes. The reality was that exports to the United States were not sufficient to enable Spain's imports from that country to be resumed on anything like their prewar scale. In 1947, high Spanish export prices combined with high priced American imports to reduce trade between both countries by almost one-half.

TABLE 5.2   SPAIN'S TRADE WITH USA, 1943–7 (in millions of gold pesetas)

Year	Imports	Exports	Balance
1935	147 000	55 900	– 91 100
1943	92 671	77 147	– 15 524
1944	111 835	134 570	+ 22 735
1945	157 549	177 573	+ 20 024
1946	162 195	159 673	– 2522
1947	107 381	75 543	– 31 838

Source: *Anuario Estadístico de España*, 1946–8.

The imbalance in trade commodity composition added desperation to any future improvement. Agricultural commodities accounted for 65 per cent of Spain's exports to the United States in 1946, while cotton, oil, machinery and vehicles accounted for 68 per cent of imports from the United States. Cotton was necessary to provide exports to countries unwilling to expend their scarce dollars purchasing cotton textiles from the United States, while oil, machinery and transport equipment were major economic bottlenecks. Spain was unable to expand exports to the United States, while it could not further reduce its dollar imports if reconstruction was not to be impaired. An expansion of exports to the United States could not be achieved through the restriction of domestic consumption or dumping mechanisms. The government had already attempted both, with little success, when the first signs of a decreasing export trend appeared. At the end of 1945 the Minister of Industry proposed to export 10 000 tons of oil (five per cent of the annual output) to the United States to increase dollar earnings. Given the extremely low level of oil output in 1945 (68.5 per cent of 1944 and 43 per cent of 1935) the measure was to be implemented secretly. Secondly, the subsidies for cork exports were answered by the United State import authorities imposing a charge (40 per cent *ad valorem*) on these same exports since November 1947. The only way to increase dollar earnings lay in a normal pattern of trade based on increased output and productivity which would enable Spanish exporters to sell on the US market.[8]

The second feature of IEME's exchange stock was the leading position of the pound sterling, which had followed a continuous increase since 1944 (Table 3.7). In the autumn of 1947 sterling holdings compensated for 60 per cent of the accumulated deficit of the European currencies plus the dollar deficit. The surplus position of sterling attracted the largest share of import demand: authorizations for sterling purchases accounted for 60 per cent of authorizations in all currencies. The large sterling and much reduced dollar holdings could, in part, be explained by the expectation of sterling convertibility announced for July 1947, under the provisions of the Anglo-American Financial Agreement of July 1946. Spanish and British officials had already agreed in principle, in February 1947, that Spain, as part of the British transferable account area, was to benefit from the announced measure. Transferable accounts were intended to become the basis of a multilateral trade settlements structure in Europe, based on sterling freely transferable among those countries which agreed to accept and hold sterling. The agreement was not signed then because it was felt that it would be embarrassing to give Spain currency spendability ahead of some of the Allied countries.[9] An official agreement, complementary to the monetary agreement of March 1947, was signed in June that year (at the time of the new trade and payments agreement). London wanted to link the Spanish economy to the international economy, or at least to the British economy, and to end its inward-looking character. The agreement, coming into force on 1 July 1947, provided for the free convertibility of the IEME's sterling holdings for current account transactions to residents of countries outside the Spanish monetary area. The prospect of a flexible system of compensation, including conversion into dollars for current transactions, may have provided an incentive for the Spanish authorities to accumulate sterling and to spend dollars beyond prudent limits.

Unfortunately, the convertibility exercise for the pound sterling collapsed in August 1947 after only six weeks. Transferability rights for sterling accounts and the right to automatic convertibility into dollars were suspended. The supplementary agreement providing for the expendability of Spain's current sterling was at first virtually placed in abeyance and then formally abrogated in June 1948. It was the dramatic end of the Spanish dream of benefiting from a multilateral payments scheme. Spain, without ERP membership, could not take part in the First Agreement on Multilateral Monetary Compensation signed in November 1947, coming into effect in January 1948, which covered France, Italy, and the Benelux countries and lasted ten months. The first monetary agreement was of little importance because the volume of settlements made under it was very small. However, it meant the first step toward more ambitious financial agreements, from which Spain was to remain excluded. Spain remained locked in a suffocating bilateral system of payments, which acted as the most effective constraint to trade promotion. The only oxygen came from the British facilities for obtaining import supplies of cotton, rubber, jute and other raw materials from the sterling area and petroleum products from British-controlled sources. This was a device which the British used constantly to improve their commercial bargaining position *vis-à-vis* Spain. Trade relations with the United Kingdom were pivotal in these circumstances, as we shall see in Chapter 7.

Other circumstances concerning some of the main trading currencies should be considered. Most of the inter-bank and commercial credits which fed the deficits shown in Table 5.1 required either immediate repayment or were exhausted. The IEME's reserves of 35.7 million escudos were necessary to cancel the Bank of Portugal's revolving credit facilities of 40 million before the end of the year. A credit of eight million granted by Crédit Suisse, Zurich, allowed for one-third of the deficit in Swiss francs. Although the credit was not to be repaid before the end of June 1948, by mid-October 1947, 96 per cent of the credit was exhausted. On the other hand, Spain had exceeded the swing allowed under the bilateral clearing (a maximum of ten million) by 5.7 million Swiss francs. This caused the Swiss to cancel all payments to Spain and temporarily end bilateral trade. With respect to Belgium, by mid-October Spain had used 71 per cent of the maximum trade deficit allowed by the National Bank of Belgium. Furthermore, it was necessary to hold part of the reserves to pay pending commercial debts. The situation was so critical that even payment of diplomatic personnel was problematic.[10]

In general, export earnings failed to meet official expectations. The authorities had apparently believed that world prices for Spanish products would rise rapidly, at least, during the first half of 1947, that continued world shortages would sustain demand for Spanish products during the same period, and that the improved water power and agricultural situation would result in increased production of consumer goods with a concommitant general decline in domestic prices by mid-1947. Accordingly, devaluation of the peseta could be avoided at least until fall or winter, though subsidies could be granted to a few isolated export commodities. None of these beliefs materialized. While foreign prices continued to rise, demand fell sharply in hard currency countries, and Spain had somewhat less available for export than was apparently anticipated. Competition from other countries was also keener in certain foreign markets.

Spain's invisible earnings were also much reduced. The difference between official and free market rates of exchange diverted the flow of invisible earnings to the black market and to other obscure operations. Despite their constant increase between 1941 and 1946, invisible earnings were way below their past contribution to the balance of payments. Problems with entry visas for visitors and complications over peseta rates did not help tourism to ease balance-of-payments difficulties, as would be the case after the mid-1950s. A preferential tourist rate (approximately 50 per cent above the commercial rate), which was initially limited to the dollar, was extended to other currencies (sterling, Swiss francs, escudos and Argentine pesos) in August 1946. When the restoration of the preferential rate of exchange, suspended in 1942, was discussed, it was feared that the country's poor tourist structure (hotels and transport facilities) would militate against any benefits and would only open a door to illicit foreign currency operations.[11] This was partially avoided by the requirement for travellers entering Spain to exchange officially a certain minimum amount of foreign currency. At the same time, foreign exchange was only granted to Spaniards for travel abroad when the journey was considered to be in the national interest. Income from tourism increased progressively but weakly from 1945 (£811 555) to 1947 (£3 million).

The extension of the preferential rate in August 1946 to capital transfers to Spain by Spaniards and to remittances did not compensate for changing at the official rate rather than on the black market. Remittances increased slightly by £710 396 between 1945 and 1947. The transfer entry in Spain's balance of payments for 1946–7 remained at 30 per cent of its 1931–2 level. The tourist rate served, however, to open the door for pressure groups to request its extension to other financial operations. In December, the application of the preferential rate was extended to cover a variety of other transactions for living expenses, fares payable in foreign currency, travelling and education expenses, private insurance premiums and newspaper subscriptions, but, as far as possible, its application was designed to avoid affecting the amount of foreign currency due to a foreign creditor.[12]

Spanish legislation continued to limit the contribution of foreign capital to capital formation, balance of payments, and productivity. In July 1947 a law reasserted the existing prohibition on foreign holdings of more than 25 per cent in Spanish companies and virtually blocked the transfer of dividends and royalties. This prohibition now affected all companies instead of only manufacturing ones. The amount could be raised to 45 per cent in special circumstances. Any higher percentages could only be authorized by the Council of Ministers, although commercial associations could never surpass ten per cent of foreign capital and in mining no more than 49 per cent. A relaxation of legal dispositions was discussed but the legislation lasted until 1957, to the detriment of foreign investment.

There had also been significant liquidation of foreign overseas assets during the Civil War and the immediate postwar, in particular in Argentina, Switzerland, the United Kingdom, and the United States. Furthermore, restrictions applying in several countries, especially in the United States, did not allow the transfer of benefits. Spanish-owned assets in the United States, amounting to some \$50 to \$60 million, remained blocked by the Truman administration and could not be used as guarantees in obtaining bank credits. After a seven-year freeze, they were released in May 1948 following the conclusion of the *Safehaven* negotiations by which the Spanish government agreed to restore gold identified as Nazi loot.[13] Until then, the Foreign Exchange Institute had serious difficulties in selling gold in various countries, due to its inability to provide guarantees that the gold to be sold had not been acquired directly or indirectly from Axis powers. In any case, the gold assets in the Bank of Spain were equivalent to Pts 1215 million at the end of 1947, one-half those in 1935, and did not cover the deficit in current account. Finally, Spanish borrowing abroad to finance imports was only partially feasible.

It is continuously argued that the Franco regime had an aversion to international financial aid. However, in the summer of 1946, the official credit policy regarded it 'indispensable' to bind 'the largest possible number of foreign interests' to the domestic economy.[14] There was only a limited flow of foreign private credits to Western Europe, and Spain hardly attracted any because of the difficulties it encountered in providing gold as collateral. Besides, foreign private credits were unattractive: they meant short-term profitable investment at high interest rates. As for long-term government loans, only Argentina was a potential creditor. Fresh bilateral financial negotiations were under way in spite of the problems concerning previous credit lines. Argentina accounted for 43.6 per cent of total imports, in particular wheat, in 1947; Spain had, thus, expanded the supply of foodstuffs from Argentina so much that by mid-October 1947, 82 per cent of the credit facilities granted by Argentina in 1946 had been consumed.[15] However, as has already been mentioned, Argentine credits could not be used for industrial purposes. The Swiss, moreover, only accepted profitable financial operations and it was doubtful whether they could grant any large credit for industrial modernization. It was also evident that they were unwilling to deviate from the general pattern adopted regarding Spain. The only country able to do so was Portugal: a major disappointment for Spain. Toward the end of May 1946, Spanish officials endeavored to obtain a loan of approximately 1500 million escudos to be provided (probably) out of the Portuguese blocked sterling balances in London.[16] The final credit facilities granted amounted to 40 million escudos. In such circumstances, there could be no hope of counting on foreign credits to purchase an appreciable proportion of the extra imports required for the rehabilitation of the Spanish economy and productive capacity (Table 5.3).

TABLE 5.3   INTER-BANK CREDITS AND GOVERNMENT LOANS GRANTED TO SPAIN, 1945–7

1945	
Société de Banque Suisse	7.5 million Swiss francs
1946	
Argentine Government	
External Redeemable Loan	400 million pesos
Revolving credit facilities	350 million pesos
Bank of Portugal	
Revolving credit facilities	40 million escudos
Crédit Suisse	8 million Swiss francs
1947	
Société de Banque Suisse	$3.5 million

Source: Own elaboration from IEME files cited in text.

Rumors regarding the possibility of dollar credits to Spanish firms were widespread. It was reported that RENFE and both the International General Electric Company and the Westinghouse Company had agreed to a $15 million credit for imports of materials for the electrification plans, to be amortized over five years. It was also rumored that loans from US firms amounting to between $20 and $40 million for raw cotton supplies were being negotiated. These rumors were grossly exaggerated and did not come to fruition in the short term. IEME officials considered that obtaining American public credits either in direct form or through the ERP was out of the question.[17] Any financial assistance from the United States, the only country able to grant

assistance on a scale large enough for medium-term industrial plans, was politically problematic; American officials, as will be shown in Chapter 6, had
constantly declared that the US government would not grant any credit to
Spain unless a change in its political regime took place. The application for
Marshall aid alone shows that the Franco regime did not have a *sui generis*
aversion to international aid, but that it wanted aid with no political strings attached. Official Spanish policy was to accept credits 'when the credit and investment conditions are economic without mortgaging or injuring other
national interests'.[18] Despite the clear needs of the economy, the Spanish administration would not accept economic and financial assistance if it risked
Franco's political regime. In other words, the Spanish government would
only accept credits free from political conditions.

As far as possible, Spain should rely on its own resources to finance the additional supplies of goods and raw materials required from abroad. Export
trade had generated 75.8 per cent of all foreign currency earnings registered
by the IEME in 1946, while it had been 66.6 per cent in 1945. The prospect of
obtaining either long- or short-term international credit was virtually non-
existent and other non-commercial earnings of foreign currency could provide little relief. Therefore, imports could only be financed by equivalent
exports, which had then to be fully promoted 'to alleviate the precarious foreign exchange position and seeing that in the near future we cannot count
upon any other assistance [the Minister of Industry and Commerce] estimates
that there is no other procedure than to stimulate exports'.[19] Nonetheless, the
salient feature of Spanish trade after 1939 was a decline of about 50 per cent
in volume. The adverse visible balance, so characteristic of the pre-1936
years and masked temporarily by heavy Allied preemptive purchases of wolfram during the war, reappeared in 1946 and continued to deteriorate in 1947
and 1948. Spain's exports could not expand greatly due to the slow recovery
of output and the comparatively high and rising cost of many domestic
goods.*

The decline in agricultural production (the sector accounted for 67 per cent
of pre-Civil War exports) held up any substantial expansion of exports. Without much greater supplies of nitrogenous fertilizers and a wider use of farm
tractors, progress toward larger output was bound to be slow. It could only do
little more than cover the additional consumption needs arising from the increase in population. The contribution of raw materials (chiefly minerals) to
exports, important during the war due to price increases (31 per cent of total
exports in 1940–4), progressively declined from 1944 as a result of the fall in
home production and foreign prices. Iron ore and pyrites, at the time two of
the country's most important basic industries and traditional export sectors,
were producing below the 1935 level, leaving little margin for increasing the

exports in the field. The downward trend of mineral production, with a few notable exceptions, could only be reversed by a rise in productivity levels via equipment. The suspension of trade with Germany and France, after the end of 1944 and the beginning of 1946 respectively, imposed important limits to the degree of recovery of Spanish export trade; before 1936, Germany and France were Spain's second and third largest consumers, taking 25 per cent of total exports. The commodity composition of Spanish export trade, dominated by agricultural produce, reduced the capacity to replace traditional export markets. It was then believed that an effective promotion of exports, following the rise of purchasing power in Europe, went necessarily through a promotion of manufactured goods, in particular textiles, chemicals, and goods from the coal and steel industry. Manufactured goods, headed by textiles, had made a striking advance aided by the keen demand created by world shortages. Compensation for the diminution in traditional exports had partially come from this side. It remained to be seen, however, how Spanish textiles and many other manufactured goods were to fare when price again became a deciding factor on world markets.

The high price of domestic raw materials was a main obstacle to the development of some competitive industries and hampered the sale of the export surpluses. When at the beginning of 1947 the IEME announced that new possibilities to place manufactured goods in foreign markets existed, it requested larger imports of raw materials to keep production prices as low as possible. The first alarm bells rang in the spring/summer of 1946 when the constant decrease in the position of foreign currency reserves revealed the weak potential of Spanish exports. The export expansion expected for 1946 had not taken place. Although the lack of recovery of some traditional markets, in particular Germany, was considered partially responsible, the major obstacle was perceived to come from the inflationary tendency of the domestic market. Discounting rationed commodities, by May 1946 Spain's wholesale prices increased between 200 and 300 per cent compared to 1939. Spain could not hope forever to place high-priced exports on the European markets. Moreover, the highly remunerative prices obtained on the domestic market made exports unattractive. Transitional measures concerning individual commodities (export subsidies combined with import surcharges) could only be considered a prelude to more general measures.[20]

Reports favored reforms to activate trade but a straightforward devaluation was not recommended for fear of inflationary effects. It was also believed that sterling convertibility would have a positive effect on Spain's balance of payments, making unnecessary, or at least postponing, any decision on the matter. The IEME authorities thought price increases affected only a limited range of products. The important decreases that had taken place between 1945 and 1946 in traditional commodities, such as nuts, mercury and iron ore, were not always linked to price effects. Mercury exports decreased as other sources of supply recovered; iron ore exports fell because of local output levels. The fall in exports was balanced by increases in olives, cork, textiles, oranges, wine and the reappearance of tomatoes and bananas. Spanish exports appeared to continue to benefit from the discrimination against hard currency which followed the collapse of the sterling convertibility and the desire to improve diets. Rather than resort to devaluation, the government adopted a variety of corrective expedients. Compensation, combined accounts, *ad hoc* subsidies, and compulsory export quotas (for cotton textiles, olive oil and lead) appeared sufficient to promote exports. A package of these measures was adopted in August 1947.

The compensation system allowed exporters of some industrial commodities which used raw or semi-manufactured goods scarce on the domestic market, to import given quantities of goods free of duty. The system attempted to increase exporters' international competitiveness through imports which were cheaper than domestic supplies. Combined accounts allowed exporters (especially of industrial goods) to retain part of their exchange earnings in order to import goods directly related to their productive activity. The compensators' imports could be authorized up to the value of either 34, 50 or, in exceptional cases, even 100 per cent of the goods exported, the exact percentage being calculated to cover export losses. The condition was that the account gave a general profit never lower than 66 per cent of the total value of exports under the combined operation, 25 per cent of which ought to be in hard currency. The system was originally designed to free exporters and importers from strict dependence upon IEME. The weight exerted by pressure groups, however, turned it into an indirect subsidy to exports. Owing to the differences in domestic and world prices exporters covered any losses incurred as a result of exporting goods below cost by importing certain goods on which to recoup the loss. The system (adopted in several other European countries at the time) has been strongly criticized by most authors. In my opinion, the system itself was essentially sound; it was only the conditions of the domestic market which made it a caricature of itself.

Trade performance in the first half of 1947 was disastrous. The first seven months accounted for 66 per cent of the deficit accumulated since 1945. Although unbalanced trade constituted a traditional feature of Spain's foreign sector, it now appeared dangerous because the reserves of foreign exchange were unable to finance any large deficit. An increasing number of Spanish export commodities, it was said, had reached price levels which, at the official rate of exchange, placed them at a crippling disadvantage on world markets. If, in 1946, only few exportable commodities were significantly affected, in 1947 production costs of some of the major export items rose, making exports increasingly difficult unless prices below cost were accepted. Woolens, it was argued, were offered at prices 60 per cent above world prices; cotton textiles, nuts, onions, lead, wines, canned fish, wolfram, and raisins at 50 per cent; oranges at between 40 and 60 per cent; olives at 40 per cent; and sherry, grapes, brandy, bananas, minerals and cork at between 20 and 30 per cent. During 1947 it was estimated that exports of cotton textiles, wines, cork, rosin and brandy would only reach 60 per cent of the 1946 level. Some citrus fruits, apricots, bananas, canned goods and iron minerals would only reach 50 per cent of the 1946 level, while olives, skins and turpentine would only reach 30 per cent. The only products Spain could beneficially export at international prices were olive oil, tomatoes, potash and iron pyrites. In these circumstances, the different expedients did not give the desired results. They created complications and inequalities of commercial return without building up exports on a firm and permanent basis.

Different sectors within the administration favored devaluation to remedy the situation. For instance, a proposal signed by all the members of the IEME Permanent Committee and presented to the Council of Ministers, via the Minister of Industry, proposed even an 85 per cent devaluation *vis-à-vis* the dollar. There seemed to be no more opportunity for transitional measures. The various subsidies and the measures adopted in August 1946 were considered by the IEME as obstacles to a normal development of trade, 'acceptable only in given circumstances'. They should be abolished as soon as possible. Subsidies could only work efficiently in exceptional circumstances. They had no flexibility to adapt prices to the changing conditions of international markets. Furthermore, a subsidy system extended to most export commodities was unlikely to be able to raise enough money and ran the risk of general retaliation. The chief commodities to which subsidies applied were cork and almonds. The subsidy funds derived largely from an *ad valorem* surcharge of 30 per cent and, in a few cases, 70 per cent, on imports of machinery. Generally speaking, the Spanish authorities were reluctant to subsidize exports directly and preferred, whenever possible, to resort to the indirect subsidy under a combined account operation.[21] Combined accounts, however, did not produce the expected results due to the permanent lack of supply in the internal market. The trading system adopted in the summer of 1946 neither promoted exports nor gave satisfaction to the internal market. It increased import prices, accelerated the inflation rate and gave rise to speculative financial operations which weakened the peseta on the international exchange markets. Straightforward devaluation might well have been the more sensible option.

Devaluation would certainly have helped exports in the long term. The problem, however, was to determine its short-term effects on the supply side and the domestic capacity to finance the immediate commercial deficit. Pent-up demand would ensure a high level of imports, and their higher price (because of the lack of reserves) would immediately raise the import bill. This, it was feared, would speed up the inflationary tendency of the internal market, which would soon reduce the price advantage gained by exporters from devaluation. Conversely, the Spanish economy was starved of imports and further import restrictions (even if temporary) were not feasible if the population were to be fed and collapse avoided. The supply of the domestic market in the short-term (even on a day-by-day basis) remained by far the most important concern: an economy characterized by a conglomeration of bottlenecks could not forego any temporary diminution of imports.

Without any substantial foreign assistance and, in the absence of hard currency reserves to finance minimal import requirements, to follow the suggested 85 per cent devaluation meant that Spanish 1946 exports had to expand by 243 per cent. Could Spanish exports expand sufficiently to cover the import bill? A general stagnation in traditional exports set in after the first three months of the year. International demand was perceived as increasing the pressure on the import of capital goods. Results at the end of the year (regarding foreign exchange earnings exclusively) confirmed this (Table 5.4).

TABLE 5.4   EARNINGS OF FOREIGN EXCHANGE BY EXPORT COMMODITY GROUPS, 1946–7 (in pesetas)

	1946	%	1947	%
Agricultural commodities	31 623 527	70	32 413 665	57
Raw materials	4 381 592	10	7 707 112	14
Manufactured goods	9 240 219	20	16 258 802	29
of which textiles	2 474 093	5	11 245 573	20

Source: AHBE, IEME, box 7: IEME's annual report for 1947.

Spain's imports could be broken down into about 800 industrial and manufactured goods, most of them indispensable to domestic industry. These imports needed to be financed by exports of perishable foodstuffs (mainly fruits, wine, alcoholic beverages and olive oil). Government officials had little hope that lower-priced exports, more than 50 per cent of which were non-essentials, would increase in the short-term. Most European countries had fostered domestic production, imposed import restrictions and distorted trade in agricultural commodities, which affected semi-luxuries such as lemons, preserved vegetables, sherry and grapes. Decreasing international demand for agricultural commodities prevented expansion of Spain's main export category; as a consequence, export returns diminished. With agricultural exports facing difficulties, once postwar Europe's immediate relief needs had passed, the export of industrial products seemed to offer the only way of achieving the supplies required. The structural modification of Spain's export commodity composition was a long-term undertaking. Devaluation and the resulting higher-priced supply of raw materials, it was feared, would have a direct negative effect on what appeared the most dynamic export sector – manufactured goods (mostly textiles). Until the national economy overcame specific import bottlenecks, thereby increasing productivity, there was no solution to Spain's export problems. The attempt to boost exports without reducing imports through devaluation appeared too drastic an option and was rejected in November 1947 by the Cabinet which, in turn, proposed a deflationary policy. The National Federation of Importers and Exporters agreed that devaluation was not the best way out; they preferred an extension of the combined accounts as a corrective measure of the exchange rate. Special powers were taken by the government to promote exports of national interest by exceptional measures, compulsion included.[22]

The Import Program was the Ministry of Industry's response to supply-side inflation. It was believed at the time that inflation was caused by the scarcity of consumer goods and the inability of crippled industrial plant to turn out the necessary quantities of goods. It was also partly caused by the lack of foreign assistance which forced the Spanish authorities to choose an inflationary path to recovery. The shortage of foreign exchange produced a shortage of raw materials, obliging manufactures to use expensive and frequently inadequate local substitutes and to meet demand by recourse to the exorbitant prices of the black market, thus inflating costs. Shortage of equipment resulted in continued re-use of obsolescent machinery which raised the cost of manufactured goods. The Import Program aimed at the regeneration of industrial plant through foreign assistance. It wanted to develop an industrial plan capable of assuring the mass-production of consumer goods. Any other action on the demand side, the end to large and persistent government deficits, fiscal reforms, rigorous enforcement of direct controls, price–wages pauses and the reduction of military expenditure, fell outside the Ministry of Industry's responsibility.

Short-term inflation was not, however, the primary objective of the Import Program. The targets selected to remove bottlenecks would add pressure to short-term inflation and the program was not designed to supply consumer goods to the economy but basic goods to heavy industry. The program of extensive railway electrification at a time of scarce capital, electrical equipment, and power could not be conceived as anti-inflationary. It might be for this reason that the Ministry of Foreign Affairs requested $600 million of interim aid to import consumer and capital goods in addition to the $451 million of the Import Program's second draft.[23] Despite the fact that the Ministry of Industry had previously felt that a cut of almost $225 million was necessary from the first to the second drafts, the Ministry of Foreign Affairs unilaterally increased the import bill to $1051 million, that is, $375 million over what the Ministry of Industry had already considered difficult to obtain.

Some thought was given in Washington to the profile of US assistance in the event of Franco being replaced by a democratic regime in accordance with the provisions of the Tripartite Declaration of March 1946. This aid program, which to my knowledge never went beyond a preliminary form, did not differ much from the Spanish version, not even on the amounts. While the Spaniards had requested a maximum $1051 million (of which $600 for immediate assistance) for a period of five years, the aid program for Spain drafted by the intelligence services of the State Department projected a $900 million aid package for three years of relief and reconstruction (Table 5.5). As in the case of the Spanish administration, the report by the Office of Intelligence Research (OIR) conceived immediate and long-term assistance working in line with the general European recovery plan.

Supplies of critically short raw materials (particularly fertilizers, raw cotton, petroleum, and coal), foodstuffs (mainly cereals), vehicles and other consumer and capital goods were considered necessary before the long-range program could bear its first fruits. This was the preliminary stage of emergency relief to assist a distressed population and to avoid the chaos from which disciplined Communist forces would take full advantage. At a second level, economic assistance would aim to restore production and consumption to at least the levels of 1935. Although these levels placed Spain among the poorest countries in Western Europe, Spain was far from reaching 1935 levels of output. Again, any restoration to 1935 levels was totally insufficient unless achieved on a per capita basis, since the population of Spain was to increase by about 15 per cent by 1950 as compared with 1935. Therefore, Washington, as the Spanish administration had suggested with its Import Program, considered economic assistance of a more fundamental character: long-term plans designed to modernize and expand domestic industries and to introduce modern agricultural methods. Although no clear distinction can ever be drawn between aid designated for immediate relief and assistance intended for rehabilitation purposes, the OIR Report of a US aid program for Spain clearly presents the three consecutive stages of economic reconstruction assumed by most governments of Western Europe after the war: emergency relief, restoration of prewar levels of output, and economic modernization. While the Spanish Import Program was centred on the second and third stages, the preliminary views of the intelligence services dealt exclusively with the emergency and restoration programs, leaving the third stage open to discussion within the overall negotiations for the ERP.

The State Department's $900 million was to address Spain's balance-of-payments difficulties. The US projected an import program of about $700 million a year over three years which represented annual imports in terms of 1935 quantities, plus extraordinary imports of wheat and coal, at 1947 prices. It was assumed that during the first year of aid merchandise exports would maintain the 1945 level at about $300 million (quite favorable if compared with 1946). During the following two years Spanish exports should increase slightly because all efforts were to be devoted to capital formation rather than to the production of export goods. Two-thirds of the net services considered as receipts were estimated to come from emigrant remittances, the remaining from shipping and tourists. It was expected that during the fourth year the balance-of-payments deficit, reduced to some $75 million, could be met by foreign investment in Spain as well as loans from the World Bank and from the International Monetary Fund.[24]

TABLE 5.5   **ESTIMATES OF SPAIN'S BALANCE OF PAYMENTS ON THE BASIS OF HYPOTHETICAL US ASSISTANCE**
(in millions of dollars at 1947 prices)

	Payments		Receipts			Estimated Loans or Grants Required
	Required Imports	Exports	Net Services	Use of Existing Credits	Total	
1st year	700	300	–	40*	340	360
2nd year	700	350	30		380	320
3rd year	700	430	50		480	220
						900
4th year	700	550	75		625	75

Source: NARA, RG 59, Department of State, Division of Research for Europe, Office of Intelligence Research, 'Considerations Relating to a US Aid Program for Spain. Preliminary Version', OIR Report No. 4405 (PV), 19 June 1947. Import values based on declared values at point of entrance in Spain. (*) Estimated balance of the credit extended by Argentina to Spain in April 1948.

The financial situation this section has tried to show – the unfavorable relation between resources and import needs – was paradoxically a transitional as well as a permanent situation of crisis. The need to halt imports was a temporary expedient and not the signal that the country was on the edge of collapse.

As the new year of 1948 started, new commercial credits became available. The paucity of exchange reserves during 1947 was provoked by the exhaustion of the commercial facilities allowed by the bilateral trade and payments agreements in the drive for higher output. Credit authorizations were suspended for good commercial reasons. Had they not been, Spain would have been deprived of its only solid base for trading relations: 'crédito de buenos y puntuales pagaderos'.[25] During the second half of 1947 imports climbed to a maximum, while exports showed a progressive incapacity to finance them. The difficult payments position in current account of 1946 became very disturbing during 1947. The Spanish administration did not request Marshall aid to rescue a country on the edge of collapse but to help it to get the dollars they needed for modernization and development.

In January 1948 a commission was set up to allocate the foreign exchange available for imports. The total resources available for the first half of the year were calculated to reach Pts 2071 million. This figure was the result of commercial credits granted through bilateral trade dealings, a few inter-bank credits, plus an estimate of export earnings. The Commission reserved the necessary money to purchase commodities under State trade (tobacco and petroleum products) and to cover the State's financial payments abroad. Both categories amounted to 20 per cent of resources. The Commission also reserved a special fund (the so-called *incidentals'* account), amounting to a further 10 per cent of the total. The Commission, after reducing the total amount of foreign exchange available by 30 per cent, distributed the remaining Pts 1500 million over six categories of essential imports (Table 5.6). Annual provisions doubled the amounts available with a very similar allocation by categories. Exchange resources for 1948 represented 40 and 60 per cent of the amount of imports required by the Import Program's first and second drafts, respectively. Exchange resources for 1948 were 160 per cent and 240 per cent of the annual import requirements of the first and second drafts respectively. However, several further qualifications seem immediately necessary.

The Import Program focussed all financial resources on raw materials and capital goods, while the Commission now had to allocate 41.4 per cent of the available resources to purchase agricultural commodities. Discounting them, the resources available for 1948 amounted to 90 per cent and 137 per cent of the total annual amount of the first and second drafts respectively. Another important consideration is that the Import Program represented investment additional to the normal trade pattern. Normal trade allocations could finance partially the Import Program. Transport and fertilizers received similar annual allocations: $32.5 million and $29.5 (chemicals) while the Import Program allocated $36.7 million and $10 million (exclusively to fertilizers) respectively. Basic industries, however, received only $9.2 million, whereas

TABLE 5.6   ALLOCATION OF FOREIGN EXCHANGE RESOURCES FOR THE FIRST HALF OF 1948 (in millions of dollars)

Categories	Quota	%
Transport	15.6	11.7
Canary Islands#	4.8	3.6
Agricultural Commodities	55.4	41.4
Chemicals and Fertilizers	14.1	10.5
Textile fiber, paper pulp, wood and dyestuffs	34.6	25.9
Metals, oils, coal, scrap, electric material	9.3	6.9
Total	133.8*	100

Source: AHBE, IEME, box 117 bis: 'Memorandum relativo al plan de distribución del contingente de divisas para el primer semestre de 1948', 30 January 1948. (*) Out of a total figure of $137 million (#) The Ministry of Industry and Commerce allocated exchange for imports into the Islands.

the Import Program had forecast $47.4 million for them, and tractors as well as machine tools disappeared from priority purchasing. And while the Import Program had assumed massive dollar assistance, the allocation Committee had to face the problem of inconvertible currencies (Table 5.7).

TABLE 5.7   SPAIN'S EARNINGS BY MONETARY AREAS OF ORIGIN, PROVISIONS FOR THE FIRST HALF OF 1948 (in percentage over total earnings)

Pound sterling	31.25
Argentine peso	30.40
Dollar	18.60
Dutch guilder	4.95
Pesetas	3.44
Belgian franc	3.20
Swedish kroner	2.40
Swiss franc	2.00
Danish kroner	1.30
Escudos	1.20
Norwegian kroner	0.53
French franc	0.40
Chilean dollar	0.06
Italian lira	0.05
Moroccan franc	0.02
Total	100

Source: See Table 5.6.

The breakdown of Spain's earnings by monetary area provides a bleak picture of Spanish room for manoeuvre in January 1948. Import requirements were to be distributed by countries exclusively according to currency holdings. Purchases in Argentina of non-capital goods corresponded to 30.4 per cent of total earnings. Only 58 per cent of dollar resources could be used for commodity trade, the rest being necessary to pay financial debts.[26] The sterling area provided greater relief, since only 18 per cent was to be reserved for non-commercial purposes. The amounts of the various kinds of foreign exchange held at any given moment had the greatest influence on Spanish import licensing policy. Licenses were granted for a certain commodity from one country and refused for the same commodity from another, which in some cases even offered better qualities or prices, because Spain was then much shorter of the currency of the latter country than that of the first. Prices meant less than the currency in which the commodity had to be paid. The financial limits of bilateralism, as we will see in Chapter 8, constituted the principal obstacle to any substantial expansion of trade. Spain's exclusion from the European Payments Union represented the most disturbing feature of the country's future relations with the different institutionalized forms of economic interdependence; this exclusion meant depriving Spain of the benefits of a system in which surpluses and deficits were balanced for each country with the whole group of trading partners, rather than with each partner separately. Spain's clearing system could be maintained as long as desired but it could not avoid a constant shortage of foreign exchange and a reduction in trade volumes.

*　*　*

The permanent weakness of the situation so far described – limited financial resources to undertake modernization attempts – meant that the Spanish economy could not stage major recovery on the basis of its own resources. Foreign trade could only provide the basis for long-term economic transformation, a slow process which implied a potential widening of the gap with more industrialized economies. Within a bilateral trading framework, Spain, as any other country in Western Europe, was forced to purchase non-essentials to obtain the quantities and qualities of essentials from a given country. In the drive to expand imports of essentials, token imports were imported at a higher quantity than the import authorities would have allowed. Conversely, the intrinsic aim of bilateral trade agreements – equilibrium in payments between two countries – meant that once a country surpassed the margin of permissible debt any further imports would have to be paid for in gold or hard currency. Spain's foreign exchange stringency meant that once the always limited commercial credit granted by a given country had been exceeded, imports from that country would have to stop. One of the factors which explains the importance of Spain's commercial relations with the United Kingdom is that the British authorities, in the face of Spain's failure to fulfil its undertakings on the so-called non-essentials, did not implement any retaliatory measure which would have reduced bilateral trade. Foreign exchange earned by exports increased too slowly to serve as a stable basis for economic modernization and growth. In 1947, for instance, they only grew by £7.6 million over 1946. Credits from Argentina added some £23 million as extraordinary resources. They could keep the economy running day by day, with recurrent stop–go measures provoked by specific bottlenecks, such as the shortage of energy supply and the inadequate transport system, which required larger investments than the Spaniards could undertake with unaided resources. Growth would have to keep pace with structural bottlenecks. So progress was being made, and there were signs that, in general, the modest advance was to continue, except perhaps with respect to the development of dollar earnings which suffered most from non-competitive prices. The important point, from a historical perspective, was that progress was necessarily slower from a comparative perspective. A higher industrialization rate could not be achieved in the absence of new machinery and raw materials from abroad.

6 Was there an Alternative Course of Action?

Spain's first official reaction to its exclusion from the European discussions on Marshall's offer was one of pride and feigned ignorance. It was 'with discretion and sense of touch and speaking on own account' that the Chargé d'Affaires in Washington was instructed to say the following: Spain, always ready for peaceful international collaboration, was less in need of aid than the rest of Europe. It would not accept Marshall aid if it conflicted with its national dignity and sovereignty. Spain had requested nothing and only aimed to be left in peace to continue its path toward 'national unity and political perfection' (sic).[1] The Spanish government would only join the European Conference for Economic Cooperation (the so-called Paris Conference, July 1947) if officially invited, and, should it join the Conference, it would only collaborate in economic matters without assuming any political compromise. The government soon changed its attitude.

THE INITIAL STRUGGLE FOR ERP MEMBERSHIP

Once the Spanish government had officially made it clear that it would not beg for dollars, the Ministry of Foreign Affairs started to beg for them unofficially. Spanish diplomacy was, however, very ineffective in the initial phase of the Marshall Plan. Apart from Portugal, which was very reticent to accept the need for aid in any case, Europeans turned a deaf ear to Spanish complaints. The American response was that Washington had voluntarily excluded itself from the meeting of the 16 future ERP members so as not to influence the deliberations; it could therefore do nothing to modify their course. It was up to Spain to improve its image in Europe if it wanted to obtain something from ERP arrangements.

After the Committee of European Economic Cooperation (CEEC) presented its general report for discussion in Washington, Spain launched a diplomatic offensive. After the first fruitless initiatives, Madrid outlined a basic array of arguments to convince the Americans of the benefits to be derived from Spanish membership. Madrid felt that a direct dialogue with the United States would have more probability of success than either with France and Great Britain or with the 16 nations as a whole. In their over-optimistic interpretation of US intentions, the Spanish government believed that once the Americans were convinced, they could make Western Europe comply.[2]

The advantages of joining the Marshall Plan were obvious. Any international relief allowing Spain to confront its economic backwardness was welcome. The effect of ERP aid on an economy structurally short of hard currencies and financing essential supplies of capital goods and raw materials against a background of world shortage, would not have been negligible. In political terms, ERP membership would have represented Spain's official return to international politics. Madrid deliberately presented the Marshall Plan in purely economic terms. Political arguments for membership would have found little support. It was more than convenient to present the Marshall Plan as a technical matter dealing with commercial policy; being a piece of planning about finances and trade, with no other ultimate goals, there was no reason to exclude Spain. This country had satisfied all its financial obligations, granted important credits to some of the participants, yet had never received assistance from the United States. Franco declared that this was a valuable record: 'It seems better business to give credits to those who will not pay them, than to provide normal credits to good creditors.'[3] The Minister of Foreign Affairs also argued that there was no reason to deprive European recovery of Spain's contribution. Clearly, on the basis of indigenous wealth and resources alone, it would necessarily be a very limited one: initially mineral raw materials, fruit and vegetables, wine, and textiles (Table 6.1), but according to the authorities, once the minimal import requirements reflected in the Import Program had been satisfied, the Spanish economy could increase twofold and even threefold many of its exports, thereby providing an 'essential' (sic) contribution to the economic recovery of Europe.[4]

This reasoning represented a mirror image of Spanish post-1945 trading experience. The miscalculation was to believe that western policy-makers would think Spain's contribution was just as important as it had been in previous years. The Spaniards were loath to admit that circumstances had changed substantially. The immediate postwar system of bilateral trade and payments was based on the reduction of dollar purchases to a minimum and the greatest possible diversion of supply sources. Spanish exports could not be considered as dollar-savings when the Marshall Plan was about to pour dollars into Europe. Spanish exports remained high-priced commodities at a time when a recovery in output was finally coming to international trade. Most important, was it necessary to include Spain in the ERP simply to obtain 27 000 tons of onions or one million tons of iron ore? What, therefore, explains the network of bilateral trade agreements constructed with Spain after 1945? The Allied declarations and the UN resolution of December 1946 did not forbid economic relations with Spain and all West European countries, except France after March 1946, traded with Spain. Whatever the importance of Spanish export commodities to European economic recovery and welfare was, they could be channelled through bilateral trade. Bilateral trade was a form of collaboration which international public opinion did not consider as a favorable sign toward the Franco regime but as a source of welfare for the receiving countries.[5]

TABLE 6.1   SPAIN'S POTENTIAL CONTRIBUTION TO EUROPE'S RECOVERY, EXPORT PERIOD 1947–8
(in thousands of metric tons)

Iron ore	1000	Hazel nuts	7
Pyrites	1000	Onions	27
Lead	10	Salted anchovies	3
Wolfram	3	Tinned Fish	7
Mercury	(*)	Paprika	2.3
Potassium chloride	50	Tomatoes	125
Rosin	15	Lemons	20
Turpentine	7	Mandarins	25
Cork	83	Oranges	618
Skins	3	Bananas¶	18
Salt	1000	Grapes	8
Olive Oil	40	Brandies**	4000
Olives¶	42	Wine**	26 500
Dried apricots	3	Cotton fabrics#	110 000
Apricot pulp¶	3.5	Wool fabrics#	11 000
Almonds	20	Rayon#	16 300

Source: MAE, Leg. 2309, exp. 2: 'Spain Must Cooperate'. (*) 'Preponderant share of west European consumption'; (¶) Different figures in ibid., 'Memorandum': 22 000 tons for olives, 3000 tons for apricot pulp, and 15 000 tons for bananas; (**) in '000 gallons; (#) in '000 yards.

Spanish propaganda constantly underlined the Marshall Plan's strong anti-communist slant and portrayed Franco as the only successful fighter against Communism. Ostracism of Spain was explained as the lasting enmity of countries with Marxist-influenced governments. Accordingly, the Franco-British Note of 3 July 1947 was the result of 'violent reaction by the Soviets and leftist press' to Spain's possible inclusion.[6] The authorities continuously declared that fifth columns were marching all over Europe. In a world of anti-communist hysteria, Spain was presented as a bulwark against Communism. Whereas France and Italy were politically vulnerable, only the violent downfall of Franco could lead to communist influence in Spain, the Central Intelligence Agency reported.[7]

Franco also argued that Spain's strategic position imposed some understanding between Spain and the United States.[8] This argument has been taken for granted by most scholars. Strategic values, however, change as the perception of the enemy and of the means of fighting it change. At the time, there was no military threat that required any specific strategic disposition toward Spain. The Soviet Union had started to demobilize its armies as early as June 1945. Between the summer of 1947 and the spring of 1948, when Spain's inclusion in the ERP was being discussed, the Russian threat was limited to Eastern Europe and the Balkans. Moreover, the United States had the atomic bomb, which the Soviet Union was thought incapable of producing for some time yet. US military interest in Spain's strategic value was consequently low. The Joint Chiefs of Staff compiled a list of candidate nations for aid based on their importance to national security and the urgency of their needs. Spain came after the United Kingdom, France, Germany, Italy, Greece, Turkey, Austria, Japan, the Benelux countries, and Latin America. Spain was strategically desirable, but not essential.[9]

As for the defense of Western Europe, the US military gave a very low rating to Spain's potential contribution in the event of war, even though it was bound to come in on the side of the West. The Director General of Foreign Policy at the Ministry of Foreign Affairs, José Sebastián de Erice, explained to the US Chargé d'Affaires, Paul T. Culbertson, that in the event of a war with the Soviet Union 'there could be no question as to [the] eventual position of Spain, although the general weakness of the country and its ill-equipped army could force a neutral status or a very limited intervention'.[10] The regime's high echelons and Franco himself had made similar declarations. Although the real value of such commitment was more than doubtful. Washington believed that hostility between Spain and the USSR was so intense that Spain could not hope to remain neutral in an East–West conflict.

Unfortunately for the Franco regime, the means selected by the Truman administration to combat the Soviet Union and the spread of Communism were political and economic, rather than military. The ERP was designed precisely to provide political stability through accelerated economic recovery. Europe required economic, political and military stability. The latter was not pressing, while Spain was not only unnecessary for the economic and political stability of Western Europe but even disturbing, as the UN debates had shown. Spain's anti-Communism embarrassed the Truman administration and put the future of its policy toward Europe at risk. The downfall of the Czechoslovak government, the only democratic government left in Eastern Europe, helped to feed Communist hysteria all over Europe and on Capitol Hill. On 30 March 1948, at the annual congressional debate and approval of ERP funds, the Republican Representative of Wisconsin, Alvin E. O'Konski, succeeded in having the House of Representatives approve an amendment to allow Spain to receive similar treatment to the other West European countries through Marshall aid. 'Let us include the country that is the most anti-Communist of any country in Europe at the present time', he declared.[11] The so-called O'Konski amendment consisted in including Spain under Title I, 'European Cooperation Act', section 3, 'Participating countries', of the Foreign Assistance Act of 1948.

Spain received the O'Konski amendment, on the anniversary of Franco's military victory, with delirium. Franco had been finally understood, the press commented. Minister of Foreign Affairs Artajo, who had been prudent not to make declarations to diplomatic representatives, asked for a general mobilization to request ERP membership. He was aware that O'Konski had opted for the most difficult of existing alternatives. Artajo had requested that the Chargé d'Affaires in Washington urge friends on Capitol Hill to propose a general reference regarding ERP membership instead of naming the European countries which would benefit from aid.[12] This more elastic formula might have allowed the subsequent incorporation of Spain. The O'Konski amendment, as Artajo feared, had a boomerang effect. The inclusion of Franco's Spain in the ERP was grist to the Soviet mill in its declarations on the true character of American economic involvement in Europe. It led the President and the State Department to restate their opposition to Franco, ending the apparent thaw in relations.

In January 1948, Marshall replied to a question before the Foreign Affairs Commission of the Congress by saying that 'there is nothing in the bill that prevents [Spain's equal treatment]' but it was up to the European nations to take the initiative. Again, at a press conference held in February, the Secretary of State expressed the view that there was no US objection to Spain joining the ERP, as long as the 16 ERP nations agreed. Marshall's declarations provoked a strong reaction from the British trade unions and Bevin asked Marshall in future to avoid any similar declaration if he did not want to put the ERP at risk in its most delicate phase.[13] The vote at the House of Representatives, bringing the question out into the open, ended any ambiguity on the matter. This episode, which has attracted the attention of most scholars in the field, is presented as representing the division between the State Department and the President, on the one hand, and strong anti-communists and military men, on the other hand. Not exclusively.

The O'Konski amendment showed that many in Washington understood the Marshall Plan as an anti-communist device and revealed that many were not only convinced but desirous of seeing Spain's international rehabilitation. This remained in the bag of wishes. The President and the State Department were perfectly aware that it endangered the delicate equilibrium reached by the 16 West European nations in eight weeks of meetings regarding four years of planning ahead. It was obvious that the amendment to the

Economic Cooperation Act making Spain eligible to take part in the ERP could not be agreed by the participating nations and it could not, certainly, be imposed upon them by the US Congress. The prolonged build-up of emotional thinking on the question of Franco Spain could not so easily be wiped away.

The political implications of the Spanish issue in Europe were uncertain. The British government had made it crystal clear that it was politically impossible for them to cooperate with Spain within the ERP. There was no need for a new clash with the Trade Union Congress and the Labour Party when there was nothing to gain and so much to lose. Hector McNeil, British Minister of State for Foreign Affairs, speaking in the House of Commons, declared that it had never occurred to Britain that Spain could form part of a Western European Union as long as it maintained a totalitarian regime.[14] A Memorandum by the British Labour Party on European Cooperation within the framework of the Recovery Program, 28 February 1948, declared that 'Spain cannot participate in the work of cooperative unity until its people are freed from the Franco regime'.[15] Bevin informed Marshall that the decision of the House of Representatives 'seems to make the whole Marshall Plan appear as a lineup behind Fascism and Reaction'.[16] Franco Spain was thus seen as undermining western democracy, the ERP, and the consolidation of a democratic front.

The French Cabinet had decided, shortly before the O'Konski amendment, on a gradual resolution of its main conflict with Spain which would not allow Franco to claim a significant diplomatic victory. The two governments agreed to the progressive opening of the border in February 1948 for passengers and postal communications, and for mercantile traffic in March. Immediately after the reopening, Paris negotiated a trade agreement with Madrid. Support for the inclusion of Spain in the ERP was too great a concession for the French to make to the Franco regime in the name of realism. Any amelioration of relations would come about not through the ERP, a highly political issue, but exclusively through the promotion of trade, an area which made far less impact on public opinion.

The other participating countries left the British and French to solve the question. The support the Spaniards received from ERP members was lukewarm.[17] Although Madrid believed 11 countries would have supported the Spanish request, no delegation accepted the invitation to discuss the incorporation of Spain presented by Portugal's representative at the CEEC's meeting of 16 March.[18] Bevin and Bidault convinced Minister Caeiro da Matta that while Spain was a cornerstone of the community of nations it was not convenient to suggest it publicly; it was preferable for Spain to send an observer and to let the working parties consider the possibility of importing pyrites and iron ore.[19] Franco himself refused to send observers.[20]

The joint session of the Senate and House of Representatives, meeting to produce the final text of the Foreign Assistance Act, on 1 April, rejected the O'Konski proposal in accordance with the State Department and President Truman. The latter had publicly declared himself utterly opposed to making Spain eligible for ERP aid. For the President, the decision was simple: Western Europe was more important to the United States than Spain, and Spain was more important to Western Europe than to the United States. European governments wanted a speedy solution to the question. Apart from this, the President did not need pressing. According to his life-long friend Acheson, 'Truman held deep-seated convictions on many subjects, among them, for instance, a dislike of Franco and Catholic obscurantism in Spain'.[21] Thus Truman signed the Foreign Assistance Act on 3 April without the Spanish clause. For his part, Marshall reassured Bevin of the US government's view that it was for the European countries setting up the OEEC to decide whether or not to include Spain.[22] However, annual congressional authorizations meant that during the life of the Marshall Plan, Congress would hold hearings on the ERP legislation, which in turn meant three new opportunities to appropriate funds for Spain. The O'Konski amendment was only the first volley of congressional support for Spain.

The commercial agreements with France, the United Kingdom and, in particular, Argentina, would undoubtedly provide partial relief of Spain's economic problems but capital equipment and long-term loans were still required for industrial rehabilitation. To counterbalance the effects of Truman's declarations, the Spanish Ambassador in Buenos Aires, José María de Areilza, was instructed to end the negotiations for a bilateral agreement which had been underway since September 1947 and to proceed to its immediate publication as the Franco-Perón protocol, which was signed on 9 April. The immediate publication of the Protocol on 4 April, even before it had been signed, was a useful propaganda device at the domestic level.[23] Perón liked to call it 'little Marshall Plan in indigenous style', «a la criolla».[24]

Juan Domingo Perón was delighted to defy Washington. For him the bilateral commercial agreement running prior to the Franco-Perón agreement was the complement to the Marshall Plan that Argentina wanted to give to the only true anti-communist country in Europe.[25] This economic agreement, by far the most important signed by Spain at the time, provided the equivalent of $200 million credit over the years 1948–51. It assured Spain of vital food imports that would have been difficult to finance otherwise. The reader should not, however, overestimate the overall importance of Argentina's credit facilities. Imports financed this way from 1947 to 1949 amounted to only 62 per cent of imports in the single year of 1949. Furthermore, the protocol was not designed, as in previous bilateral agreements, to help finance the extra imports required to rehabilitate the Spanish economy. These remained matters in which the assistance of the United States was necessary.

ALTERNATIVE COURSE OF ACTION

The Marshall Plan was based, among a variety of other things, upon the assumption that economic growth was a precondition for stable and democratic governments. In the case of Eastern European countries, the general agreement was for participation provided these countries abandoned the near-exclusive Soviet orientation of their economies. In the case of Spain, a similar alternative would have been to move toward the abandonment of economic inward-looking policies, but without the need of immediate political change. The modification of Spain's political structure would have then been left to blossom from the economic growth expedited by American assistance. Had the Truman administration not made economic assistance conditional on political transformation, Spain might have anticipated economic stabilization and liberalization by a decade. Yet, in order to receive Marshall aid, becoming a respectable democracy was not the only option open to Spain. There was another, equidistant from both full exclusion and full political evolution, which may have brought more effective results than the policy the United States chose to adopt.

The Truman administration failed to use its strong bargaining position as leverage to impose political and economic changes in Spain. The initial American policy toward Spain – made explicit by Acheson in April 1947, that only after Franco had been overthrown and replaced with a more liberal government would Washington aid Spain – changed only slightly at the end of the year. However, between November 1947 and January 1948 the State Department had become progressively convinced of the need for normalization of relations between Spain and western democracies, particularly the United States.

The most important think-tank within the State Department, the Policy Planning Staff (PPS), affirmed in October 1947 that the policy of ostracism had tightened the dictator's rein while impeding the recovery of the Spanish economy. Franco had turned international ostracism into a monster demonstration of domestic support and belt-tightening, the supreme proof of patriotism.[26] Consequently, Washington needed a new policy: 'Instead of contributing to the rapid deterioration of the economic situation, as we are doing at present, we would provide the opportunity for Spain to develop its resources and play a normal part in the revival of world commerce and industry'.[27] George F. Kennan, head of the PPS, advised an immediate relaxation of official restrictions to trade, shortly to be followed by the opening up of the possibility of financial assistance for general economic rehabilitation. The situation appeared clear to Kennan. Depriving Spain of the benefits of international economic relations could push the country to the edge of disorder and civil strife, an explosive situation bringing no benefit to anyone except the well-organized communists. Depriving Western Europe of Spain's economic contribution, albeit limited, seemed unnecessary. This famous PPS's report was presented to the newly-created National Security Council in December 1947 (as NSC 3) and was approved by Truman on 21 January 1948. Although Marshall and Truman in essence approved the PPS's recommendation, its real implications were not fully absorbed.[28]

The only real effect of Kennan's call was a modification of policy on the Spanish question at the United Nations. When in mid-November 1947 the General Assembly proposed the reaffirmation of the December 1946 resolution, it failed, in part due to effective opposition from the US delegation. Believing that the US attitude in this matter had led to complacency on the part of certain Spanish officials and had probably encouraged the Ministry of Foreign Affairs to set down Spain's official position with relation to the Marshall Plan, the US Embassy in Madrid decided to dampen Spanish ardor. The original US intention was to work out a fully coordinated program involving political as well as economic problems in Spain before Spanish officials could be given 'even a glimmer of hope that we are prepared to modify present policies'. This attitude was adopted even though Culbertson himself, the US Chargé d'Affaires no less, stated that 'Spain at least offers to meet the first essentials of the Marshall Plan objectives, namely, to help not only herself but the other countries of Europe who normally depend upon Spain as one source of supply'. Indeed, the US embassy felt that 'with appropriate assistance the Spanish economy can and should be put on a productive basis' and hoped that 'some formula – Marshall Plan or otherwise – will be possible by which Spain will be saved from possible economic chaos, with resulting political and social problems'.[29] The State Department none the less insisted upon political respectability in Spain prior to any economic assistance.[30]

The Americans adopted limited and insufficient measures to help the Spanish economy during the early months of 1948. As a first step toward gradual relaxation of existing trade restrictions, Spain was placed on an equal footing with all other European countries with respect to export controls. A second step was eliminating political objections to private credits granted by American banks to Spanish entrepreneurs and their government.[31] The Spanish government had already been thinking of a three-stage plan to obtain American credits and now rushed to agree on details. There would be, initially, an agreement between an American pool of banks and its Spanish counterpart on a short-term credit of $300 to $500 million with a guarantee of annual supply of certain commodities. The Export-Import Bank of Washington (Eximbank), the international lending agency of the US government, would then gather all private credits and enlarge them to a given amount. The total credit line would, finally, reach a maximum with the incorporation of Spain to the ERP. A figure of $1000 million was initially proposed by some officials. The Spanish administration held little hope of accomplishing all three stages, but it would have been satisfied with accomplishing just the first. It would have provided a useful basis for negotiation. This deal would have provided a sufficiently large amount of money to give room for manoeuvre; and it spared the inconvenience of sporadic private aid while retaining versatility, elasticity and flexibility. The US commercial counsellor in Madrid, Mr Randall, the first to be approached on the matter, requested and immediately obtained a twofold guarantee. First, there would be a freer selection and allocation of the goods to be exported to Spain. Second, given the normal administrative delays in any industrial and commercial deal with any Spanish counterpart, the Spanish pool of banks would obtain beforehand a formal promise of delivery of licenses and goods from the Ministry of Industry. While Randall thought he had obtained a modification of the Spanish economic system, Spanish officials maintained that these concessions were 'without substantial importance'. Top Spanish civil servants travelled to Washington to visit banking figures, the Eximbank and the State Department, the main actors in the three-stage process. They received the same response from all their interlocutors: no long-term credits would be granted by US banks. Apart from oil companies, American private capital was not interested in investing in Europe, and long-term credits required prior political approval through Eximbank intervention. There was, thus, no other way to obtain short-term private credits than to offer gold as collateral and, as a result, private credits were granted in extremely limited amounts because of the scarcity of Spanish gold.[32]

Uncoordinated, piecemeal, private short-term credits could not serve as a stable basis for redressing the economy. Moreover, they were likely to have no effect on economic policy and certainly none on the political course of the country. The measures adopted by the Truman administration did not help unblock the problem of raising the productivity of domestic industrial plant, leaving unresolved the country's dollar shortage. Spanish production would continue to be internationally uncompetitive until a large range of competitive goods could be incorporated into its production lines. It was a vicious circle which could only be broken by an infusion of investment. The lack of Spanish recovery and modernization continued to hamper bilateral trade. The State Department, however, would contemplate neither direct nor indirect financial assistance to Spain unless the latter provided *convincing* evidence of economic and political liberalization.[33]

On the economic side, the Americans complained of excessive intervention and the priority given to the public sector in import allocation; it was these two facts which, according to Washington, would explain the limited flow of private credits to Spain. The answer from the Spanish officials was immediate:

It is precisely the scarcity of financial resources to purchase the supply required by the Spanish economy that imposes intervention. The latter is not a whim but a necessity. As financial resources improved, formulae similar to those in practice in other countries would be looked for.[34]

They argued that the extreme features of the import licensing policy were a consequence of the fact that Spain was able to earn only a part of the foreign exchange needed to meet its essential import requirements. The Minister of Foreign Affairs declared that the Spanish government agreed with a liberalization of its economic policy, although it required previous financial commitment.[35] Franco told Truman's special ambassador to the Vatican, Myron C. Taylor, early in March 1948, that there was no obstacle in principle to a reduction of public intervention if the necessary financial backing was granted.[36] Without the latter, Franco saw the risk of a situation similar to that of Italy and France, where Communists were free to spread the revolutionary virus. Indeed, the same line was taken at the Council of Ministers, where financial and monetary stabilization were argued for as distinct possibilities if international backing was granted.[37]

One might have expected that an initial clash between Spaniards and Americans over one particular point concerning the Import Program, namely, that it did not aim at a restoration of the role of private initiative but the reinforcement of the public sector. The INI was getting an excessively large share of the limited foreign exchange available for the import of essentials and the Import Program aimed at extending this situation to American aid. The reduction of State interference in private enterprises, especially through the INI, Artajo explained, was a 'situation [that] could be worked out'.[38] There seemed to be little problem in reaching an agreement about how assistance might have been invested, despite the clear State priorities of the Spanish administration, as long as the assistance was real.

The only straight negative coming from the Spanish side was political liberalization. The Spanish administration agreed to collaborate with the United States in every way as long as they left it to run its own political house. Franco explained to the US Chargé d'Affaires that his government wanted an end to political isolation but 'they [were] not now going [to] modify politically in order to obtain these ends'.[39] The Spanish government argued that the international community had not appreciated previous attempts to provide a more liberal political structure. The Charter of the Spanish People of 1945 in principle enumerated the rights and responsibilities of the Spanish citizens and their relationship to the State. In July 1945 Franco had reshaped the political composition of the cabinet by replacing phalangist leaders with representatives of monarchism and Catholicism. The Referendum Act of 1945, conceived as a means of allowing citizens to participate in the governing process, was employed in 1947 to ratify the Law of Succession and the lengthy statement of intentions which constituted the Labor Charter. The years 1946 and 1947 opened with diplomatic representatives protesting that the harder Spain worked to liberalize its government the more the Allies complained. The reality was the Spanish government gave no grounds for thinking that its regime intended to evolve, however gradually, in a more liberal direction. They showed no signs whatsoever of envisaging an enlargement of civil and political liberties.

There was a mutual miscalculation on both sides which allowed little progress. On one hand, the Americans (and British) had wrongly judged that eagerness for Marshall aid would be so keen that Franco would be forced to implement political liberalization: 'We heartily shared the British feeling that the continued exclusion of Spain [from ERP] would serve as an inducement to General Franco to bring about substantial political and economic changes in order to qualify for inclusion.'[40] On the other, the Spanish government considered that, in the progressively deteriorating international situation, strategic considerations made assistance to Spain inevitable, without it having to move one inch in the political direction asked by the Allies. The Spaniards argued that progress was up to the United States. The State Department thought that progress was definitively up to Spain. A compromise proposal came from the Spanish government: Spain could not comply with the political requirements of the Americans but this was not necessarily the case on the economic side. By insisting on the political proviso the Truman administration brought about deadlock: 'Positive economic assistance for [Spain] should await, and serve as an inducement for the taking of concrete steps toward liberalization.'[41]

Many had previously expressed doubts about the wisdom of this policy. On the American side, Culbertson recommended the fostering of political and economic evolution through Spain's ERP membership and some American companies had declared their readiness to assist the Spanish economy if ERP backing was provided. On the European side, the Quai d'Orsay and the Foreign Office were of the opinion that the US government should find a way round the obstacle barring assistance to the Spanish economy. Even Juan Negrín López, who headed the Popular Front government of the Second Republic (May 1937–9) and who was leader in London of a minority socialist group with a manifest pro-communist tendency, opposed economic sanctions and requested the inclusion of Spain in the ERP. Relief of the Spanish people and economy was more important, he argued, than any political capital Franco might construe from it.[42]

When it became clear that the ERP was to be a reality without Spain, the Spanish government offered the possibility of reaching a bilateral agreement outside of but parallel to the ERP, which would provide assistance without the political inconvenience of ERP membership. 'It does not matter much', Minister Artajo argued, 'whether the money comes from one corner or another, whether it arrives in the form of credit or in any other form, whether it is granted through the Marshall Plan or through any other plan.'[43] After discussion with Franco and his Cabinet, Artajo informed the US Chargé d'Affaires that the 'Marshall Plan was of less interest to Spain than an individual deal with the United States'.[44] The first official declaration regarding the Spanish offer of military bases to the United States was soon to come:

Spain wants and needs help but she wants it on a basis of a bilateral arrangement with the United States and not under Marshall Plan aid. If Spain could receive such aid as to give solidity to her economic structure, liberalizing action could and would be taken and Spain would be prepared to meet such reasonable conditions as [the US] might be prepared to suggest... Could some understanding be reached between the two countries, [the US] could, if so desired, have bases in the Canary and Balearic Islands and facilities on the Spanish mainland.[45]

This was not necessarily the preferred course of action. Spain's ERP membership would have meant obtaining dollar credits without the need to deal directly with the United States. Madrid had feared from the outset that the United States could impose a much higher price in the context of bilateral dealings than if negotiations took place within a multilateral framework.[46] ERP membership offered a greater appearance of complete international rehabilitation of the Franco regime than any bilateral deal. Finally, the major inconvenience which ERP membership involved – in the Spanish government's perspective – did not disappear with the bilateral deal: Spain losing some of its freedom of action in case of military conflict. In sum, Spain's apparent preference for bilateral negotiations was due to necessity having been excluded from the multilateral framework; it was the only way to obtain foreign financial assistance without political liberalization.

Given the pressing needs of the Spanish economy in the late 1940s, positive assistance to Spain – granted outside of the Marshall Plan structure – could have worked as leverage to obtain an effective coordination between economic and political liberalization. The Spanish government perceived the United States as holding out a fairly empty hand of friendship. The Americans were calling for immediate action in return for which the Spaniards may have received nothing because any action they implemented might have failed to convince Washington. The problem is whether political liberalization was to be a precondition of any further move. 'In fact,' Culbertson told Marshall, 'economic stability and liberalization may well bring with it political stability and liberalization.'[47] The State Department refused to see things from this perspective.

Had the State Department thrown out the ideological and emotional leftovers from the war in their Spanish policy, a means to encourage economic stability in Spain could have been found without much public announcement. In the early 1950s, when the Truman administration came to accept a Spanish contribution to western defense, means were found to bring Spain within the security system without the need for Spanish adhesion to either NATO or the Western European Union. When the Americans adopted this policy economic liberalization was subordinated to strategic requirements. In the late 1950s, when the Spanish economic situation progressively deteriorated, international aid for economic stabilization was not conditional upon parallel political liberalization. It was assumed that political liberalization would follow from economic liberalization. Could a policy similar to those adopted in 1953 or in 1959 have been implemented in 1948? Could the economic bonanza that supposedly stemmed from mid-1950s American aid and the implementation of the Stabilization Plan have taken already place around 1948?

Some of the circumstances which supposedly favored the implementation of economic and financial stabilization in 1959 were already present a decade earlier. On the one hand, the Spanish administration was already conscious that an inward-looking economy could not promote sustained growth and, on the other, foreign exchange reserves in the second half of 1947 were as heartbreaking as at the end of the 1950s. It is incorrect to state that the Spanish administration took 20 years to recognize that the economic system designed immediately after the Civil War was ineffective. In fact, whatever ideological commitment toward autarchy existed before 1945 was mostly dropped after that date. It emerges from the different programs in place and from the Import Program that the Spanish government explicitly recognized the essential role of imports to develop the industrial capacity of the nation. The period up to the end of 1947 was considered transitional to new policies which were never implemented due to the lack of financial support. A technical team was ready in 1947 to redress the domestic economy and to end its international isolation. The idea of financial and economic liberalization reached the Council of Ministers in 1948. The main element which existed in 1959 but not in 1947 was the granting of foreign financial assistance.

The question now lies in determining how effective the policy of ostracism toward Franco was. This policy, of which the exclusion from the ERP was a part, failed in achieving its objective, namely, encouraging a political change which might have led to the disappearance of Franco and his regime. It had no deleterious effect on the Franco regime and, if anything, it strengthened the dictatorship by providing a cohesive rallying cry against foreign intervention. This policy, however, diminished the possibilities of any further economic liberalization as the conglomerate of bottlenecks subsisted and lucrative vested interests rooted deeper. Without resources to purchase essential equipment, fuel, fertilizers and other raw materials, and capital goods, the recovery and further modernization of Spain was held in abeyance for many years.

Although the ERP's economic contribution to West European economies was not as startling as is often claimed, it undoubtedly allowed them to maintain high levels of investment and imports of capital goods (machinery, vehicles, iron and steel, and iron and steel products) from the United States. The importance of ERP is not to be gauged uniquely in terms of the absolute value of ERP-financed imports as a proportion of total imports. The commodity composition of these imports was of greater importance to the importing economy. In addition, the Marshall Plan released important funds for investment through the counterpart funds. Counterpart funds and ERP-financed imports were of relative importance to those sectors which bore the main burden of reconstruction and helped governments to widen bottlenecks in the recovery process. Marshall aid had provided a solution to the European dilemma of financing the dollar imports of equipment at the same time as securing the necessary domestic investment.

It is impossible to know what would have happened had the United States not provided aid for, say, French reconstruction. However, one observation might prove pertinent to the Spanish case. When preparing the discussions for the negotiation of the lend-lease, Jean Monnet warned the Americans that without a large credit, French reconstruction would take longer and operate within a closed economy:

Il nous faudra alors adopter une ligne politique tendant à utiliser au maximum nos propres ressources; à développer la production de produits synthétiques quel qu'en soit le prix de revient intérieur; à utiliser la puissance de production industrielle de l'Allemagne.[48]

Supply was the crucial factor. While in most western countries the value of imports was much higher than exports and recovered prewar levels faster than exports, this was not the case in Spain. In most West European countries the deficit bore little relation to the size of their resources in gold and foreign exchange but was, rather, related to their ability to obtain access to international aid. Most countries were gambling on the provision of more American aid. This was a risky game, especially because it was being played when the Americans were insisting on an end to any extraordinary financial aid by the end of 1947. Although the structural causes of the dollar deficit were complex and could not be solved by the Marshall Plan alone, the Marshall Plan allowed Western Europe to continue importing American goods to sustain high levels of capital investment in spite of their payment difficulties. While other countries continued their expansionist domestic policies, Spain was left on the verge of international bankruptcy.

*   *   *

There is a commonly accepted set of views on postwar Spain which can be summarized as follows. First, the Franco regime opted voluntarily for international economic isolation which, in turn, contributed to the exasperating slowness in recovering pre-Civil War levels of output and welfare. Second, foreign trade was hardly considered in terms of economic growth; it merely served to satisfy the regime's clientele through the manipulation of administrative requirements (such as licenses and quotas). Economic interventionism was hand-in-glove with the isolationist option of the Franco regime and interventionism was extreme because it had to serve the goals of autarchy. Third, the Franco regime could have followed a path similar to that followed by other European countries had it opted to do so. Finally, that the Spanish administration made no move to link itself to the institutionalized pattern of European economic cooperation before 1957.

Yet, the Spanish administration did consider linking the Spanish economy with the international economy. The economic authorities had accepted, as early as 1945, the idea that in the long-term prosperity depended on a return to more open economies within a relatively free multilateral system of trade and payments. The administration studied the possibility of joining the Bretton Woods system, offered its participation through UNRRA in the relief of Europe, contributed through a complex network of bilateral agreements to the economic reconstruction of Western Europe and applied for Marshall aid to soften the extreme features of intervention and trade restriction. The will to join the Marshall Plan shows, in itself, that isolation was not the aim of Francoist economic policy.

Equally, the Spanish administration was perfectly aware that Spain's weak trading position was the major bottleneck to economic growth. It is far from clear whether policy options similar to the rest of Western Europe could have been adopted in Spain without the benefits of massive financial assistance. No other means were available to absorb the necessary convulsions which any stabilization and liberalization would have provoked in a traditionally closed economy. However, it is also far from proven that, had it received foreign economic support, the Spanish government would have dispassionately moved toward a liberal economic policy. Nobody did so in Western Europe at the time.

Spain's principal foreign economic problem in the post-1945 period was of a clear-cut nature: 'In what conditions could it be assured a supply of raw materials and goods necessary for the national economy on the basis of the export of national produce and the rationalization of all available financial resources.'[49] The exclusion of Spain from the ERP arrangements deprived the Spanish economy of the necessary margin to accelerate economic recovery and modernization. While the Franco regime had survived isolation and came out stronger than ever, ostracism only delayed Spain's economic recovery.

The solution of the short-term problems of the country's economy weighed too heavily on the long-term plans for industrialization and capitalization and represented an obstacle to the reconstructive economic process. Any significant financial assistance would have been of extraordinary value in overcoming bottlenecks and stimulating growth. Argentina's aid came at a critical time for Spain and helped to ensure the supply of foodstuffs. However, Spain could not find a feasible market overseas for its agricultural exports and Argentina could not fulfil its requirements for manufactured goods from Spain. Argentina soon ran out of funds, while Spain did not pay for its Argentinian imports. The trade relationship built up between both countries was, of necessity, short-lived. It took Spain away from *primum vivere* but did not finance capital equipment, the main hindrance to the creation of a more competitive industry.

The Import Program was a priority plan for allocation of scarce supplies for temporary relief and for modernization. It wanted to overcome a conglomeration of bottlenecks which hampered recovery: the loss of German technical collaboration on which many of the vast industrial schemes were based, the foreign exchange shortage, in particular of dollars, the need to reinforce its energy and power supply, the transformation of the rail system with the electrification of the network and an increase in coal imports, the obtaining of regular supplies of raw materials, such as petroleum and raw cotton, and the purchase of capital goods. Meanwhile, the Import Program was to reduce the country's dependence on food supplies through an increase of productivity in the countryside. Only with Marshall aid could Spain have purchased an appreciable proportion of the extra imports considered essential for the full recuperation of the country's economy and productive capacity.

Appended to the modernization objectives of the Import Program was a list of political wishes from which needs were deduced. In this sense, the program for national reconstruction became a mixture of economic reality and political desirability, conceived in a sort of daydream where international economic and political difficulties were largely ignored. The Marshall Plan appeared to the Spanish administration as an opportunity to correct the country's obsolete economic structures and strengthen Franco's political regime. For their part, the United States and its western partners were concerned about the domestic political implications for themselves of any Spanish ERP connection; so to benefit from Marshall aid, Spain was required to dismantle the Franco regime. A kick-Franco-out-of-power policy preceded all other considerations. The needs of the Spanish economy and population were not considered independently of the country's political circumstances.

Spain's non-participation in the ERP had cut off the possibility of international financial assistance for economic reconstruction purposes. If there was no way to pay for imports other than by exports, imports and exports were to be kept in balance. Furthermore, the alternative means to recovery were to continue with intervention, priorities, rationing, price control, labor allocation, export set-asides, import quotas, on the one hand and, budget balancing, credit restriction and high interest rates, on the other. The Marshall Plan partially avoided increasing trade controls as the only other response to the 1947 financial crisis, by permitting a level of imports from the United States of investment goods appreciably higher than could otherwise have been the case. Spain, however, with no dollars other than those earned from exports, had to have recourse to trade controls and an economic policy constrained by the need to maintain a constant equilibrium in the country's balance of payments. Spain's exclusion from the ERP meant holding down imports for Spain, keeping pace with exports (particularly dollar imports of capital goods), and continuing the rationing of domestic consumption. The increased import of valuable investment goods, which participation in the Marshall Plan could have made possible, would have created some room of manoeuvre for the government's economic policy.

The interesting aspect of this research is to reveal that the Spanish administration, conscious that involving Spain in the Marshall Plan was not feasible because it would have indicated international plenary absolution for the Franco regime, proposed that the United States grant aid to their economy outside the ERP framework with a commitment to progress toward economic liberalization. The proposal was permanently rejected because it would have reduced the value of the American commitment to a coordinated plan for recovery. Washington did not consider the practical implications which might have derived from the Spanish proposal: to synchronize economic assistance with impulses toward economic liberalization and, subsequently, political transformation. The Spanish administration agreed with the objectives of liberalization and modernization but rejected the political conditions linked to the granting of US assistance. Washington asked too a high price for the government to consider seriously their proposals. Once the latter had declared itself to be prepared to go along with economic and financial spring-cleaning if backed by foreign assistance, it would have been more sensible to provide assistance to Spain conditioned upon an effective commitment to work progressively toward trade liberalization and the dismantling of autarchic industries. Political transformation could have been left to be induced indirectly by the improvement of the country's economic conditions and subsequent economic growth.

Washington failed to test how far it could go in extracting economic concessions in return for assistance. It limited itself to demanding political concessions without providing any convincing guarantee of financial assistance. The promise of Marshall aid remained so ambiguous, imprecise and conditional upon many uncontrolled factors that no economic leverage was exerted by the United States to force through its own policies in Spain. The potential for economic stabilization and liberalization was never explored. If the Americans had translated their political problems with the Spaniards into technical ones which would have been easier to settle they might have been able to expect some returns. The exclusion of Spain from the ERP and, more particularly, the American inability or unwillingness to provide a substitute mechanism of assistance while demanding substantial political and economic changes in Spain, is a good example of how the gap between ambition and feasibility deprived the American policy of effectiveness to solve the Spanish problem. The United States continued to be uninterested in what has been called a 'non-democratic nationalistic modernization'.[50] The Truman administration refused to admit the Spanish official theory that liberalization and modernization should only apply to the economic sphere. The result of this for Spain was a 'capitalist stagnation without democracy'.[51]

The Truman administration continued to deploy the Marshall Plan as a political stabilizer: economic aid was designed to support democratic political parties in power. There was no room for non-democratic governments. Internal as well as external threats justified economic aid to governments with questionable democratic credentials, such as in Greece and Turkey, while

Portugal's dictatorship never represented a major problem for public opinion. This was not, evidently, the case with Spain. Periodic discussion of the Spanish question in the United Nations and the press had distorted the question out of all proportion, building an emotional issue which blocked policy options. Spain appeared to the Americans as an isolated case to which the rule of political stabilization could not be applied and for which no specific policy could be conceived at the State Department.

A point of departure for this book has been to consider the non-democratic nature of the political regime and Franco not leaving office as given factors. Therefore, an alternative research perspective is proposed here. Had the western Allies displayed a less ideological attitude and had Spain received ERP financial support, regardless of Franco's political regime, its economic retardation might have been overcome sooner, making possible in 1948 what the most famous Stabilization Plan made possible a decade later. Spain's high-policy makers might have been stimulated to introduce financial and monetary measures to stabilize its money system and exchange rates. They might have been forced to adapt some discipline in trade and exchange rate policies to encourage an expanding trade with Western Europe, with as extensive free trade as possible.

The problem-solving capacity of the Spanish administration in foreign economic policy up to this point was high. After the world war, it had efficiently used the economic and administrative resources then available in foreign economic policy. It had become a creditor at the time of general scarcity of hard currencies as a means to promote trade and to link the United Kingdom and France to the Spanish economy despite political considerations. It had paid off all its financial debts in an attempt to appear as a serious commercial partner. It had taken advantage of the postwar worldwide scarcity of supply and hard currencies to place the Spanish export commodities presented as hard currency savings and make an important contribution to economic recovery and diet improvement. It had promoted trade relations through the recreation of the traditional network of bilateral trade and payments agreements between Spain and the West European countries. Trade relations were presented as mere technical dealings to obtain a non-political supply of necessary goods. This specific trade pattern was fully effective and the Spanish economy reaped the maximum advantage which its output capacity allowed.

In the crucial period between the summer/autumn of 1947 and the end of 1948, the Spanish administration perceived that the economically favorable period of Europe's economic recovery had ended. Traditional exports were not performing as expected and a change in the pattern of international demand was taking place against Spain's export trade commodity composition.

This was when the trade tools used since the end of 1944 were clearly perceived as less profitable. It was then that foreign economic assistance desired to overcome the poor state of the national economy – in particular supply and investment shortages – appeared viable and the various plans to increase industrial output were gathered into a single plan for economic reconstruction. It was then, in sum, that exclusion from the Marshall Plan made Spain the *rara avis* of Western Europe.

Spain's exports during the immediate postwar years were based not on Spanish economic potential but on the dramatic short-term needs of Europe's relief and reconstruction. They certainly served to maintain a level of foreign currency income to satisfy minimal import requirements. They have served even to stabilize Franco's political regime in the international sphere, but were insufficient to accomplish the necessary modernization of the economic structure for sustained growth. Reconstruction of the country's economy required larger financial resources than those provided by bilateral trade channels, or otherwise, as happened, recovery would take longer. Recovery of pre-Civil War levels of output and modernization of economic structures were the two sides of the same problem, more so when Marshall aid searched for higher productivity levels in the recipient countries. For instance, the recovery of pre-Civil War agricultural output still left the problem of keeping up with the increase in demand resulting from a steadily growing population and a rising standard of living. Marshall aid appeared as the optimum solution to secure large foreign financial assistance and a subsequent increase in trade levels, both of which were permanent objectives of the Spanish administration. The crux of the second half of the 1940s was thus, the limited resources of foreign exchange available.

The American financial resources available through the Marshall Plan changed the terms of European economic reconstruction and, thus, Spain's relations with Western Europe. Before June 1947, the logic of separate, often conflicting, national reconstruction plans permitted dealings with Spain to obtain whatever Spain had to offer. When Marshall called for a coordinated plan as a precondition of receiving a large package of economic assistance from the United States, bringing Franco's Spain in would have provoked undesirable domestic criticism from all corners. The inclusion of Spain was difficult to defend to public opinion in France and Italy and more, particularly, to the US Congress, since what was presented as being at stake was democracy and the most cherished values of western civilization. Fruit and vegetables, pyrites, iron ore, cork, tungsten, were no longer single commodities after Marshall's offer, but components of an ambitious political program. Trade became an instrument to achieve major political, economic, social and ideological goals. It was no longer a goal in itself.

The point is not that Spain had little to offer to European reconstruction. Neither that, if Spain had joined the CEEC, it would have added a new shopping list to the 16 separate estimates of needs drafted in Paris, the maximum cooperative effort the Europeans were able to undertake at the time. The point is that Western Europe did not consider it necessary to obtain the possible contribution from Spain through the ERP. Public opinion was strong enough to discourage any attempt in that direction, while bilateral trade could fulfil the task of channelling Spanish goods for economic reconstruction without risking domestic upheaval. The Franco regime's exclusion from the ERP was possible because Western Europe and Spain had developed a network of bilateral agreements necessary to obtain what the Spanish economy could offer to European reconstruction.

Excluding Spain, however, meant Western Europe finding other means to avoid the collapse of the Spanish economy, in particular its foreign sector upon which the foreign supply of essentials depended. The appearance of disorder and civil strife at the western corner of Europe, possibly stemming from a drastic deterioration of economic conditions, did not appeal to western policy-makers, especially since the Marshall Plan was to save the continent from political and social turmoil. The policy adopted by the West European countries was to avoid carrying out further discrimination against the country such as to leave the Spanish economy on the edge of collapse.

Part III
Bilateralism within a Multilateral Context, 1949 to mid-1950s

7 Avoiding the Collapse of Spain's Bilateral Trade Channels

Scholars have paid a disproportionate amount of attention to Spain's relations with the United States, to the detriment of Western Europe. USA–Spain relations have been placed within the so-called high politics and the United States is viewed as the main source of financial relief to the Spanish economy during the 1950s, when Argentina had disappeared as a creditor and public assistance provided by Europeans was negligible. Western Europe, on the other hand, has been pictured more as a source of distress than of relief and perceived as a scattered bloc dealing with such low politics as trade and technical matters. However, US assistance to Spain was not significant until after 1955 (Table 7.1).

After 1947 the Spanish government repeatedly requested approximately $1300 million (in addition to normal imports) in the form of a short-term import program for economic modernization and stabilization. The different interpretations of the interdependence between the granting of military base facilities and the commitment to assist in the improvement of Spain's economic and military situation delayed the conclusion of the base agreement until September 1953. Early in the negotiations, the Spaniards discovered that large-scale economic development was of no interest to Washington. On average, US economic assistance (including private banks loans) represented approximately $49 million per year between 1950 and 1955 (accounted for primarily by expenditures for foodstuffs and cotton imports from the United States). This amount was far from the most modest estimates of Spanish import requirements in assistance from abroad. In fact, the physical resources for the import programs needed to place the Spanish economy on a sound footing were no longer available from the United States.

The total of economic assistance from the United States to Spain between 1950 and 1955 was a drop in the ocean of Spain's needs. Most of the weaknesses of the Spanish economy were structural, impossible to overcome in the short run. The small amount of dollar aid had a very limited effect on domestic productive capacity, which would have continued its slow transformation and modernization even without dollar assistance. An immediate cessation of US assistance would certainly have worsened Spain's

131

dollar position but not irreparably, since the authorities would have offset it by reimposing rigid import controls on dollar goods. The Spanish economy would have probably adjusted to a sudden termination of US aid, just as it had adjusted to the loss of other transitory advantages such as the Argentine aid and the stock-piling programs following the outbreak of hostilities in Korea.[1]

TABLE 7.1   FOREIGN CURRENCY EARNINGS BY EXPORTS AND LONG-TERM CAPITAL INVESTMENT, 1948–55 (in millions of dollars)

Years	Exports fob (1)	Trade Balance (2)	Private Capital (3)	3 % 1	Public Capital (4)	4 % 1	3+4 % 1	Long-Term Capital B. (5)	5 % 1	2 + 5
1948	375.1	−62.5	5.3	1.4	177.4#	47.3	48.7	+167.7	44.7	+105.2
1949	407.3	−15.3	28.7*	7.0	74.2#	18.2	25.3	+87.9	21.6	+72.6
1950	405.6	+61.9	13.5**	3.3	–	–	3.3	+8.4	2.1	+70.3
1951	498.0	+116.8	4.5	0.9	17.9♩	3.6	4.5	+3.0	0.6	+119.8
1952	458.2	−52.2	6.9f	1.5	11.5♩	2.5	4.0	+3.5	0.8	−48.7
1953	483.1	−56.5	25.0f	5.1	13.6♩	2.8	8.0	+30.9	6.4	−25.6
1954	464.4	−91.3	32.2	6.9	60.2‡	13.0	19.9	+46.8	10.1	−44.5
1955	446.2	−112.4	57.9	13.0	106.0‡	23.8	36.7	+154.6	34.6	+42.2

Source: Chamorro *et al.*, *Las balanzas de pagos en el período de la autarquía* (Madrid, 1976), and own elaboration. Chamorro *et al.*'s data on private capital have been augmented with the part of the credits granted during 1949 and 1950 by private US banks and effectively delivered in those same years. This might imply some overlapping and, consequently, an overvaluation of private capital during both years. Public capital has been modified regarding the distribution of the credit authorizations for a value of $65.2 million voted by the US Congress in August 1950. The long-term capital balance includes payments of interest and commission due to Argentina and, after 1954, Eximbank credits. It comprises equally aid granted under the provisions of the 'Defense Support Program' (after 1954), the 'Public Law 480' and the 'McCarran Amendment' to the Mutual Security Appropriations Act of 1955. Aid offered by the National Catholic Welfare Conference and distributed by «Cáritas Española» has not been considered. The amounts of American economic aid under the Pact of Madrid have been adjusted according to different official US sources and OEEC reports on the Spanish economy. There are important differences between the figures used here and those given as US aid in other sources. The amounts of economic aid quoted here correspond to effective deliveries and expenditures, and not, as frequently quoted, obligations, appropriations, or end-authorizations, which disregard whether the amounts granted (either loans or grants) were effectively delivered. Military assistance is not considered because it did not represent a transfer of resources to the civilian economy and did not affect the external asset and liability position of the Spanish government. For the most part, military aid represented a transfer of military end-items that presumably would not have been acquired without this aid. Furthermore, the difficulty in measuring the net addition of resources to the civilian economy brought by military aid (which in the form of end-items did not enter national accounts), makes it necessary to neglect it altogether. Finally, commercial credits, frequently of a short-term nature, are not considered.

(*) Includes $19 million out of the two-year $25 million loan granted by the Chase National Bank of New York and $1.5 million from the Société de Banque Suisse of Geneva; AHBE, IEME, box 164: 'IEME. Balanza General de Pagos del año 1949'. (**) Includes $3 million corresponding to the Chase National Bank of New York, $9 867 319 from the National City Bank of New York and $645 039 from the Société de Banque Suisse; ibid. box 65: 'Balanza General de Pagos del año 1950'. (f) Including two short-term loans (18 months) totalling $24 million granted by the Eximbank (early in January 1952 and in mid-April 1953) for the purchase of raw cotton outside the amounts authorized by the US Congress in August 1951; PRO, FO 371/113024: Dispatch 334 from British Ambassador John Balfour to Secretary of State for Foreign Affairs Anthony Eden (October 1951 to April 1955), 'Annual Report of Spain for 1953', Madrid, 1 January 1954. (#) According to AHBE, IEME, box 164: 'IEME. Balanza General de Pagos' for 1948 and 1949, Argentine credits for 1948 and 1949 amounted to $177 368 331 and $74 208 995, respectively. (♪) Expenditures corresponding to the $65.2 million loan authorized in August 1950. (‡) Distribution of American aid in 1954 and 1955. Year 1954: Eximbank credits for a total value of $10.9 million, $24.3 million under the terms of 'Defense Support Program', $20 million for the purchase of wheat through the Commodity Credit Corporation, and $5 million under the terms of 'Public Law 480'; latter two figures from AD, DE-CE 1945–60, vol. 371: OEEC C(56)201, 'Conseil. Association de l'Espagne aux travaux de l'Organisation. Rapport du Groupe de Travail spécial du Conseil', Annex A, 'La situation économique de l'Espagne', Paris, 25 July 1956, p. 35. Year 1955: Eximbank credits for a total value of $3.3 million, which was the remainder of the $62.5 million of the congressional appropriations for Spain voted in August 1950, $31.2 million and $16.4 million under the terms of the 'Defense Support Program' and 'Public Law 480', respectively, and, finally, $55 million provided under the terms of the 'McCarran Amendment'.

Regardless of labels, high politics were ineffective in providing relief to the Spanish economy and political system during the very difficult times of the first half of the 1950s, while trade was rather more effective. From this perspective, although not being on the list of declared foreign policy priorities, Western Europe constituted the essential element of Spanish foreign economic policy after World War II. Most countries in Western Europe considered bilateral trade with Spain independently of political considerations. This attitude had been temporarily overshadowed by the strong ideological commitments made at the time of launching and securing the Marshall Plan. Once the ERP was a reality, most West European governments took the line that they continued to disapprove of the Franco regime as a political system but were willing to cooperate economically, as they did with other countries whose system of government they disapproved.

In a meeting early in October 1948 with his French and British counterparts (Robert Schuman and Ernest Bevin), Secretary of State George C.

Marshall, confessed not to knowing how to effect political or economic change in Spain. The Spanish economy had received no assistance, but Franco was strengthened not weakened by the policy of ostracism. The Allied policy represented a difficult compromise between complete isolation and economic boycott on the one hand, and an attempt to get close to and influence the Spanish government, on the other. It had the disadvantages of both and the effectiveness of neither. Bevin and Schuman immediately agreed with Marshall. Any step that could be interpreted as recognition of the Franco government would involve serious political complications for their respective governments, but 'so long as we were only dealing with trade and similar questions that were not political, there was no difficulty'.[2] Public opinion in the west was that the Spanish problem could only be solved by the removal of Franco and his replacement by a democratic government. A temporary solution, however, could be effected through trade and technical cooperation. Most West European governments seemed to share the sentiment that assisting Spain's economic recovery was necessary and maybe even a step toward advancing its return to the democratic fold, but that to join hands with Franco compromised their political and moral positions. This would have caused difficulties with democratic forces and even within governments themselves. They agreed with the idea that relations with Spain should be dealt with as a technical matter, leaving aside political issues.[3]

For Europeans, trade contributed to the relief of the Spanish economy and escaped public criticism. On the one hand, bilateral trade would take place outside the popular ERP and, thus, it could hardly be perceived as strengthening Franco's authoritarian regime. On the other hand, bilateral trade would channel what Spain could offer the economies of Europe, and foreign exchange so earned would prevent the collapse of the Spanish economy. Aside from some reservations of a political nature against Franco's regime, the need to help Spain in its economic rehabilitation and, after June 1950, to obtain from that country some strategic raw materials for rearmament programs seemed obvious.

Before the establishment of EPU, bilateral agreements were the basic instrument for channelling and financing trade among countries of the non-dollar world and of the OEEC. At the time of Marshall's speech in Harvard, the number of trade and payments agreements in force was about 200. Even the Marshall Plan, launched as the definitive step toward European unification, was implemented through bilateral agreements between the United States and each of the beneficiary countries. In 1948, 61 per cent of the payments related to OEEC foreign trade were made through bilateral agreements.[4] Intra-European trade remained almost at a barter stage based on discrimination, quantitative restrictions, direct controls over foreign exchange, and other trade barriers until trade liberalization, backed by an effective mechanism for setting off balances multilaterally, was fully effective. Even then, bilateralism continued.

Spain had been an efficient part of the network of bilateral agreements that allowed the resumption of intra-European trade among soft-currency countries without waiting for the solution of the chronic hard-currency shortage. However, contrary to what became the future European pattern, Spanish trade continued to be conducted exclusively on a bilateral basis throughout the period under consideration. Spain's main trading features were quantitative restrictions, a narrow licensing system, the administrative concession of foreign exchange at a multiplicity of exchange rates, and several practices directed to the promotion of exports (compensation, combined accounts for exports and imports, import surcharges combined with export subsidies), all of which were conducted through bilateral agreements for trade and payments. Whether bilateralism was an option consciously adopted by the Francoist State as a function of domestic interest groups or part of its ideology, is of no interest here. For our purposes, the basic choice was between autarchy and maintaining the existing bilateral system while trying to make it more flexible and beneficial. Between 1948 and 1959, Spanish participation in the organizations promoting trade liberalization and multilateral settlements of outstanding balances was barred from consideration in western capitals. However, bilateral agreements represented the first step away from national autarchy and toward the resumption of international trade and payments. The absence of a bilateral agreement with a non-dollar country frequently meant that trade with this country took place only under rigidly balanced barter arrangements, if at all. In such cases, bilateralism becomes a trade-creating device.

After 1949 and until the mid-1950s, export trade maintained the responsibility for financing imports of machinery and raw materials necessary for reconstruction plans. The government's appeals for foreign assistance, which could have provided imports with no drain on reserves, went mainly unheard. Although confronted by perennial shortages of basic foodstuffs and blockages in industrial production, borrowing from abroad to finance imports was not a feasible option. Spain's non-participation in the financial aid arrangements for European countries (the OEEC distributing US financial aid and the EPU's automatic credits) ruled out the possibility of international financial assistance for purposes of economic reconstruction and growth. With no access to Marshall aid, with few remittances from emigrants, and reduced income from tourism, Spain was obliged to keep imports strictly within the available means of payment derived from visible exports.

When foreign currency earnings had to rely on exports, especially of food-stuffs, Western Europe deserves special attention in order to understand Spain's foreign economic policy during the final years of the 1940s and the early 1950s. Europe was the natural market for Spain's export items and the main source of manufactured goods. The OEEC countries accounted for 56.3 per cent of Spain's exports and 46.6 per cent of its imports from 1949 to 1955. While Spain's exports to Western Europe suffered from the variability of agricultural crops and measures for domestic protection, imports from OEEC countries constantly increased their proportion of Spain's total imports; from 19.8 per cent in 1947 to 69.5 per cent in 1955. Trade with Western Europe thus appeared to be strategic for overcoming some of the bottlenecks to sustained economic development. The EPU was the leading customer as well as taker from the Spanish monetary area throughout the early 1950s (Table 7.2).

TABLE 7.2   DISTRIBUTION OF FOREIGN TRADE OF THE SPANISH MONETARY AREA BY MAIN MONETARY AREAS AND MAIN PARTNERS, 1950–5 (in percentages)

Monetary Areas	Exports				Imports			
	1950	1953	1954	1955	1950	1953	1954	1955
EPU Area of which:	55	64	61	64	52	63	61	59
– Sterling area	24	19	21	19	15	14	14	15
– Germany	3	13	11	15	4	12	11	10
– France	7	8	7	8	8	11	9	11
Dollar Area of which:	21	15	15	17	24	21	23	24
– USA	15	11	10	10	15	12	18	19
Latin American countries outside the dollar area	7	4	4	7	11	5	5	6
Rest of the world	17	17	20	12	13	11	11	11

Source: AD, DE-CE, 1945–61, vol. 371: OEEC Council, doc. C(56)201, 'Association de l'Espagne aux travaux de l'organisation. Rapport du groupe de travail spécial du conseil. Appendice à l'Annexe A', Paris, 25 July 1956.

It is worth considering that Spain's total exports expanded very weakly; exports augmented 19.8 per cent between 1948 and 1955. This was an extremely low performance if one considers that world exports increased 56.2 per cent and continental Western Europe's total exports (excluding

Yugoslavia and Finland) increased 145.7 per cent in that same period. Nevertheless, the argument here is one of quality. While Spain's trade relations did not allow rapid trade expansion or economic transformation, they did avert economic collapse. During the period from 1948 to 1955, Spain's imports increased 28 per cent (continental Western Europe's imports increased 72.6 per cent) and helped the Spanish economy to proceed to an important rate of expansion in the 1950s, the first postwar period of economic growth. Spain's bilateral agreements with the United Kingdom, France, Germany, and the smaller European countries provided for substantial increases in the shipment to Spain of a variety of essential capital equipment items, including railroad equipment, trucks, electrical equipment and a vast range of industrial machinery.

That Spanish bilateralism did not collapse within the context of increasing multilateral cooperation in trade and payments requires explanation. Records of bilateral trade talks prove to be an important source because concessions from individual countries in terms of extending a similar OEEC treatment to Spain on specific commodities were an important subject when negotiating the signing or renewal of trade and payments agreements. The OEEC's primary purposes were to increase the resources of food and raw materials outside the dollar area and to return the OEEC economies to a state which would allow them, without requiring continued dollar assistance, to move toward a worldwide non-discriminatory trade system and to the general convertibility of currencies by 1952/53. It should not be surprising, therefore, that some thought it inevitable to include a country which was geographically inseparable from the group and had rich deposits of high-grade iron ores, potash and pyrites, as well as zinc, lead, mercury, wolfram, cork, rosin, and many other raw materials. National delegates to the OEEC wondered more than once, although always outside the Council room, whether Spain could be excluded from the program of viability when some of its products were in high demand and many of them were still irreplaceable except against dollar expenditure.[5]

In general, trade with Spain was conducted on the basis of precisely defined goods, mostly so-called essentials accompanied by less essentials as counterpart to which each partner agreed to issue licenses up to a quota (specified either in quantity or value) during the period covered by the agreement (usually one year). Essential imports were those commodities considered necessary to feed the population and to implement public plans for general economic rehabilitation. Consequently, import licenses were generally granted only for the more essential needs to prevent the drain of the country's scarce reserves of convertible currencies and gold. As a general rule, the Spanish authorities reserved foreign exchange for import of foodstuffs and tobacco, industrial raw materials (in particular petroleum products, cotton,

wool, rubber, wood pulp, phosphate, copper), machinery (particularly hydro-
electric plant, mining machinery, industrial equipment, public works machinery, motor vehicles, tractors and agricultural machinery, railway material, and scientific and precision instruments), chemicals, and, lastly, a limited
number of drugs. Licenses were generally not issued for goods which could
be manufactured in Spain regardless of price and quality. Imports of competitive goods were allowed in only when domestic production was manifestly
inadequate to meet demand. Less essentials were goods of a range of consumer and capital goods, which varied from country to country and in time.
Their common characteristic was that they were of secondary importance in
the use of the always limited foreign exchange resources. Licenses were
granted for less essentials to secure export and import quotas for essentials.
Without some form of restraint, Spain probably would have spent nothing on
imports of less essential goods since it was chronically short of foreign exchange.

Bilateral trade agreements were complemented by payments agreements
which defined the method of financing trade. The system by which outstanding balances (after the two central banks had offset their mutual claims and
debts) required settlement in gold and/or hard currencies at relatively brief
intervals was replaced by one providing for longer periods. The new system
also provided for the introduction of the so-called swings, whereby exporters
in the creditor country received payment without having to wait for importers
in the debtor country to make full payment into the corresponding account so
as to save the debtor the need of paying in dollars and/or gold. The swings, or
mutual credit margins, established the amounts of inconvertible credit within
which Spain and its partner limited their respective debtor and creditor positions to avoid settlements in either gold or hard currency. Frequently, swings
were not paid at the end of a bilateral agreement's life, and thus acted as long-
term reciprocal commercial credits, instead of financing temporary swings in
bilateral balances of trade. Spain maintained swing credits with all continental OEEC countries except Austria.

Reciprocal swing credits provided limited flexibility in trade. On the one
hand, Spain could import from the partner without the need to maintain a
strict bilateral trade balance until the deficit in the clearing account reached
the authorized limit. On the other hand, most European countries did not have
to limit their sales to the value of Spanish purchases of their goods. Increases
in the credit margins favorable to Spain were difficult to obtain because the
Spaniards could not provide any satisfactory exchange guarantee, and commercial partners found it very difficult to obtain settlement of any substantial
Spanish deficit. Contrary to the EPU agreements, where the credit element
was provided by the clearing union mechanism independently of the amounts

and number of transactions involved, or the sterling agreements which did not require a bilateral balance of trade between any two particular countries, the Spanish monetary area benefited only from limited credit lines established on the basis of a routine anticipation of periodic fluctuations in the bilateral balance of trade.

Within this framework, a bilateral balancing of trade was compulsory, once all quotas were utilized and credit swings allowed by the partner exhausted. When the bilateral balance exceeded the agreed credit provisions, the debtor country was committed to settle the difference in gold or dollars (the so-called gold point). The credit margins authorized were normally respected by Spain, which tried to conserve its dollar holdings for imports from the dollar area. Frequently, however, the balances in excess of permitted swings were usually not adhered to in practice. As we shall see, in the desire to maintain trade with Spain, Europeans expanded the swings, provided additional short-term commercial credits, and improved the conditions under which certain commodities were exported by Spain. Those countries lacking a trade agreement with Spain carried on bilateral trade on global compensation accounts.

There was no country in Western Europe that rejected trade with Spain. Most interesting is the case of France, which had previously adopted extreme retaliatory measures. Official French quarters had come to the realization that a policy of open hostility toward Spain was not in the best interests of France itself. The French government therefore decided to reopen its frontier with Spain. Since bilateral trade had been at a standstill for two years after February 1946, the French decided to link the reopening of the border with adopting the necessary steps to recover the commercial ground lost.[6] A few weeks after the agreement to open the border progressively, negotiations had been concluded and a bilateral trade and payments agreement was signed in May 1948. This replaced a barter system installed immediately after the reopening of the common border. The reopening of the frontier and the new commercial agreement enabled Spain to get vital supplies of phosphates as well as some coal, a wide range of chemicals, electrical goods, motor vehicles, and other transport equipment, and to renew exports on a considerable scale to a traditional market for minerals and agricultural products. Imports from Spain grew from Ff 20 million in 1947 to Ff 4209 million in 1948, while exports went from three million to Ff 863 million. France immediately became a major consumer of Spanish exports in 1948. This occurred despite the fact that all bilateral trade was nil in January, that the border progressively opened only after mid-February, and that the bilateral trade agreement was not signed until May. The recovery of trade was absolutely spectacular.

Once political obstacles had been overcome, economic difficulties came to the forefront. They explain the slow growth of French exports to Spain until 1950. Among these difficulties was a levy introduced in June 1948 on imports of some non-essential goods. The levy was imposed on a discriminatory country basis (for instance, 20 per cent of the peseta value for French goods, 30 per cent for British, and 40 per cent for Swiss).[7] The continued rise in Spanish export prices during 1948, as a result of the over-valued peseta, made its trading situation with all countries increasingly serious. The list of goods that required subsidizing for export to the European markets progressively lengthened. Prices for Spain's most important export goods (iron ore, pyrites, potash, and oranges) were generally not higher than world prices, but prices for desirable but less essential goods were, in many cases, 50 per cent or more higher than world prices.[8] As early as October 1948, the French–Spanish agreement was failing to work because the margin to be covered by the subsidy proved too great. At the time of renewal, in June 1949, only 65 per cent of the volume of trade forecast during the April–May 1948 negotiations was accomplished. Spanish trade with Italy and Switzerland was virtually in a state of suspense because the surcharge had proven too high also, and exports to the United States fell to 50 per cent of the 1946 level.

The United Kingdom was the only country with which Spain was able to maintain any substantial volume of trade at the time, avoiding political interference by favoring a policy of working agreements with Spain on trade and payments. The monetary agreement of March 1947 and the supplementary agreement of June 1947 (concerning free convertibility of sterling), which should have governed payments between the Spanish monetary area and the sterling area up to April 1949, were abrogated by the bilateral trade agreement of June 1948 and the payments agreement of December 1948, when Spain instituted the multiple exchange rate system. The trade agreement was extended until June 1949, when a new trade agreement was signed and complemented with a payments agreement in December 1949; a new bilateral trade agreement was singed in June 1950. As far as possible, the Spanish Minister of Industry and Commerce stressed, bilateral trade should 'always be conducted on a plane of mutual understanding and advantage entirely divorced from the political scene'.[9] For their part, the British tried 'to keep questions of politics and trade apart, and to conduct the latter on purely business principles'.[10]

If politics presented no major problems, economics did. The consultative committee established to keep under review the course of bilateral trade faced the same problems as others: trade did not reach the level which was expected to result from the agreements concluded. It soon became clear that the gap between the peseta subsidy fund and the import program's cost could not be bridged except by substantially increasing the existing surcharge. Such a step might simply have stopped trading. Alternative mechanisms, such as combined accounts, failed to promote Spanish exports. No real change in prices could be expected in normal circumstances until the peseta was devalued. Nevertheless, keeping imports from Spain within the limits of the subsidy fund meant the restriction of Spanish purchasing power which would have resulted, in turn, in a lower level of imports. In London the solution to increase Spain's sterling holdings was to grant additional credits and swings, to purchase additional useful commodities which did not require subsidies, and, more importantly, to implement a non-discriminatory policy with regard to Spain's main export commodities.

The conciliatory British attitude was not insignificant. Anglo-Spanish trade was an essential part of Spain's economic and financial machinery. According to official trade statistics, trade with the United Kingdom was higher than with any other country in the world. This fact alone would justify paying special attention to the significance of the British market for the Spanish economy and its fluctuations. To this should be added the very important feature that Spain, by virtue of its payments agreement with the United Kingdom, could automatically and freely transfer its sterling earnings for purposes of direct current transactions, not only in the British Isles, but in the whole sterling area (from which most of Spanish purchases of petroleum products, rubber, cotton, wool, wheat, and jute came) and in the so-called transferable accounts area, that is, in the majority of the soft currency countries. In addition, Spain could benefit from administrative transferability, that is transfers of sterling with the specific consent of the Bank of England, on the understanding that Spain continued to make adequate provision for financial transfers to the United Kingdom and for imports from the United Kingdom and the sterling area as a whole.[11] Administrative transferability referred to some hard currency areas. Because the British wanted to reestablish sterling as a medium for international settlements, transferability of sterling for current transactions expanded consistently either by a widening of the transferable accounts area or by the administrative action of the Bank of England. Countries within the dollar area were the only ones almost permanently excluded from sterling transferability.[12] Therefore, if Spain were to improve its sterling position, it might be able to pay for increased imports from the biggest multilateral trading area in the world. The pound sterling was as important as the dollar, and was treated as a currency almost as hard. But from a structural economic point of view, there were more possibilities for increasing the country's sterling earnings through export trade than with regard to dollars. The use of sterling, as the British commercial counsellor in Madrid expressed, was 'called to play a crucial role in filling the important gaps created by Spain's shortage of dollars and the obvious limitations of narrow bilateral trading with other countries'.[13]

Under these circumstances, it is important to note that the British gave Spanish exports, in particular agricultural commodities, a rather liberal treatment even before trade liberalization as promoted by the OEEC applied. The expansion of Spanish exports in the British market before 1950 (Table 7.3) was due exclusively to the promotion of agricultural commodities. Spanish agricultural products imported by the Ministries of Food and Supply had few restrictions because of the need to meet minimum consumption requirements. Private importers needed no specific permission – in British licensing system terms, Open General License (OGL) – to import major Spanish goods. The Board of Trade offered OGLs to a wide range of consumer goods supplied by those countries where there was no risk of hard currency loss. This included the sterling area, most OEEC countries – except the Federal Republic, Switzerland, Belgium, and Luxembourg – and certain other non-dollar countries, including Spain. This move was taken before any multilateral European payments system came into operation. Imports not under OGLs (such as mandarins, grapes, lemons, onions, plums, apricots, melons, and peaches) were subject to Open Individual License (OIL), that is, licenses issued to individual importers on a source-discriminatory basis. For the first four commodities mentioned, individual licenses for imports from Spain were freely granted, and Spanish goods were not placed at a disadvantage in the British market. This was due to the fact that they did not compete with domestic horticultural production. Otherwise, licenses would have been withdrawn during the season of peak home production (block licensing) in the interest of domestic crops.

TABLE 7.3   BRITISH TRADE WITH SPAIN, 1947–9
(value in thousands of sterling)

	Imports						Exports					
	1947	%	1948	%	1949	%	1947	%	1948	%	1949	%
Total	25 571	100	30 966	100	33 639	100	7388	100	13 644	100	11 924	100
Class I	18 316	71.6	24 138	77.9	26 677	79.3	154	2.1	229	1.7	185	1.5
Class II	5042	19.7	4543	15.1	3703	14.4	692	9.4	3293	24.1	4270	35.8
Class III	2212	8.6	2272	7.3	2743	8.4	6498	87.9	10 068	73.8	7419	62.2

Source: *Annual Statement of the Trade of the United Kingdom with Commonwealth countries and Foreign Countries.* It includes Canary Islands and Spanish ports in North Africa. Value of total imports, not of articles retained in the United Kingdom. Class I: foodstuffs, drink and tobacco; Class II: raw materials, minerals, fuels and lubricants; Class III: manufactured goods.

The low performance of British imports of manufactured goods was related to the low economic interest offered by Spain's goods. It was not a result of the non-inclusion of Spain in the token import scheme for manufactured imports, which can be considered the only major relaxation in the strict licensing arrangements for imports of manufactured goods before the OEEC's trade liberalization program. The exporters from the countries included in the scheme were allowed to send a fixed percentage by value of their prewar exports (between 20 and 40 per cent) for an agreed list of products (about 200 commodities), mainly consumer goods, but including also some goods for industry.[14] Although not formally admitted (it could not be justified on political grounds), Spain benefited from the token import scheme through *ad hoc* arrangements. The Spaniards had been anxious for the United Kingdom to grant import quotas on a number of less essential products. In order to satisfy them, the British should have granted quotas on a scale likely to give Spain better treatment than a number of OEEC countries that faced British domestic protection, particularly on high-quality pottery and textile goods. However, had the United Kingdom refused every concession, it would have obtained no quotas for essentials: iron ore, potash, pyrites, zinc concentrates, rosin, mercury, and wolfram. The Board of Trade suggested that, since Spain's interests were confined to a few items, some of which received import quotas already, by granting token import quotas to a few goods, such as cotton textiles, chemicals, porcelain, toys, shoes, and tobacco, they covered the Spanish list without great economic effort. This was finally agreed upon by the Foreign Office and Treasury officials.[15]

Spain's exports of raw materials to the United Kingdom did not increase because of low output. Although the world supply of raw materials had improved from previous years, the dominant rule was to obtain as much non-dollar supply from the greatest possible diversity of sources. Potash provides a good example of the logic of this attitude. A worldwide shortage of potash was reduced in 1947 when Palestine potash appeared on the world markets and the Soviet zone in Germany reappeared as a potash supplier. However, the US pressure after November 1947 for an embargo policy as part of a general containment strategy against the Soviet Union and its satellites posed an uncertain threat to the latter source of potash.[16] Spanish potash was left as the only substitute when a shortage of potash was accentuated in 1948 by the interruption of supplies of high-grade Palestine potash. That year Spain traded large quantities of potash in exchange for ammonium sulphate from Belgium, potatoes from the Netherlands, and pulp from Scandinavia. The United States was also knocking at the door for supplies against payments in dollars at exceptionally attractive prices. The main British concern regarding Spain was to obtain a fair share of its exports of raw materials, which it did (Table 7.4).

While the total volume of exports to the United Kingdom, especially of agricultural produce, continuously expanded, direct imports into Spain from the

United Kingdom increased more slowly and many of the less essential manufactured goods diminished. This situation differed from the great expectations created by the British commercial counsellors in Madrid, who saw great
opportunities for British producers in the Spanish market.[17] Spain's main
trading problem with European countries was its inability (or unwillingness)
to purchase a greater amount of less essentials. In general, bilateral agreements were based on the assumption that essentials (capital goods and certain
raw materials) were supplied by commercial partners at a certain level of purchase of less essentials. Although the problem caused by a low level of imports of less essential manufactured goods was not exclusively Spain's, it
was an important factor in Anglo-Spanish commercial negotiations.

**TABLE 7.4   BRITISH IMPORTS OF SELECTED
RAW MATERIALS, 1949–50**

	1949	1950
Pyrites (tons)	230 323	195 829
Spain	227 342	179 901
Iron ore (tons)	8 692 897	8 412 876
Sweden	3 103 819	3 441 802
Algeria	1 585 947	1 481 057
Spain	807 297	750 239
Spanish North Africa	491 176	433 526
Tunisia	453 567	468 590
France	368 611	373 021
Mercury (lb)	1 430 586	4 119 097
Spain	874 505	3 532 807
Italy	104 352	528 822
Yugoslavia	98 110	–
Potash (tons)	394 193	397 982
France	160 638	157 614
Spain	53 494	56 419

Source: PRO, BOT 11/4722: Notes on estimates of
essential supplies.

The system of quota lists established in trade agreements in June 1948 was
the first attempt at increasing the rate of Spanish purchases of less essentials.
The first set of lists enumerated the commodities that each government wanted to import from the other and the maximum allocations allowed by each
country in case of a scarcity. A second set of lists referred to less essential
goods, for which the importing authorities were bound to issue import licenses.

List drafting revealed the conflict-prone nature of bilateralism; the partner country was anxious to obtain Spanish raw materials and Spain was anxious to sell articles of secondary importance to foreign importers, and vice-versa. The lists established approximate quantities and values, but they did not commit either government to the prices to be paid.[18] From the outset the Spanish import authorities complied badly in licensing quotas of British less essentials as prescribed in the agreements:

> The Spanish tendency was to spoil every trade agreement by buying all the essentials and pleading poverty when they were asked to take less essentials. When goods offered had no interest for them they had no money but they could suddenly produce money if copper or iron and steel were offered to them.[19]

The Spanish tried, as did all, to use their currency holdings for imports of essentials to the near exclusion of other goods of a less essential nature but which trade partners were anxious to export. Since sterling holdings to pay for essentials were low, the Spanish authorities reluctantly granted licenses for less essentials. British merchants in Madrid, fearing competition in the fields of machinery and transport equipment, criticized their government 'for not taking more Spanish produce and for not insisting that Spain shall only buy manufactured goods in exchange'.[20] Some in London were of a different view. The Board of Trade was being increasingly pressed by British manufacturers of less essential goods over the lack of Spanish licenses for a wide range of goods. They drew special attention to these commodities because they had difficulties in all markets. The Board of Trade considered sanctions to force the Spanish to fulfil their undertakings for less essentials in the trade agreement, although it recognized that the 'armory of threats' was limited.[21]

The most important bargaining tool at the disposal of the British was to remove transferability benefits, that is, to deny Spain the use of its sterling earnings to make payments to third countries for current transactions. As far as the rules of sterling were concerned, however, Spain had behaved 'in an exemplary manner'. The largest part of Spain's sterling earnings was automatically absorbed by purchasing essential and traditional sterling imports, which included coal, capital equipment, petroleum products supplied by British companies, and imports of essential raw materials from Commonwealth countries. In addition, sterling transferability sanctions were inconvenient at a time when British policy was to make sterling more rather than less convertible. Any administrative modification such as the one proposed could not be done 'without upsetting the overall world implications' of the use of sterling as an international currency. Consequently, the British Treasury and the Bank of England maintained that they could not use a financial sanction of this magnitude in countering the shortcomings of commercial practices.[22]

The Spanish authorities argued that they were short of sterling and wanted to use their reserves to the best advantage, that is for the import of raw materials and capital goods. The fulfilment of less essential purchases depended directly on how well they could obtain their basic needs and still earn a surplus of the necessary currency. The Under-Secretary of Foreign Economy and Commerce, Tomás Súñer Ferrer, promised that, in return for the understanding attitude of the British, who had allowed extensive use of sterling to buy large quantities of essentials at a difficult time, the Ministry of Industry and Commerce would issue licenses for a considerable volume of less essentials. Licenses were granted for railway materials, machines, machine tools, electrical machinery, but only a few were granted for less essentials (motor cars and commercial vehicles). From a commercial point of view, although Spain failed to admit more less essential goods, it imported ever greater quantities of raw materials and capital goods from the United Kingdom. Any overall reduction of trade due to discriminatory action would have been felt most in Spanish imports of less essential goods. No discriminatory action could improve Spain's sterling holdings, which was exactly what the discussion was all about. Finally, it is important to note that the Board of Trade did not consider excluding Spain from OGL. This was not surprising, because the British policy toward Spain was in strict accordance with the general tendency to extend quota removal to non-OEEC soft-currency countries when it did not lead to balance-of-payments difficulties involving loss of gold and dollars.[23]

The British, then, decided to expand imports from Spain, including less essential goods, on a unilateral basis, provided they obtained what they considered a reasonable share of Spanish raw materials. Coal remained by far the most important item from the Spanish point of view, followed by tin-plate, copper, fertilizers and supplies of petroleum products. It is important to bear in mind that Spain drove a hard bargain over its essential raw materials in the face of strong European competition for British coal, sterling transferability rights, and non-discriminatory treatment when the OEEC moved toward new forms of multilateral economic cooperation.

THE OEEC TRADE LIBERALIZATION PROGRAM: AN OBSTACLE TO SPANISH TRADE?

The founding convention of the Organization for European Economic Cooperation was signed in Paris in April 1948. It was then seen as the first step on the path toward European Unity.[24] The OEEC's tasks were to promote a common reconstruction program, to remove trade restrictions between the participating countries, and to ease financial barriers. As soon as it was feasible, the OEEC moved from the allocation of aid to the implementation of trade liberalization through the removal of quantitative restrictions. These were believed to be a far greater impediment to free trade than tariffs, which had lost most of their protective incidence due to widespread changes in international prices. Moreover, there was a specific institution to deal with tariffs as limitations on trade (the General Agreement on Tariffs and Trade, instituted in Geneva in 1947). The existence of GATT and the deep disagreement among the members of the European Customs Union Study Group in 1949 indicated that if progress were to be achieved at the OEEC level, efforts had to be concentrated on removing quantitative restrictions.[25]

Trade was conceived as a means of integration and, thus, it was necessary to stop the proliferation of trade barriers and discriminatory practices. A program for trade liberalization was the OEEC's main working tool, although the adoption of the non-discrimination principle caused considerable difficulty as long as European currencies remained non-transferable among themselves. A Code of Liberalization of Trade, approved in Paris in August 1950, came into force simultaneously with the signing of the agreement establishing a European Payments Union (EPU) in September; the transferability of European currencies provided by the EPU substantially diminished the pressure to discriminate against any specific European partner for payments reasons. The OEEC Code was a code of behavior for merchandise trade between the OEEC member countries prescribing principles of equal treatment on liberalized as well as non-liberalized trade; those countries with economic or financial difficulties were exempted from immediate implementation of the 60 per cent liberalization target, and not obliged to take all of the measures for the liberalization of trade. In October 1950, the OEEC Council agreed to raise by February 1951 the liberalization percentage to 75 per cent of imports on private account from the OEEC area – which included the metropolitan countries of Europe that were members of OEEC and their dependent overseas territories – on the basis of 1948 trade levels, in each of the three major categories of goods into which trade was divided: raw materials, manufactured goods, agricultural products and foodstuffs. By the end of 1951, the measures were to be applied without discrimination in respect of non-liberalized commodities originating in other OEEC countries.[26]

Spanish economic authorities looked anxiously at the developments taking place in Spain's major trading area. When the trade liberalization program came into operation, the OEEC countries and their dependent overseas territories accounted for 45 per cent of Spanish imports (equivalent to a total value of $167.2 million) and 69 per cent of Spanish exports ($199.8 million). Spain had a trade surplus with the OEEC countries and a trade deficit with their dependent overseas territories, but showed a surplus of roughly $33 million with the group as a whole. It was Spain's only trading surplus with any area that could partially compensate for the overall deficit with the rest of the world ($64.6 million). Spain's largest adverse balances were with South America ($92 million) and the United States and Canada ($18 million). Among the OEEC countries, Spain had a large trading surplus with the United Kingdom, Germany, and France.[27]

Initially, the official position adopted by the government regarding the OEEC was a combination of resignation for the dollars not received, a declared lack of interest, and an affirmation of political independence. What could be considered a normal pattern of public behavior by an ostracized country came, on this occasion, with authentic relief: 'Spain could not now logically adhere to these more liberal systems'.[28] As a matter of principle, however, it was necessary to watch the implications of any external event affecting major export markets and suppliers. In this specific case, Spain's non-participation in European trade liberalization would render it even more difficult to maintain the already unsatisfactory level of exports, which was of extreme importance for the nation's economic development and political stability. Some countries proposed that the Spanish authorities suppress lists and give greater freedom to bilateral trade.[29] The Spanish position was that any decision to free a given commodity from controls was to remain necessarily on the bilateral level and not be extended to all partners. Nevertheless, the Spanish economic authorities immediately learned that bilateral negotiations with Spain's main European partners were intrinsically linked with the ongoing process of trade liberalization.

At the time of the renewal of the June 1948 trade agreement with Spain, the British authorities suppressed individual import licenses for a long list of products, extending OGLs to the bulk of agricultural commodities subject to bilateral trade. By May 1950, all the items which the British imported from Spain were on OGLs (except sardines, tunny, bananas, and raisins).[30] The Spanish foreign economic attaché interpreted this as result of the trade liberalization policy undertaken by the United Kingdom together with the rest of the OEEC member states.[31] The effects of this important liberalization measure were visible in the increase in agricultural exports taking place in 1950–1.

Encouraged by this liberal attitude, the Spaniards tried to obtain similar treatment from France, their second largest consumer of agricultural produce. The French government had already responded to the difficulties in bilateral trade by increasing imports of citrus fruit to allow the Spanish to

import French motor vehicles and railway material.[32] However, it was impossible to obtain from Paris any formal compromise to treat Spain as an OEEC
country. There is hardly any record of trade meetings that did not include a request from the Spanish delegation for more favorable import-licensing treatment. In France, unlike the United Kingdom, there was strong domestic
opposition to the liberalization of imports from Spain. French continental
and North African territories produced a range of products which competed
directly with Spanish exports, especially fruit. Their natural response to the
seasonal nature of supply and price markets was the establishment of a highly
sophisticated system of protection, the so-called *calendriers*, which were
highly prejudicial to exports of fresh fruit and vegetables and which, therefore, constituted the first target of the Spanish negotiating team.[33]

Calendriers consisted of an import timetable which took into account the
timing of domestic and North African production. Countries entered international trade to meet requirements at different times of the year and stopped
imports when domestic harvests reached the market. This protection took the
form of either seasonal modifications in tariff levels, quota volume and licensing, or the halt of imports when the authorities perceived possible damage for the market conditions of domestic crops. This implied an immediate
and unilateral action to stop imports of a given commodity when the minimum price was reached or the home crop harvested. Quota volumes could be
perfectly spelled out in bilateral trade agreements using the hypothetical timing of local crops. Since the estimates were made much in advance, they took
account of similar conditions of supply and demand within the importing
country in previous years but not those of the actual campaign. If there was no
exact coincidence between the calendrier's dates and domestic output campaigns production, there could either be a massive supply shortage or massive importation at the end of the fixed dates, with consequent price
distortions. Pressure from French and North African agricultural organizations, therefore, made it tremendously difficult to increase imports from
Spain. It is not surprising that under these circumstances, the Spanish commercial authorities expected OEEC discipline to break the pressure from
French agricultural organizations. Indeed, import liberalization was perceived by the French farming community as a threat to its bargaining position
vis-à-vis industrialists and as a direct threat to domestic protection. For the
Spanish government, the OEEC could help Spain indirectly in those cases,
such as France, where Spain's bargaining power was nil due to the strength of
agricultural pressure groups. French industry was aware that the Spanish
capacity to import capital goods depended upon the volume of imports from
Spain. Due to the pressure exerted by some industrial groups during the bilateral negotiations of October 1950, the French delegation agreed to extend the

OEEC liberalization measures to Spain.[35] The agreement signed for the period November 1951 to October 1952 represented an increase of 50 per cent over the previous agreement in the value of the trade flows between the two countries; oranges accounted for 53 per cent of Spain's exports to France. In return, Spain had to spend a fixed quota of its earnings in francs to purchase manufactured commodities classified under a special list.[36] In real terms, however, calendriers stood in the way of the promise to extend liberalization, especially for fruits and early crops.

Trade with Germany was still recovering when the OEEC liberalization program was being elaborated. The recovery of Germany's economy and the end of the Allies' physical control over its resources created great expectations about the future capacity of the Federal Republic to absorb Spanish goods. The Spanish authorities had expected that the transfer of trade negotiations from the occupying military authorities to new agencies after the birth of the Federal Republic would lead automatically to a proper trade agreement. However, the administrative complexity involved in setting up the Federal government after September 1949 caused the last quarter of the year to elapse before the list of commodities to be included in the following year's agreement was decided. Despite the existence of the Federal government, the exhaustion of most quotas led to negotiating an additional agreement with the Allied High Commission. It was signed in November 1949. Negotiations for a proper bilateral trade agreement took place in March, and further administrative difficulties postponed the signing of the agreement until June 1950. The German import list of commodities amounted to $43 million whereas the Spanish list totalled $48 million. In spite of the efforts made to make the two lists even, it was not possible because the Germans advanced a number of insuperable objections to fixing large quotas for the bulk of Spain's traditional exports. French and Italian agricultural exports obtained preference in the restricted and high-priced German market. During the first six months of 1950, Spanish exporters operated within the 1949 quota allocations. The German interpretation was that the new agreement could not begin operating until it had been definitively signed. By contrast, the Spanish authorities, with a pent-up absorption capacity for German products, authorized imports to the maximum swing allowed ($5 million), which caused a radical alteration in reciprocal payments during the following months. From a balance of approximately $2 million in favor of Spain at the end of February 1950, an unfavorable $5 million deficit was reached in September. As the commercial attaché in Bonn expressed it, 'the so-called liberalization policy of the German Government [...] has operated against Spanish exports, which have been treated, to our way of thinking, in an unjust way'.[37]

In general, initial trade liberalization caused a deterioration in Spain's balance of payments with the EPU monetary area. Earnings in all the currencies mentioned in Table 7.5 (except Belgian franc, Danish kroner, and, significantly, dollar-trade with Western Germany) decreased. Export earnings in these currencies decreased from 80 per cent to 68 per cent over total export earnings. Expenditures in all these currencies decreased except in the case of the Belgian franc, escudo, and, again most significantly, dollar payments to Germany. The result was to pass from a surplus in balance of payments with the EPU area of approximately $7.9 million in 1949, to a $15.4 million deficit in 1950; from a trade balance surplus of $14.3 million to a deficit of $6.6 million.

TABLE 7.5   SPAIN'S BALANCE OF PAYMENTS WITH THE OEEC MONETARY AREAS IN 1949–50 (in pesetas)

	Credits		Debits	
Year	1949	1950	1949	1950
Total	4 680 157 700*	3 602 841 587	4 529 789 630[♪]	3 969 844 129
Trade Balance	2 974 486 591	2 909 877 364	3 681 538 512	3 228 194 662
Pound sterling	1 302 658 159	1 022 965 152	1 172 836 986	1 095 740 480
French franc	485 971 217	402 289 028	539 142 228	412 610 366
Belgian franc	129 204 522	130 546 384	131 691 951	144 343 089
Swiss franc	167 310 883	109 298 993	157 272 583	99 416 003
Dutch guilder	170 650 490	122 592 376	170 373 346	143 072 202
Swedish kroner	134 820 306	124 647 944	131 316 504	127 805 438
Danish kroner	90 262 170	132 973 100	95 222 066	91 557 722
Norwegian kroner	60 920 759	49 853 940	57 098 800	48 164 413
Lira	58 205 594	3 965 731	76 295 549	11 620 522
Escudo	38 733 641	36 005 477	31 264 588	35 774 114
Dollar Germany	87 533 238	124 610 168	75 836 863	218 812 218
Dollar Italy	595 339	–	4 241 953	–
Total OEEC	2 725 026 031	2 259 748 293	2 638 575 622	2 428 916 567
as % of general total	58.2	62.7	58.2	61.2
Trade Balance in all currencies mentioned	2 384 287 785	1 970 589 954	2 227 628 554	2 043 340 733
as % of total trade balance	80.2	67.7	60.5	63.3

Source: AHBE, IEME, boxes 163 and 164: IEME's general balance of payments for 1949–50. (*) Pts 1 037 063 504 of which were credits granted by Argentina, US and Swiss private banks; (♪) Pts 147 960 331 of which were credits granted by US and Swiss banks.

Fortunately for Spain, although the liberalization percentages increased progressively (from 50 per cent in December 1949 to 75 per cent in February 1951), trade liberalization was reversible because countries facing balance-of-payments difficulties and other serious economic disturbances were allowed to suspend the application of the liberalization measures. When the deadline of February 1951 appeared, the process of liberalization stagnated and was soon followed by widespread deliberalization due to the deterioration of balance of payments, which was produced by stockpiling and price increases following the outbreak of war in Korea. The balance-of-payments difficulties, which the Code itself considered a legitimate reason for suspending liberalization measures, became the escape clause for avoiding any radical removal of non-tariff restrictions. Major importers invoked the Code and reestablished import licenses for OEEC exports: Germany in February 1951, the United Kingdom in November 1951, and France in February 1952.

The retreat toward protectionism was particularly disturbing in the first case because it was only in 1951 that Germany's total exports to the OEEC countries surpassed the prewar level, causing increasing payments difficulties to its partners. This case shows how bilateralism was beneficial to Spain, especially during a period of import restrictions. Exports to the German market increased in 1951 because Spanish trade was insulated from the increasing difficulties within the EPU (Table 7.6). The desire to expand German exports to Spain required, in turn, imports from Spain to produce the necessary earnings, which, incremented with short-term credits, could pay for the value of exports to Spain. Exports and imports were tightly inter-linked. In 1951, the reciprocal credit swing was increased from $15 million to $20 million worth of deutschmarks. This was not due to the need to cover a temporary debit in the trade balance, but primarily to extend an additional unilateral loan to Spain.[38] At the same time, the structural tendency to move toward an export surplus in trade with Spain induced the German economic authorities to grant 'substantial liberalization, particularly for the import of citrus fruit'.[39] This early German interest in treating Spanish agricultural exports liberally was intended to improve Spain's export performance. The capacity of the Spanish market depended on this to absorb larger quantities of goods from Germany. The dynamic pattern of Spain's export trade toward Germany (compared to Italy's) after 1951, was linked to an official policy designed to encourage imports from Spain in order to attain overall trade increases without altering substantially the credit swing originally established.

During the implementation of the 1951/52 bilateral trade agreement, the Federal Republic completely liberalized a long list of Spanish agricultural export commodities, including citrus fruit, in accordance with the liberalization lists presented to the OEEC Council.[40] This represented unilateral liberalization toward Spain because Spain did not adopt any import liberalization measures in return. By mid-October 1952, at the negotiations for a renewal of the trade agreement, the Spanish asked for an extension of all the liberalized

lists submitted to the OEEC since January 1952. Again, the Federal government agreed to extend to Spain the liberalization in agricultural products that
Germany had conceded within the OEEC. Spain was allowed to export the
most important commodity items in bilateral trade and most of the products
partially liberalized already without the need for import licenses and with no
limit other than the demand capacity of the German market. Whenever Spanish products competed with domestic production, temporary prohibitions
were raised, but these, in general, affected all exporters, OEEC members
included (except grapes which were totally liberalized for OEEC countries).
The Council of Ministers in Madrid was informed that the extension of liberalization benefits was an 'important concession' from the Federal Republic.[41]

TABLE 7.6   GERMANY'S IMPORTS FROM ITALY AND SPAIN, 1950–2
(in millions of deutschmarks)

Year	1950[a]	1951[b]	1952[c]	1953[d]	[b]%$_a$	[c]%$_b$	[d]%$_c$
Total Trade							
Italy	507	549	643	743	108.2	117.1	115.6
Spain	48	145	229	319	305.6	157.7	139.3
Total Agricultural Trade							
Italy	268	273	354	422	101.8	129.7	119.3
Spain	17	65	126	209	372.2	192.9	166.8

Source: *Der Aussenhandel der Bundesrepublik Deutschland* (various years).

Although the Germans had extended OEEC liberalization measures to
most of the Spanish agricultural exports, increased export quotas for non-
liberalized goods, included new products in the quota list, and increased the
swing to $20 million by October 1952 in order to assist Spain's debtor posi-
tion, the expected expansion of reciprocal trade did not occur. Spain limited
purchasing to what its authorities considered essentials (materials for the
coal and steel industry). Although creditor countries were anxious not to
curtail exports or to bring pressure on Spain to balance trade in a downward
direction, they were forced to put an end to bilateral trade when the amount
on non-transferable pesetas had been excessively accumulated in the clearings accounts. The Spanish formula for increasing bilateral trade was the automatic extension of liberalization to Spanish trade and an increase of the
financial swing, which altogether would increase Spain's payment capacity.[42] The Germans thought of a working arrangement with EPU, although
they never specified how to implement it without joining the OEEC.

Spanish EPU membership would have fulfilled the German desire to import from Spain regardless of Spanish exports to Germany and the state of the Spanish reserves. The impossibility of applying to Spain the benefits of the EPU mechanism, and inasmuch as free dollar settlements were not forthcoming, forced a reduction of German commercial discrimination against Spanish exports via the unilateral extension of the OEEC liberalization measures.

At the end of March 1953, the liberalization percentage in relation to goods imported from OEEC countries increased to 90 per cent. The Spaniards demanded the corresponding extension to their exports of the new OEEC liberalization measures since the one then applying to Spain was 'a little more restrictive'.[43] Six months later, as a result of the increased bargaining power that Spain acquired through its participation in the European conference of ministers of agriculture, the Spanish trade negotiators asked the Germans to extend to them trade liberalization measures in terms similar to the OEEC members and to increase the quotas on products not subject to liberalization.[44] An increase in the list of liberalized products for Spain was difficult to produce in clear-cut terms, for political reasons. Nevertheless, Spain obtained immediate increases in the quotas of juices and concentrates of citrus fruit, table grapes, melons, and artichokes from the level set by the trade agreement then in force. By these means, by 1953, West Germany became the most important supplier to the Spanish economy (11.6 per cent of total imports) and the second largest (after the United Kingdom) consumer of Spanish exports (13 per cent of total exports). The excitement was so high that the Spanish Minister of Agriculture suggested the formation of a Bonn–Madrid axis![45]

This liberal treatment temporarily changed in 1954, showing the Spanish that reverses in trade liberalization also affected them. In February 1954, Germany published a liberalized list covering 92 per cent of its private trade with OEEC countries on the base year 1949 but it was not automatically extended to Spain. On the new list, there were some export products which Spain could not or did not want to increase, while other products under specific quota restrictions were of great interest to Spanish exporters.[46] In August 1954, Germany made extensive liberalization concessions and, after April 1955, it finally included wine and citrus fruit. The result of this liberal attitude toward Spain's agricultural export trade was a spectacular increase in exports to the Federal Republic from 1949 to 1956. In that period, the value of exports to Germany multiplied nine times and agricultural exports 9.8 times, while German imports from Italy multiplied three times and agricultural imports 4.3 times.[47]

Trade restrictions were also imposed by the British Conservative government on the grounds of balance-of-payments difficulties. The measures adopted in November 1951 and again in March 1952 were directed in particular at the liberalized EPU trade. As a result of these restrictions, the liberalization percentage dropped from 90 per cent of British 1948 private trade with the OEEC in November 1951, to 61 per cent in December, and to 44 per cent a year later. Minister Arburúa presented import restrictions as proof of the failure, inefficiency, and bad service given to dollar assistance, the objective of which was to promote trade not to restrict it.[48] His implication was that, had Spain received dollar aid, it would have been put to better use.

Action was planned to restrict imports on a larger scale than that which actually took place. The quotas announced should have reduced imports to 38 per cent of the equivalent 1951 import level of the items under restriction but, in fact, total imports in 1952 amounted to 54 per cent of the 1951 level. The strategic stockpiling program instituted by the Labour government following the Korean War had slowed down, but reduction in the import of raw materials was not very great. On average, import restrictions were thought to affect non-foodstuffs more strongly than foodstuffs, but the effect was more strongly felt in the latter group. Commercial performance in 1952 was disastrous for fresh fruit, imports of which dropped to 19.4 per cent of the 1951 level. Excluding this category, total 1952 private imports of the restricted food items from

TABLE 7.7 COMPARISON OF QUOTAS AND IMPORTS FROM THE RELAXATION AREA OF THE ITEMS AFFECTED BY THE CUTS OF NOVEMBER 1951 AND MARCH 1952↔ (in thousands of sterling, cif)

	Imp. '51 (A)	Quo. '52 (B)	Imp. '52 (C)	B%A	C%A
Food					
Biscuits (1) #	14 305	2 040	10 602	14.26	74.11
Fondant (2) #	8 257	800	2 657	9.69	32.18
Cocoa products #	2 241	732	1 675	32.66	74.74
Preserved fruit and veg. #	2 715	1 077	1 703	39.67	62.73
Tomatoes (3) #	23 851	10 415	13 720	43.67	57.52
Canned meat #	57 924	26 723	29 198	46.13	50.41
Nuts and natural oils #	15 471	6 350	6 590	41.04	42.60
Sugar fat mixtures #	8 546	2 570	3 609	30.07	42.23
Fresh fruit #	15 948	4 791	3 090	30.04	19.37
Un-rationed Cheese *	8 868	4 500	9 666	50.74	109.00
Other foods	6 738	3 095	4 683	45.93	69.50
Total Food	164 864	63 093	87 193	38.27	52.89
Non-Food					
Carpets #	7 522	2 345	907	31.17	12.06
Apparel and dressed furs #	5 350	2 413	5 026	45.10	93.94

TABLE 7.7 (contd.)

	Imp. '51 (A)	Quo. '52 (B)	Imp. '52 (C)	B%A	C%A
Office machinery #	1 456	480	672	32.97	46.15
Sport and leather goods #	1 828	920	840	50.33	45.95
Imitation jewellery #	1 770	775	1 252	43.78	70.73
Furniture and glassware #	4 014	1 510	2 305	37.62	57.42
Paper goods and stationery #	4 012	1 720	1 369	42.87	34.12
Textile yarns (4)*	73 150	12 566	40 846	17.18	55.84
Matches *	1 384	685	1 180	49.49	85.26
Building materials and glass*	1 849	845	1 376	45.70	74.42
Other manufactures	4 319	1 572	2 206	36.40	51.08
Rape seed and oil *	1 223	810	2 106	66.23	172.20
Total Non-food	107 877	26 641	60 085	24.70	55.70
Total	272 741	89 734	147 278	32.90	54.00

Source: Values of quotas and import values of restricted items compiled from basic figures supplied by W.M. Corden, 'The control of imports: A Case Study. The United Kingdom Import Restrictions of 1951–2', *Journal of the Manchester School*, vol. 26/3 (1958) 190. Original values of quotas from *Board of Trade Journal* (24 November 1951) 1070, (19 April 1952) 787, and (31 May 1952) 1092. (↔) Excluding items for which no comparable import figures are available. (#) Items affected by November 1951 cuts. (*) Items affected by March 1952 cuts. (1) Biscuits, chocolate, raw cocoa; no quotas published for these items for the second half of 1952. (2) Fondant and cake mixtures; no quotas published for these items for the first half of 1952. (3) Tomato and fruit juice, pulp and purée and vegetables in brine; quotas for these items were issued for 12 months to June 1953; import figures are therefore given for the same period. (4) Textile yarns, piece-goods and manufactures.

all sources amounted to 56.5 per cent of food imports of the same items in 1951 (Table 7.7).

Spain tried unsuccessfully to avoid British restrictions, arguing that trade with Spain would not involve the United Kingdom in any loss of either dollars or gold. The Spanish economic authorities urged their British counterpart to encourage rather than restrict imports from Spain, since these had not contributed to the difficulties in the second half of the year which had forced the extensive trade controls. Again, during the trade talks held in Madrid in December 1952, the Spaniards had a new opportunity to point this out after the renewal of dispositions for import restriction had been adopted in March 1952.[49] Despite the failure of these demands, Spain came out of the experience more advantageously than the average pattern (Table 7.8).

Spanish behavior in relation to import restrictions in the British market differed from the general pattern with respect to both the importance and the

TABLE 7.8   BRITISH IMPORTS FROM SPAIN, 1950–3 (in sterling)

Year	1950 (a)	1951 (b)	1952 (c)	1953 (d)	c%b	d%b
Total	33 753 685	50 712 714	41 243 761	36 431 568	81.3	71.8
Class I	25 106 390	34 948 007	29 805 243	28 316 571	85.3	81.0
Fruit	10 765 012	17 742 104	13 308 382	13 258 457	75.0	74.7
Bananas	545 696	1 449 899	1 313 780	879 159		
Grapes	1 368 266	1 295 577	697 990	1 101 439		
Oranges	4 848 730	8 845 268	7 996 269	7 505 449		
Almonds	1 552 008	2 182 464	993 172	949 363		
D and P fruit#	857 851	1 625 176	866 815	713 542		
Nuts*	297 980	414 287	49 701	119 401		
Vegetables	11 494 632	13 614 880	13 840 006	11 579 879	101.6	85.0
Wine	2 501 274	3 460 109	2 447 963	3 105 153	70.7	89.7
All other	345 472	164 914	208 892	373 082	126.7	226.2
Class II	3 703 450	7 071 316	7 752 992	4 740 400	109.6	67.0
Class III	4 939 599	8 631 635	3 682 494	3 368 517	42.7	39.0
Chemicals	881 508	3 313 469	1 392 119	1 439 260		
Textiles	2 481 718	3 297 782	917 693	214 635		
Clothing	–	104 908	24 252	53 189		
Vehicles	211 546	217 500	274 000	2943		
Wood/Cork	167 862	1 100 293	670 845	567 090		
Pig Iron	–	–	89 467	637 664		
All other	1 196 965	572 829	190 787	370 781		
Miscellaneous	4246	27 756	3032	6080		

Source: *Annual Statement of the Trade of the United Kingdom with the Commonwealth Countries and Foreign Countries.* Including the Canary Islands. Value of
imports, not of articles retained in the United Kingdom; # Dried and preserved fruit;
* Barcelona and hazel nuts.

distribution of the effects. On the one hand, while the value of British imports of
restricted items from Spain in 1952 was 81 per cent of the value of these same
items in 1951, in the general pattern the relation was less favorable: 54 per cent
on average of the 1951 level. Therefore, the first conclusion to be drawn is that
Spain suffered less than average from import restrictions. On the other hand,
the disparity between foodstuff and non-foodstuff commodities was much
more striking. While, on average, both categories suffered the restrictive effect
to a similar extent, in the Spanish case, non-food items (mainly textile manufactures) suffered the effects of the restrictions much more strongly. Exports
of raw materials were not affected. A further decrease in the level of exports to
the United Kingdom during the period of restriction was deliberately avoided.[50] The liberal treatment given by the British to the principal Spanish export

commodities at the time of general restrictions was so obvious that, in December 1952, the Minister of Foreign Affairs expressed public appreciation.[51]

After 1952, the level of Spain's agricultural exports continued to fall for another year but only slightly and considerably less than those of Italy (Table 7.9). Spain did not suffer much either from early liberalization or from import restrictions regarding its main export commodities in the British market. Anglo-Spanish commercial relations at the time of restrictions show that the British authorities did not want to deprive Spain of sterling earnings and jeopardize mutually beneficial trade relations. The choices confronting the British were to give flexibility to a bilateral system which lacked it, to proceed through compensation operations, or to do without bilateral relations with Spain. The answer to this dilemma was the rapid bilateral trade recovery which took place in 1954. By 1955 Spain had already recovered pre-1952 export levels. This was important because the United Kingdom was the largest consumer of Spanish agricultural exports and because sterling transferability provided a little oxygen for Spain's asphyxiating bilateral system of international payments.

TABLE 7.9   **BRITISH TOTAL AND AGRICULTURAL IMPORTS FROM ITALY AND SPAIN, 1949–53 (in thousands of sterling)**

Year	1949	1950	1951[a]	1952[b]	1953[c]	$^b\%_a$	$^c\%_a$
TOTAL IMPORTS							
Italy	37 466	51 072	83 148	45 481	42 963	54.7	51.7
Spain	18 698	33 754	50 713	41 244	36 432	81.3	71.8
AGRICULTURAL IMPORTS							
Italy	22 198	25 433	31 372	14 990	19 114	47.8	69.3
Spain	26 677	25 106	34 948	29 805	28 317	85.3	81.0

Source: *Annual Statement of the Trade of the United Kingdom with the Commonwealth Countries and Foreign Countries.* Including the Canary Islands.

Similarly, in the French market, OEEC liberalization worked to the advantage of Italy only during 1950. This was not the case in 1951, nor in February 1952 when France suspended previous liberalization measures and imposed import restrictions. In 1951, the Spanish export performance in France was already more dynamic than the Italian one. In 1952 and 1953, Italian exports to France had suffered significant setbacks compared to 1951 as a result of French import restrictions. In contrast, Spanish agricultural exports experienced important increases in 1951 and especially in 1952 and 1953, despite restrictions, while

French imports from Italy continued to drop. In 1953, French total imports from Italy dropped by 35 per cent from the 1952 level and Italian agricultural exports dropped 14.6 per cent. By contrast, French imports from Spain decreased by seven per cent whereas agricultural exports increased by ten per cent (Table 7.10).

TABLE 7.10   FRANCE'S TOTAL AND AGRICULTURAL IMPORTS FROM ITALY AND SPAIN, 1949–53 (in millions of French francs)

Year	1949[a]	1950[b]	1951[c]	1952[d]	1953[e]	$\%_a$[b]	$\%_b$[c]	$\%_c$[d]	$\%_c$[e]
TOTAL IMPORTS									
Italy	17 653	38 071	49 571	35 077	22 815	215.7	130.2	70.8	46.0
Spain	12 900	9850	13 548	18 099	16 833	76.4	137.5	133.6	124.2
AGRICULTURAL IMPORTS									
Italy	3934	9763	9786	7274	6214	248.2	100.2	73.3	63.5
Spain	11 229	7983	9384	12 997	14 282	71.1	117.5	138.5	152.2

Source: *Tableau général du commerce extérieur. Commerce de la France avec la France d'Outre-Mer et les pays étrangers* (various years); the figures refer to commerce général d'importation.

These figures show that France gave different treatment to its agricultural imports from Spain and Italy during the period 1949 to 1953. The result was that, while Italy multiplied by 0.8 its agricultural exports to France between 1949 and 1953, the figure for Spain was 1.3. While agricultural commodities accounted for a very high percentage of Spain's total exports to France throughout the period, Italy's remained low. During the period of restrictions, despite the opposition shown by organized French agricultural producers, Spain enlarged its agricultural exports, while Italy, theoretically favored by common OEEC and EPU membership, did not. In 1952, Spain became France's major food and agricultural supplier. The Netherlands had held this position up to 1951. At a time of restrictions, trade between France and Spain continued to expand. This was in contrast to France's experience with many OEEC countries. This point is important, because France did not officially grant Spain any of the liberalization measures adopted in line with the OEEC.

The price information available does not give any advantage to Spain's agricultural exports over Italy's. By comparing Spain's wholesale prices with those of the major producing and trading countries in two important export commodities, oranges and wine, it can be concluded that lower prices do not explain Spain's success in competing with Italy.[52] The plethora of price distortions from which domestic agricultural commodities and trade prices suffered at that time should make the historian extremely careful when considering this information in terms of trade competition. Notwithstanding this, there seems to be evidence that the advantage that Spain's agricultural exports enjoyed over Italy's during the period under discussion was due to a political desire to reduce discrimination against Spain's main trading commodities.

Nevertheless, the reduction of discriminatory trade practices toward Spain by the French was far from complete. The bilateral trade agreement signed in October 1953 spelled out import and export commodities with quota indications (set either on a value or volume basis). Specifically, in the case of oranges, calendriers referred not only to the timing of exports but to quantities specified according to transportation means and French ports of entrance.[53] A new temporary levy of ten per cent *ad valorem* was imposed on liberalized commodities coming from OEEC countries. This was extended to Spain, and, in the case of oranges, was added to the actual levy of 35 per cent *ad valorem*. During the long negotiations for the new bilateral trade agreement (finally concluded in November 1954), North African producers pressed for a quota on Spanish oranges of a maximum of 170 000 tons. The final arrangement was fixed at the previous level of 200 000 tons, while maintaining the 35 per cent *ad valorem* levy. The Spanish delegation had succeeded, at least, in obtaining the suppression of the compensatory tax of ten per cent applied to orange imports of any provenance since the spring.[54]

In terms of trade liberalization regarding Spanish exports to other countries, the situation was as follows. Norway's free lists applied fully to Spain after January 1951. The bilateral agreement of June 1955 explicitly stated the extension of the OEEC free lists to Spain. Ireland extended the benefits of the OEEC measures to Spain as early as December 1951. After May 1953, during the annual period of application for a trade agreement, Sweden authorized imports from Spain without quantitative restrictions. However, it was always clearly specified that, in case of difficulties, quotas were to be reimposed. A similar attitude was adopted by the Dutch after June 1953. Denmark did so by means of the bilateral agreement of July 1953. Spanish imports into Greece were authorized without quantitative limits following the OEEC rules (at least) after July 1954 (and possibly a year earlier). Belgium imposed a calendrier system for those products competing directly with its domestic production, as it did with OEEC countries, and, following common Benelux agreements, imposed customs duties on oranges and other commodities. However, the Belgian trade delegation frequently offered to drop some of these measures provided Spain increased accordingly its purchases of less essentials from Belgium. By July 1954, Belgium and Luxembourg granted Spain OEEC import treatment. Switzerland followed the Belgian example by imposing a calendrier system for those foodstuffs competing directly with its domestic production, and additionally imposed maximum quotas for wines and olive oil in a clear concession to Italy. In retaliation, the Spanish–Swiss bilateral agreement of November 1954 kept important raw materials under quota restrictions, such as pyrites, iron ore, wolfram, and lead. Germany, the Netherlands, and Italy did not put Spain on an equal footing with the other OEEC countries, but conceded the importation of those agricultural commodities liberalized within the OEEC without quantitative limits. The United Kingdom extended *de facto* OEEC treatment to Spain, though it was never formally stated.[55]

By the summer of 1956, the level of discrimination against Spanish exports was low, particularly for agricultural exports. At that time, Denmark, Greece, the Federal Republic of Germany, Ireland, Norway, Sweden, Switzerland, and the United Kingdom extended to Spain the liberalization measures implemented within the OEEC. The others conceded OEEC treatment to Spanish agricultural exports. Nevertheless, these concessions were never complete and were always subject to unilateral modification. France was the major exception, maintaining a strong discriminatory policy toward Spain, in particular in the agricultural field. The negotiators for Spanish membership of the European Economic Community during the 1980s continued to suffer from French discrimination.

EXPLAINING A PARADOX

Spain's bilateralism was not the liability that an impartial observer might have assumed in a world supposedly moving toward multilateral trade and payments. In general, bilateralism for Spain's main exports was rather successful against trade liberalization. This was so, on the one hand, because it was in the field of agricultural and food products that the OEEC trade liberalization scheme failed most spectacularly to remove the barriers to free trade; on the other hand, the OEEC liberalization did not produce any major change in raw materials trade. When the OEEC trade liberalization hit the wall of protectionism, the return to bilateralism was immediate, and it became a normal practice for which Spain was well equipped. When bilateralism flourished during the period of restrictions and, in particular, during the rearmament boom, Spain benefited most because it had kept intact all the instruments of bilateral bargaining.

The economic and political circumstances which made agriculture a sector deserving special protection resulted in a lack of OEEC discipline in imposing trade liberalization. The wartime experience acted as a stimulus to reducing dependence on foreign supplies as part of the concept of national security pursued after 1945.[56] All Western European countries aimed at the maximum possible degree of self-sufficiency. Population increases and the resultant higher rate of food consumption, the worldwide shortage of foodstuffs, bal-ance-of-payments difficulties during the reconstruction period, an extended import substitution rationale, and the need to save hard currencies for indus-trial reconstruction first and then for rearmament all served to promote do-mestic production at any cost. In political terms, the maintenance of high-cost agricultural production that was protected from external competition by tariff and non-tariff barriers and dependent upon government subsidies and guarantees of selling prices, was necessary to gain farmers' political support for stable democratic reconstruction. This was especially true in countries with coalition governments and in those countries where the countryside had played a significant role in bringing about the collapse of liberal governments and the rise of fascism and totalitarianism. By the time the first OEEC liberal-ization clauses were implemented, agricultural protection was part of the nascent welfare state. Most countries were unwilling to abandon agricul-tural protectionism despite relatively inefficient and high-cost production.

Freer trade was more easily promoted when domestic protection and in-creases in output were compatible with more liberal trade policies. But agricul-tural output per capita in Western Europe reached prewar levels by 1950/51. Then, trade liberalization faced the full force of the devices set up to provide protection for domestic agriculture. The extremely seasonal nature of produc-tion, the wide fluctuations in crops from year to year, and the perishable nature of the product made further liberalization difficult. Not only did all importing countries suspend imports of fresh vegetables and fruits for specific periods; they made these products the first items for de-liberalization as soon as bal-ance-of-payments difficulties required it. Under these conditions, it was not surprising that (except for 1950) the liberalization percentages for agricultural commodities were consistently the lowest of the three categories (Table 7.11).

Most European partners could meet the first liberalization target without difficulty because it did not materially affect levels of protection. Most of the quantitative restrictions removed were obsolete as means of protection. The first target consolidated those situations in which restrictions were no longer necessary or effective, such as non-competitive raw materials and other es-sential supplies. Nevertheless, six countries had already failed to meet the re-quirements for liberalization (Iceland and Turkey, completely, and Austria, Denmark, Germany, and Norway were deficient in some category). Further targets were reached less promptly because they affected products effective-ly protected by non-tariff means.

By June 1950, the OEEC countries had removed quotas on a higher pro-portion of their 1948 private trade in foodstuffs than in manufactured goods. This was because the OEEC program did not affect trade on government ac-count, which was widely practised in agricultural trade. While the liberalization scheme applied exclusively to private trade, 54 per cent of total intra-Europe-an trade in agricultural commodities in 1950/51 was purchased by govern-ments, state agencies, or state-controlled enterprises; this figure was 39 per cent for raw materials.[57] Those countries with extensive state purchasing programs diverted a considerable portion of trade from liberalization. By using the Ministry of Food's long-term contracts and purchases, the United Kingdom, the largest importer of European agricultural products (36 per cent of total intra-European trade in agricultural commodities in 1948), excluded 39 per cent of its total trade from the threat of liberalization. Moreover, the participating countries could transfer any import from private to government trade, as long as the commodity had not been the subject of consolidation. Be-tween 1950 and the end of 1951, little progress was accomplished despite the reduction of government purchasing as several major materials were handed over to private traders.

TABLE 7.11   TRADE LIBERALIZATION PERCENTAGES ACHIEVED BY THE OEEC WITH RESPECT TO PRIVATE TRADE IN THE THREE DIFFERENT CATEGORIES, JUNE 1950/APRIL 1954

| Year | 1950 | | 1951 | | 1952 | | 1953 | | 1954 |
	Jun	Dec	Jun	Dec	Jun	Dec	Jun	Dec	Apr
Private Trade	55.3	67.5	65.6	62.1	63.4	65.8	71.4	76.6	76.7
Raw Materials	59.5	77.4	76.3	74.8	72.8	67.8	74.9	84.9	83.0
Manufactured Goods	49.5	59.1	60.0	58.9	59.9	61.8	71.9	74.0	73.6
Agricultural and Food Products	57.4	67.4	58.9	50.8	55.0	55.6	60.9	66.8	71.6

Source: F. Boyer and J.P. Sallé, 'The Liberalization of Intra-European Trade in the Framework of OEEC', *International Monetary Fund Staff Papers*, vol. 4/2 (1955), tables 1, 3–6. Position recorded on the last day of the month, except 1 April 1954.

The initial percentages of liberalization referred to total imports in the three categories. This allowed industrial lobbies to preserve their own pro-tection by pushing up the levels in raw materials and agricultural goods. When the trade liberalization percentage increased and member countries were committed to free equal percentages in each of the three broad categ-ories, restrictions on trade in agricultural products hardened and the liberal-ization of farm products lagged. When in October 1950 the OEEC Council agreed to raise the liberalization percentage to 75 per cent by February 1951, it referred to total imports in direct concession to widespread agricultural protectionism. The liberalization percentage corresponding to agricultural trade for the OEEC area as a whole as of December 1953 was lower than that reached in December 1950. The percentage was raised in April 1954 as a result of British liberalization measures. However, the overall liberalization percentage for agricultural products remained the lowest of the three categories.

Finally, the fact that the OEEC and its liberalization program were not connected with tariff problems diminished the effectiveness and credibility of that institution. By the time the OEEC was prepared to motivate trade liberalization by the removal of quantitative restrictions, tariffs were once again effective instruments for domestic protection and trade bargaining in Western Europe. Some countries increased their tariff levels in anticipation of the OEEC's trade liberalization measures and GATT rounds. The immediate effect of trade liberalization was frequently compensated for by reactivating tariffs to levels that, in many cases, surpassed prewar levels. Low tariff countries, in particular Denmark and the Netherlands, with large exports of agricultural commodities, complained.[58] They had to make great efforts in the industrial sector obtaining no compensation in agricultural trade from their partners. Liberalization in this commodity group remained confined to bilateral bargaining.

These deficiencies in the OEEC's trade liberalization scheme were of particular importance for Spain, in whose export trade agricultural produce had the largest share. The situation described above affected Spain also in the long term, because it was excluded from future initiatives at agricultural integration. The fear that trade liberalization could expose French agricultural surpluses to foreign competition became manifested in a plan for protected foreign markets for the high-priced French export products. Traditional European exporters found that the OEEC was unable to open traditional markets. Increased domestic output without productivity improvements had caused closed markets and decreased outlets. This led to a Dutch proposal (the Stikker Plan of Action, named after the Dutch Minister of Foreign Affairs Dirk U. Stikker) presented to the OEEC Council in July 1950 for the complete removal of all trade barriers (including state trade and tariffs) from which a sectoral initiative for agricultural integration developed. The inability of the OEEC to secure a freer intra-European flow of agricultural products when agricultural surpluses appeared in almost all countries stimulated the movement for agricultural market integration, which became a real threat to Spain's main exports.[34]

Spain's behavior when liberalization was most ineffective resulted from its bilateral trade and payments with Western Europe. In a basically barter system of exchange, Spain imposed upon its commercial partners the need to preserve a certain level of imports if trade flows were to be maintained. Most of the Spanish exports consisted of only a small range of commodities; any discriminatory measures adopted against them would end trade relations because of Spain's consequent inability to pay. Bilateralism, paradoxically, protected Spain when commercial partners imposed import restrictions due to balance-of-payments difficulties.

Spain's specific commodity mix of agricultural exports allowed it to escape to some extent from controls and discrimination. From 1949 to 1952, oranges alone accounted for 53 per cent of the value of all French imports from Spain, while, during 1953 and 1954, fruit accounted for 71 per cent of total Spanish exports to France. In the case of the United Kingdom, only two products, tomatoes and oranges, accounted for 56 per cent of the value of British imports of foodstuffs from Spain from 1949 to 1953. Spain's main export commodity –oranges– and the early timing of some of its horticultural crops, did not compete directly with other importing countries' production. Trade in these commodities was therefore either liberalized or subjected to seasonal restrictions. In the latter case (except in France), by the time the domestic season started and imports became more restrictive, the bulk of Spanish production was already placed.

Italian agricultural export trade was more varied than the Spanish. It included a larger variety of fruit and vegetable commodities grown in most European countries for which liberalization had made much less headway. These products attracted a large share of the protectionist measures by which individual countries sought to build up their own production; they constituted a sector ready for de-liberalization as soon as there was an excuse for it. Furthermore, the possible damage caused to the Italian balance of payments could be compensated for partially by better performance in the manufactured goods sector or by the contribution of emigrants' remittances.[59] Spain did not benefit from any of these factors. Aside from agricultural commodities, there was not much left to import from Spain as a means of expanding trade. The important contribution of raw materials to exports during World War II (31 per cent of total value of exports in the period from 1940 to 1944) and the demand boom following the outbreak of war in Korea (20 per cent of total exports in 1950–3) were considered temporary situations outside the normal contribution to exports (approximately a proportion similar to the period from 1946 to 1950, 14 per cent). Spanish industrial policies protected an inefficient industry with high costs and out-of-date equipment.

Imposing restrictions or discriminatory measures on Spain's main export commodities would have immediately entailed a reduction in the Spanish import bill. That automatically made less essential imports the first items to be put into quarantine, leading to a diminution of Spain's earnings of foreign currency. British and French manufacturers were anxious to sell Spain items such as road vehicles and other transport, communications, and electrical equipment, for which Western demand was not increasing as fast as other commodities. They forced their governments to maintain the maximum possible level of trade with Spain in spite of political or economic considerations. Otherwise, their market share in Spain would have been lost to the advantage of other European competitors.

French industry had progressively increased its share of Spain's imports of capital goods (especially in the electrical and railways industry). This required compensation since export–import quotas were intrinsically linked. French diplomats recognized the 'effort soutenu pour acheter en Espagne le tonnage maximum d'agrumes', in spite of opposition from French continental and North African producers, in order to maintain the Spanish market for some semi-manufactured goods in crisis.[60] When Spanish diplomats presented a long list of complaints about French policy toward Spain, the French government tried to demonstrate its previous good-will by arguing that the 'French market had been open to Spanish export products despite the complaints of North African interests'.[61] At the beginning of December 1952, bilateral talks took place in Paris between the National Confederation of French Producers and a delegation of Spanish businessmen. They agreed to the creation of technical committees in matters such as transport and electricity to promote the expansion of bilateral trade. A third committee on agriculture was set up with the intention of supporting Spanish participation in the European conference of agricultural ministers and increasing agricultural exports.[62] French industry then had no second thoughts about an immediate promotion of Spain's agricultural exports to provide the necessary financial means to promote the export of manufactured goods to Spain.

The pattern of bilateral trade indicates that France opted not to offer Italy the market share left by imports from North Africa, as might have been expected. The advantages of bilateralism and concentrated export trade were such that any discriminatory treatment of, for instance, Spanish oranges, would undermine the entire bilateral trade, including trade in essentials. Therefore, France, although mindful of North African pressure, had to open the French market to Spanish agricultural products. The financial protocol of 7 April 1953 granted Ff 15 000 million credit to cover purchases from French industry of certain equipment and material made by the companies of the Spanish National Institute for Industry, RENFE, municipal authorities, and private concerns. The protocol was announced together with the French acceptance of Spanish participation in the European conference of agricultural ministers.[63] This 'continuous effort' to satisfy at least some of the Spanish agricultural export requirements, plus the credits granted by the Bank of France ($10 million at the end of 1953, increased to $12 million before 30 June

1955), allowed an increase in French exports to Spain; from Ff 7000 million in 1949 to Ff 24 000 million in 1953. Spain moved from being the sixteenth largest recipient of French exports to the tenth.

Discriminatory actions or sanctions against Spain's exports to the United Kingdom were hotly debated in the British Cabinet. The Board of Trade had been forced to consider them under pressure from an influential lobby built around less essential exports to Spain. From June 1952 to June 1953, the British Cabinet considered that Spain should not be forced to import less essentials (which amounted, on average, to only ten per cent of total British exports to Spain) for fear of causing a serious contraction in overall trade that would affect all of British industry. The British could not restrict imports of Spanish goods, especially agricultural produce, beyond a certain point because of the immediate impact this would have on the capacity of the Spanish market to absorb larger quantities of goods from the United Kingdom and the sterling area.

No economy in Western Europe could afford to obstruct the trade of raw materials from non-dollar sources. The tendency for the production of manufactured goods to increase faster than the output of raw materials was a general postwar phenomenon. Because the shortages of local resources relative to manufacturing capacity were acute, trade of raw materials was relatively free. The initial impact of the liberalization scheme on trade in raw materials with sources outside the OEEC was rather modest because, before its inauguration, member countries had already been importing about as much as could be obtained externally. It was only natural that, throughout the scheme's operation, the liberalization percentages correspondings to raw materials were consistently higher than the percentages for the two other categories and permanently higher than the targets set by the OEEC Council decisions. Had it not been for balance of payments reasons that led some countries (France, Turkey, and Iceland) to maintain a substantial portion of their imports of raw materials under quota, a practically complete liberalization of trade on private account would have been achieved in this sector by the end of 1953.[64]

Neither the OEEC liberalization program nor import restrictions had an effect on Spain's exports of strategic raw materials. The dominant rule remained to secure a proper share of Spain's raw materials. Spain's reserves of pyrites – a source of sulphur and copper – were then the largest in the world. Spain also had the largest reserves in southern Europe of iron ore, hard coal, lead, zinc, copper, fluor-spar, tungsten, mercury, potash, tin, magnetite, and lignite. These minerals were vital to industrial output and the rearmament programs after June 1950. The outbreak of war in Korea led to a violent outburst of activity to increase stocks of raw materials and gave impetus to bilateral negotiations to secure raw materials from Spain and other suppliers.

Most West European countries developed mounting debts within the EPU, in particular with those countries constituting alternative sources of supply to Spain, like Sweden and Portugal, and could not afford to become even more dependent on US aid for rearmament. They welcomed the chance to obtain these raw materials indispensable to their industries from a non-dollar source.

Did Spain's exclusion from the institutional arrangements for trade and payments in Western Europe place Spanish exports of manufactured goods at a higher level of discrimination than EPU members? Between 1951 and 1959, according to a comparative study of Spain, Italy, and Portugal, the performance of Spanish manufactured goods to the United Kingdom, the Federal Republic of Germany, and the Netherlands was much poorer than those of Italy and Portugal. The proportion of manufactured goods in total Spanish exports increased only to the Netherlands, although not significantly and it was subject to constant fluctuations; it decreased on the British market, although by only a little, while it decreased importantly on the German market. In the case of Italy and Portugal, this same proportion increased substantially in exports to the Federal Republic, significantly in the case of the Netherlands, and moderately concerning the United Kingdom.[65] Narrow bilateralism did not promote exports of manufactured goods, particularly after the most intense period of import restrictions in different countries.

Nevertheless, it can be legitimately argued that if Spain had been able to benefit from the OEEC free lists in the sector, the inadequacy of Spanish industry to provide those products for which West European import demand grew rapidly during the 1950s (apart from considerations of quality and price) would have substantially reduced potential gains. The OEEC liberalization measures would have been of little benefit to the kind of less essential manufactured goods made in Spain. Institutional factors are important in explaining why Spain did not benefit more from the rapid growth of intra-European trade in the early 1950s. More important, however, is the Spanish trade commodity composition characterized by a low proportion of manufactured goods in total exports and by the predominance of textiles, which could not expand to meet the European demand in engineering, chemicals, and other industries and services. Spain's principal export categories appeared highly concentrated in a few items that remained almost invariable throughout the period here considered: fresh and preserved fruit and vegetables, nuts, wine, and olive oil, iron ore, pyrites, potash, rosin, cork, mercury, turpentine, tungsten, chemicals, wood and cork manufactures, and, finally, textiles.

In contrast to the stationary situation recorded for Spain, Italy substantially increased the proportion of manufactured goods in its total volume of exports due to its industrial modernization and specialization in engineering, chemical, and clothing sectors (responsible for 63 per cent of the increase in Italian exports between 1950 and 1960). When world import demands were unleashed, Italian industry was more diversified and better equipped to face international competition than the ill-equipped, high-priced, over-protected Spanish industry, whose main function was to supply the domestic market. These factors did not depend on the institutional arrangements governing international trade. Expansion of trade continued in a stable trend that was certainly favored by liberalization and the multilateral settlements mechanism of the EPU. Until the 1960s, exports of Spanish manufactured goods stagnated because it was not until the late 1950s that Spain acquired a noticeably diversified industrial structure. This was in accordance with the long-term logic of an industrial import-substitution policy. Time was needed to develop domestic industries to replace imports or produce substitutes and reduce the foreign exchange needs of the economy, and it would be longer still before import-substituting industries could generate new exports of manufactured goods.

One possible explanation for the slow modification of industrial structures and the stagnation in exports of manufactured goods was the low level of import trade. This was due in turn to the low capacity of foreign currency earnings through export trade or tourism and almost non-existent foreign assistance to finance balance-of-payments deficits. The country's import capacity depended on its potential to export basic commodities. The initial weakness of the Spanish manufacturing sector required a greater contribution from imports than that which exports actually financed. The permanent shortage of reserves and the consequent need to link imports to the country's limited foreign currency earnings through export trade and tourism retarded reconstruction, limited industrialization, forbade modernization, and delayed the required industrial transformation of the Spanish economy until the late 1960s.

In the meantime, the protected Spanish market deprived industries of the advantages of specialization and economies of scale. Furthermore, the discrimination with respect to the allocation of scarce foreign exchange and capital resources, between export industries and import substitution industries, which was first declared temporary but then forced endlessly, led to the weak promotion of traditional exports. As a result, balance-of-payments difficulties increased in magnitude. If the import substitution policy and export promotion appeared to be competitive instead of complementary activities in raising Spain's GNP over this period, this was because Spain could devote only a very limited amount of resources to the production of export commodities. The structure of the Spanish economy and the effects of certain economic policies on the development of the various industrial sectors are more important factors than any foreign discriminatory devices. To confirm this, however, requires a detailed study of the changes taking place in Spain's industrial development and in the pattern of western demand, which is beyond the scope of this research.

8 Financial Diplomacy: Spain and the European Payments Union

Trade was not restricted exclusively by means of tariff and non-tariff barriers, but also by the way payments were arranged. Before the EPU was established, several payments mechanisms – mutual credit provisions, limited transferability of sterling and other currencies, and drawing rights, that is, the US Treasury making dollars available to offset net debt balances accruing in bilateral trade – attempted to free intra-European trade from the rigidity of bilateralism between inconvertible currency monetary areas. However, the various intra-European payments and compensations agreements in force until June 1950 did not adequately foster the potential growth of intra-European trade.[1] The limitations of the payments system under which European trade was conducted contributed to making liberalization more painful. The small credit facilities granted between pairs of countries and the requirement to settle bilateral deficits with payment in gold or hard currencies hampered the expansion of trade. For liberalization to develop on a non-discriminatory basis, a fully multilateral payments system was needed which could automatically offset monthly surpluses and deficits and allow access to short-term credit facilities. Once experts had begun working to this end, commodity liberalization was substituted by fixed percentages of trade.

After hard negotiations, the terms of the EPU were agreed by the OEEC Council in August 1950 and the final agreement was signed in September.[2] The EPU became the first multilateral European payments system. It lasted until most European currencies could be fully converted to the dollar in 1958. The most salient feature of the EPU was its full multilateral clearing system for OEEC countries and their dependent territories. The system made European currencies transferable on current account transactions and offered protection against the dollar. The US government accepted a payments union which would discriminate against dollar exports not only because it heralded a general convertibility of currencies but because the EPU represented the first significant step on the road to European integration.

Access to the EPU's automatic system of credits and multilateral clearing further differentiated the OEEC member states from Spain in trading terms. While European currencies became transferable against each other, the peseta remained a non-transferable currency until 1961. While the EPU mechanism allowed deficits between one member state and another to be financed with surpluses earned from a third member country, the bilateral clearing system that governed trade between the Spanish and other monetary areas meant that Spain's deficits with individual countries could not be compensated by surpluses earned elsewhere (except for the sterling area) because the surpluses were not necessarily earned in transferable currencies.

Payments difficulties affected Spain's import system more than anything else, including the desire to foster and protect an expanding national manufacturing industry. Spain's import licensing policy was determined mainly by the overriding need to keep imports within export earnings. In the absence of adequate reserves of gold and hard currency, Spain was forced to impose rigid controls on imports. With no other means of paying for imports than export earnings, import licensing was based on essentiality and on availability of domestic substitutes. This was particularly pressing in years when inadequate rainfall, with resultant crop failures and restricted industrial output, caused import requirements of basic foodstuffs to increase and exportable quantities of agricultural and industrial goods to decline. It was by necessity a restrictive licensing system because no substantial improvement in exchange holdings could alter it and imports of capital equipment needed for industrial expansion could increase endlessly. The need to conserve exchange acted as a greater incentive to direct licensing, control of foreign exchange transactions, and progressive devaluation of the peseta through a system of multiple exchange rates (rather than official straight devaluation), than any policy of economic self-sufficiency.

The EPU favored multilateral payments among OEEC members. Spain stayed trapped in the straitjacket of bilateral clearings. Within the EPU it was no longer necessary to maintain a strict balance of individual payments with every single member but with the Union only. Countries showing a deficit with the Union received automatic credits in EPU units (equivalent to the gold content equal to US $1 in 1950) up to a certain amount beyond which they received some credits and had to pay a part of the deficit in gold. The proportion of gold increased as the accumulated deficit grew; beyond a certain limit, no further credits were granted. That there was no obligation to settle fully in gold and dollars allowed all prospective debtors to sign the EPU agreement. Creditor countries, on the other hand, extended credit to the EPU up to a certain amount of their claims upon the Union; they then received an increasing proportion in gold. For them, the prospect of future exports compensated for the prospect of financial loss.

According to the EPU agreement, each country had a quota amounting to 15 per cent of its total value of merchandise trade and invisible transactions with the members of the Union and their dependent territories in 1949. National quotas expressed in EPU units of account were the basis used to calculate the automatic credits and gold payments on a sliding scale. The initial debt or credit for a value of less than 20 per cent of the size of a given country's quota was covered completely by credit to the debtor country by the Union or to the Union by the creditor country. If the debt or credit position reached a value between 20 per cent and 40 per cent of the original quota, the debtor was to receive 80 per cent as credit and be required to settle 20 per cent in gold or dollars, while the creditor was to provide 50 per cent as credit to the Union and receive 50 per cent in gold or dollars from the Union. This rate was maintained until the creditor country reached a position in which its credit with the Union reached the total amount of its original quota with the Union. However, debtors running up increasing deficits would have to pay their debts in dollars in an increasing ratio as the deficit mounted, with a decreasing amount of credit until the initial credit/gold–dollars rate was completely reversed. The overall percentages were that debtors should receive and creditors extend 60 per cent of the value of quotas in credit, while paying or receiving the remaining 40 per cent in gold or dollars. The settlement mechanism was designed as an incentive to equilibrium at the highest level of commodity trade possible.

The OEEC and EPU constituted the hub of commercial and financial relations in Western Europe. The EPU alone represented 60 per cent of Spain's total trade. One Spanish source, early in 1951, presented access to EPU as 'bringing undeniable benefits' and 'a priority in Spanish foreign action'.[3] Spanish officials estimated that Spain's total volume of visible and invisible transactions with the OEEC area amounted to $581 584 080. This produced a theoretical quota of approximately $88 million, which would have placed Spain right after Denmark and before Austria and Portugal in the EPU quota ranking.[4]

These figures were approximate in the absence of full information on invisible payments and receipts, and were cited only as an indication of Spain's likely position in the EPU. The balance of payments drafted by the IEME gave a total value of $474 million of visible and invisible transactions with OEEC countries and dependent territories in 1949 (excluding dollar trade with Germany and Italy). This resulted in a quota of approximately $71 million, the figure accepted by the Spanish delegation to the OEEC years later.[5] Establishing the national quota was not an insignificant matter. Depending on how much of the quota had been used up in a cumulative position from the incorporation of the Union, settlements were graduated in a mixture of automatic credits and gold/dollar payments. A $88 million quota was maintained in the draft response to the original British idea of setting up a working party between Spain and the EPU.[6] The British presented the question to the Spanish delegates at the trade talks before the renewal of the bilateral agreement in April 1951. There is no proof, however, that either Sir Hugh Ellis-Rees, the British member of the Managing Board of the EPU, or the British Treasury was ever informed of the Spanish position.

With a quota of $88 million, Spain would then be entitled to obtain an automatic and unconditional credit of 20 per cent of its quota, $17.5 million. This was less than the total amount of authorized bilateral deficits that Spain enjoyed at that time, $31.781.[7] The more realistic quota of $71 million leads to a widening of the gap between the EPU automatic credits ($14.2 million) and the bilateral swings. The relatively high value of the bilateral credits granted to Spain proves the real effort made by the European nations to favor trade and payments relations with Spain to a level which could, at least, partially compensate for the latter's exclusion from EPU. This example and the treatment given to Spanish exports while the OEEC liberalization program applied, shows how the Europeans implemented their original intention of finding the bilateral means to provide assistance to Spain without arousing political dissent over Spanish membership of any European organization.

The total possible EPU credit available to Spain could reach 60 per cent of the quota ($53 million) conditional upon the already mentioned scale of payments in gold or dollars to the Union to a maximum of $35.2 million or 40 per cent of the Spanish quota. This was the maximum financial risk in which the Spanish authorities could get involved in joining the Union. If Spain surpassed the quota they could ask to receive part of the capital fund of $350 million (allotted from the ERP appropriations) supporting the Union. Alternatively, they could ask to adopt special restrictive measures and suspend temporarily the fulfilment of its obligations as a member; or, Spain could withdraw from the Union altogether. In strict credit terms, Spain was not necessarily better off within the EPU than carrying on its bilateral swings. The benefit of EPU membership came from the automatic credit provisions and multilateral settlement mechanism which freed trade from the caprices of bilateralism.

The essential question then, was whether the EPU's facilities could have compensated for the necessary changes that Spain's EPU membership would have involved in its economic practices. The Spanish domestic economic policy and general trade and payments practices conflicted in large measure with the obligations that Spain would have expected to assume as a member of the OEEC and the EPU. A considerable technical difficulty blocking entry to the OEEC/EPU would have been Spain's complicated system of multiple exchange controls. While the manipulation of exchange rates for both imports and exports was an infringement of the rules of the International Monetary Fund rather than those of the OEEC itself, it was a clear discriminatory device contrary to OEEC practices. The abandonment of the multiple exchange system would almost certainly have entailed a fairly drastic devaluation of the peseta, to which the government was strongly opposed. The fact that Austria held two exchange rates made Spanish officials believe that a multiple exchange rate was certainly not at variance with the orthodox practices of member countries. Nevertheless, the Spanish officials assumed that an impulse in the simplification of the system of special rates of exchange was necessary.[8] In fact, when such a simplification was adopted in November 1951 (with the implementation of revised regulations concerning the operation of the so-called free exchange market established in July 1950), Minister of Commerce Arburúa described the EPU as 'the most interesting organization from the foreign, financial, and commercial points of view'.[9] He welcomed a simplification of exchange rates, but the elimination of the multiple exchange system was considered impossible until the Spanish economy could export sufficiently without producing domestic scarcity and find other means to keep the price of raw materials low enough to contain inflation.

The intensive trade controls practiced by Spain ran counter to the EPU's commitment to trade liberalization. The objective of export controls was to channel earnings; import controls were to make the best use of available foreign exchange. Given the permanently low level of convertible currency and gold reserves, the Spanish licensing system was of necessity discriminatory because it was designed to reduce as far as possible the immediate burden on hard currency reserves. The abolition of quantitative restrictions on imports in the private sector would have involved the virtual abandonment of the import licensing system in the form in which it operated. The Spanish economic authorities argued that Spain could not be asked to comply immediately and fully with all the OEEC obligations when countries who were strongly aided by the United States (Greece, Austria, and Turkey) themselves found it hard to implement liberalization. Indeed, those countries which managed the 60 per cent stage of liberalization had also had massive injections of dollar aid. Spain had no US aid; how could it realistically be expected to meet even modest targets? But the question was never asked, and so we cannot know what the OEEC Council's response would have been. Doubtless some laxity in the form of escape clauses and exemptions would have been applied to Spain as a late entrant, but even a minimum compliance with OEEC practices would have involved a radical change in Spanish trade practices despite the fact that 30 per cent of Spanish trade was on government account (Table 8.1).

Bilateralism within a Multilateral Context

TABLE 8.1 SPAIN'S IMPORT TRADE FROM EPU COUNTRIES AND THEIR DEPENDENT TERRITORIES UNDER PRIVATE AND GOVERNMENT ACCOUNTS, 1948

Class	$	% over the group (i.e. private or government account)	% in total trade on imports	% over total
Agricultural Commodities				
Private Trade	4 603 505.9	31.0	3.98	2.76
Government Trade	10 229 494.5	69.0	20.09	6.15
Total Class I	14 833 004.4	100		
Raw Materials				
Private Trade	44 761 753.0	53.0	38.75	26.89
Government Trade	39 732 309.7	47.0	78.03	23.87
Total Class II	84 494 062.7	100		
Manufactured Goods				
Private Trade	66 160 661.4	98.6	57.27	39.75
Government Trade	957 545.6	1.4	1.88	0.58
Total Class III	67 118 207.0	100		
PRIVATE TRADE	115 525 920.3		100	69.41
GOVERNMENT TRADE*	50 919 349.8		100	30.59
Total Trade	166 445 270.1			100

Source: AHBE, IEME, box 54: 'Importación española de los países de la OECE Año 1948'; AGA, C/36863: Dispatch 1956, Spanish Delegation to the OEEC, Paris, 30 January 1956; and AGA C/36820: 'Importaciones en 1948 procedentes de los países de la UEP y sus zonas monetarias afiliadas'. (*) Commodities under government account were, mainly, wheat and other foodstuffs purchased by the Supply Commissariat, tobacco under State monopoly, petroleum products imported by CAMPSA, cotton, coal, and other raw materials for public enterprises.

Furthermore, the modest surplus of approximately $14 million with the OEEC as a whole, in the context of a total commodity trade deficit of $64 million in 1949, was based on a very strict import control system, which would have had to be greatly modified, if not largely abandoned, had Spain become a member of OEEC. The year 1950 ended with an overall trade deficit of approximately $29 million. This was due, however, to a large contraction of imports (by $41.4 million) and exports (earnings decreased by $6 million).

Considering that the poor export performance might have been due to discrimination from OEEC liberalization, the key element was the future prospects for an expansion of exports to European markets. If Spain had implemented import liberalization, it would have undoubtedly increased the total import volume and consequently raised the import bill, because it would have allowed Spanish importers to purchase from the country offering the best conditions and prices irrespective of the state of bilateral balances. The answer to the question of whether the Spanish economy – which had been starved of imports during the previous 15 years – would be able to finance even the slightest rate of import liberalization, could only come in connection with the benefits that the country expected to obtain on the export side.

The extension of trade liberalization to Spanish export commodities, in compensation for Spain liberalizing import trade, proved of scarce immediate benefit. Access to the escudo and sterling areas in conditions similar to any OEEC member country was already a reality after the unilateral declarations of Portugal, the United Kingdom and Ireland. Both monetary areas accounted for 36.4 per cent of Spain's total earnings by exports in 1950 (Table 7.5). Only an increase in exports to France and the Federal Republic could be regarded as a real improvement. As to France, it was difficult to increase exports beyond the level already reached because it was a market that managed to stay well protected despite all the efforts made by potential beneficiaries to break French tariff and non-tariff protection in the sector. In the German case, any prospect for an export expansion was quickly eclipsed by the suspension of the liberalization measures decreed by the Federal government in February 1951. An extension of OEEC treatment to Spain, thus, did not involve the prospect for any large export promotion in Europe's main markets.

In the rest of the EPU area, if Spain had become an OEEC partner the volume of Spanish exports would have probably increased less than imports from there. While the value of Spanish exports continued to increase owing to the rising world prices of raw materials, Spain could think of partially mitigating the effect of import liberalization on the balance of payments. No one in Madrid forgot, however, that favorable export prices were temporary and independent from OEEC membership, while liberalization, once adopted, was a long-lasting process. The OEEC countries were already taking the major part – in some cases the whole – of Spanish exports of industrial raw materials, and had no pressing need to absorb a greater amount of fruits, wine, and other future export prospects. Assuming that the technical difficulties standing in the way of entry into OEEC were overcome, the likely effect of OEEC membership on Spain's economic relations with the Union would have been to eliminate Spain's balance-of-payments surplus with the OEEC area by encouraging Spanish imports from the OEEC countries rather than exports to them. A large increase in traditional exports to the OEEC markets was not possible. The primary products exported by Spain depended on weather conditions and the availability of natural resources, and were characterized by low price, wide demand elasticity, and price oscillations. A more diversified industrial economy was necessary to hope for a large increase in exports to the OEEC markets which could minimally compensate for the import increase expected to result from Spain's membership of OEEC. It is not surprising that the Spanish government was unwilling to accept any commitment to carry on the program for trade liberalization which OEEC/EPU membership entailed.[10]

The economic cost of Spain's membership of EPU was unforeseeable but, undoubtedly, larger than the original quota attributed to Spain on the basis of its 1949 trade values, unless Spain was treated as a special case qualifying for aid. The level of aid that would have come directly from the United States, if Spain had been seriously considered as a candidate for membership of EPU, is difficult to estimate. Aid from the United States had been a necessary condition for final agreement on the actual terms of the EPU. Consequently, to the Spanish minds, Spain should also be helped to enlarge its payment capacity (or its deficit position). With $350 million from congressional ERP appropriations, the US government contributed to the EPU's initial working capital (completing the initial deposits of members' own currencies). Washington also provided special aid to the United Kingdom to offset any gold and dollar losses incurred in allowing accumulated sterling balances to be used in multilateral settlements. Likely persistent creditors received conditional dollar aid as compensation for the grants they were about to make to the other countries. Moreover, initial credit balances were allotted by the US government to prospective debtors to counteract initial debit balances during the period from June 1950 (when the EPU came retrospectively into effect) to 30 June 1951. Initial credit balances in the form of grants were allotted to Greece, Austria, the Netherlands, Norway and Iceland, while Turkey's was in the form of a long-term loan (through Marshall aid allocations). Initial debit balances oscillated between 9 and 255 per cent of the original quotas of the aforementioned countries. If political factors had been important in determining the initial credits balances, equally important was the prospective cost of implementing trade liberalization measures. Accordingly, it was obvious to Spanish officials that their country should move toward the highest percentage in the oscillation mentioned, though no exact amounts were given.

The British Economic Intelligence Department (EID) argued that in the event of Spain joining EPU, aid to Spain – both direct from the United States and in the way of EPU facilities – would probably be about $112.5 million. Since British officials had calculated that, on the basis of 1949 trade figures,

Spain was to receive a quota of about $55 million, the amount corresponding to direct US aid would then have been about $57.5 million.[11] According to ·British officials, the potential amount of US aid backing Spain's EPU membership was similar to the total amount of credits granted to Spain by US commercial banks plus the Eximbank administered loans. British information about the amounts of American assistance having already reached Spain was too optimistic. The actual loans granted by private US banks were much further reduced and Eximbank loans were not yet effective. There are no grounds to sustain the contention that Madrid preferred to obtain dollar aid by means of bilateral negotiations with the United States, because the EPU credits would have involved substantial modification of economic practices.

It was far from obvious that direct US aid, which the government was still hoping for in return for the bases, would necessarily come at a cost considered more bearable than the OEEC price. By March 1951, the Spanish experience in negotiating the Eximbank loan made it perfectly clear that the conditions for aid to Spain on a bilateral basis involved the same unpleasant changes in economic practice as those involved in the OEEC rules and obligations. Without major political and economic changes, it could expect no major direct economic assistance from the United States in the short term. In September 1951, the Embassy in Spain and the Temporary Economic Survey Group of the Economic Cooperation Administration recommended Spain's EPU participation as a device to accelerate its economic recovery. The State Department reminded them that in order to benefit from the EPU arrangement, OEEC membership was required. The granting of American aid through the OEEC framework was barred by the requirement of the unanimous consent of OEEC member states to Spanish membership, which was unlikely to be achieved in the short term.[12] The Europeans understood that Spain's OEEC membership would take place once prior economic and political liberalization had taken place in Spain. Nevertheless, had the Spanish government undergone a change of heart and genuinely liberalized its economy, there would still have been little economic inducement for the US authorities to extend aid to Spain through the OEEC rather than to strengthen the US bargaining position over the desired military facilities. The truth was that the Spanish administration had no alternative but to obtain economic assistance on a bilateral basis subject to the unilateral conditions imposed by the US negotiators.

Spain's contribution to the OEEC would not have been great, but this in itself would not have been a deterrent to membership. Extension of the area of multilateral trade and payments might have been welcome in the European capitals and there was no doubt that Spanish adherence to OEEC was a step in the right direction. Individual countries might have seen some advantages in it for if Spain liberalized its imports it would no longer be able to discriminate unilaterally against its European competitors. However, it appeared very likely that Spain would be a structural debtor in EPU, at least for some time, and be unable to liberalize very far. In that event, Spain's free list would have been unlikely to contain any significant number of the goods which were then causing difficulties for most European nations in their relations with the Spanish authorities. Spain could not have been expected to trade with OEEC countries in any manner significantly different from the existing bilateral basis. Non-discrimination by means of a system of global quotas for EPU imports in the non-liberalized sector might have proved impossible to implement.

The opening of the Spanish market and the increase in Spanish purchasing from Western Europe resulting from EPU financial backing would have not presented any serious advantage given the low purchasing power of the Spanish economy compared with the rest of Western Europe. Spain's natural tendency to develop a structural deficit meant that the opening of its domestic economy would be a long-term process. It would be some considerable time before Spain could reach anything similar to the average level of trade liberalization elsewhere in the OEEC. It was also clear that, if obliged to abandon the elaborate system of discriminatory import controls and licensing, Spain, a non-GATT member, would probably have updated its tariff levels for domestic protection. Spain would have then become a new recruit to the high tariff camp in which the OEEC was unarmed to act. From the trading point of view, therefore, the only effect of Spain's joining the OEEC and EPU would have been, at best, to subject itself to the usual pressure from the OEEC to bring its economy into a state which would fulfil the obligations of membership. This was too small a reward for the distortions that Spain's closer contacts with OEEC/EPU without the sufficiently completed political rapprochement might have produced within the OEEC itself and within different governing coalitions in some countries.

The British believed that Spain's accession would be advantageous only if it created additional pressure for the redirection of Spanish investment plans into the mining and extractive industries. By so doing, Spain would help overcome the scarcity of raw materials (which were at the time largely exported to the OEEC markets) needed for the OEEC members' defense programs following the outbreak of the Korean War. The likely investment policy of the Spanish government, however, was in agriculture for balance of trade and dollar savings reasons and in electricity supply, transport and heavy industry. Any such priority investment would be of no benefit to the OEEC countries. The possibilities of expanding mineral and metal production in

Spain, however, were rather limited due to the expenditures involved. Large-scale exploitation required very heavy capital outlays and the employment of foreign technicians and engineers. A program of this sort could not be carried out except by the joint action of the United States, Spain, the OEEC countries, and international private companies. This would require a complete change in official Spanish policy on foreign investment. Restrictions affecting foreign investment were not limited to the 25 per cent limit on foreign capital in new firms and the prohibition of foreign control of management. Foreign investments were greatly affected by labor regulations that kept personnel on the pay-roll when production was low because of power shortages or other bottlenecks; by foreign exchange rates and exchange controls that made production unprofitable on world markets and the procurement of foreign supplies very difficult; and by the threat of official price controls on export trade.

The scope for modifying such controls was rather limited. The first two regulations might have been more easily modifiable than granting foreign firms employment and exchange privileges not enjoyed by domestic firms. The stabilization of employment in periods of reduced production was an important device for protecting underpaid wage-earners. The only alternative was to increase unemployment benefits, which would have to be met from public funds, thus increasing the inflationary deficit. A system of realistic flexible exchange rates necessary to give market security to exporters could scarcely be established as long as the peseta was likely, at any time, to lose its purchasing power rapidly as a result of inflation. Even if one accepted the fact that Madrid could consent to a redirection of investment without major economic assistance, it could not be assumed that any future expansion of raw materials' output would necessarily provide a correspondingly larger exportable surplus. When foreign demand and international prices rose, impetus was also given to the general expansion of domestic industrial activity. No great increases in the output of iron ore in Spain was expected and exports from the Riff mines in Spanish Morocco, although increasing slightly, were limited after June 1950 by the expanding requirements of the Spanish iron and steel industry. Despite industrialization plans, there was little likelihood that Spain's mineral exports would ever again attain the importance they held in 1929. Only larger and more efficient production at reasonable costs could have permitted increased exports. Furthermore, international distribution of any surpluses would have been governed largely by production and requirements in the United States. A majority of OEEC countries argued that an expansion of trade in certain raw materials could well be achieved under trading arrangements without the need to incorporate Spain in the OEEC. Early in May 1951, Spanish representatives suspended discussion concerning EPU membership. They did not like being told how to behave financially, but undertook to continue studying the question.[13] At the same time, the governments of OEEC and EPU member states appeared to lose interest in Spanish membership.

Spain thus continued to have no access to the benefits that OEEC membership would have provided. Consequently, Spain had to maintain an equilibrium in its bilateral balances of payments with those OEEC countries expected to show a deficit in order to avoid payments in gold. This meant a reduction in Spanish imports from most OEEC suppliers and an increase from currency areas with accumulated amounts in the IEME, the Portuguese escudo and the Italian lira, independently of other considerations, such as price and quality. On the contrary, Spain's 1951 surplus with most soft currency areas (about $26 million, including $8 million surplus with Germany) was, for the most part, used to liquidate debit positions from 1950 or was carried over into 1952.

In October 1952, rumors from Paris announced that Spanish membership of the EPU was to be discussed; the Spanish Ambassador denied it.[14] Portugal had quietly mentioned the convenience of Spain taking part in the EPU, but never requested it officially. Germany had played with the idea for some time, but it did not go beyond talks in February 1953. The German Director-General of Foreign Trade, von Maltzan, and the President of the EPU, Hans Karl von Mangoldt, offered their collaboration in initiating a rapprochement with the EPU should a favorable indication come from Madrid.[15] Von Maltzan's advisers speculated that Spain's EPU quota would be $64.5 million (accepting 1950 as the base year); Spain would have to pay off 40 per cent in gold and/or dollars ($13.2 million), receiving credits for 60 per cent of the quota value ($19.8 million).[16] The Spaniards remained non-committal about the matter until a real possibility for joining the OEEC appeared.

As had been the case in 1951, in April 1953 the Europeans granted Spain automatic credits at a scale which partially compensated for its exclusion from EPU benefits. The Spanish quota was established at $60 million on the basis of 1948 which entitled Spain to receive $36 million in credits and pay $24 million in gold and/or dollars once its quota was exhausted. Bargaining the base year, a quota near $100 million could be obtained for Spain, which implied a maximum credit of $60 million and gold and dollar settlements of $40. The $88 million quota used in 1951 on a 1949 basis would have provided credits for a minimum of $52.8. Thus, according to all possible combinations of years, the EPU would allow a maximum amount of credit to Spain of $52.8 million against the $61.6 million provided by bilateral agreements with EPU members (Table 8.2).

TABLE 8.2   SWINGS ALLOWED TO SPAIN BY WESTERN EUROPE, APRIL 1953 (in dollars)

FR of Germany	20 000 000	Netherlands	2 105 000
United Kingdom	11 200 000*	Portugal	1 739 000
France	8 000 000	Norway	1 400 000
Denmark	3 623 000	Finland	1 000 000
Belgium	3 000 000	Sweden	967 100
Turkey	3 000 000*	Greece	500 000
Italy	2 500 000	Iceland	280 000
Switzerland	2 310 000	**TOTAL**	**61 624 100**

Source: MAE, Leg. 6285, exp. 3, carp. 4: 'Plafonds de Acuerdos Comerciales Vigentes con países de Europa, America y Oceanía', the IEME Vice-Chairman to the Director-General of Economic Policy at the Spanish Ministry of Foreign Affairs, 24 April 1953. (*) Refers   to maximum facilities, though these countries had expressed their desire to reduce their individual credit swings: the British authorities wanted to reduce from £4 million to £3 million, Turkey from $3 million to $1.5 million, and Portugal too but no figures were given; MAE, Leg. 5912, exp. 2: 'Informe sobre la Unión Europea de Pagos (UEP)', 25 April.

To Spanish minds, the conclusion was obvious: there was no immediate advantage to joining the EPU when the liberalization of import trade would worsen the balance of payments to an extent which could not be offset by all possible credits from EPU. Although it seemed improbable that Spain would be forced to reach the 60 per cent target, when Austria was allowed not to liberalize and the United Kingdom reached 46 per cent in February 1953, even the Spanish proposal for their own schedule (starting with 30 per cent in each of the three sectors), would have greatly affected the import bill. Again, as in 1951, the Spanish attitude was much influenced by the belief that Spain's export trade would not substantially benefit from liberalization because it had reached its volume limits already. An additional problem was that Spain would lose 'the bargaining power that has given some good results before when countries are forced to buy Spanish products in order for Spain to buy their goods'.[17] In other words, Spain resented losing some of the advantages of import discrimination and bilateral bargaining.

Washington shared the conviction that commercial credits were the alternative to Spain's OEEC/EPU membership. When Minister of Commerce Arburúa solicited assistance to move closer toward the OEEC liberalization practices, the US administration rejected going alone on the basis that several European countries were also in a position to help less developed economies. Thus, it was decided to enlist the participation of Germany, the United Kingdom, the Netherlands, and France in long-term development credits to Spain for the purchase of capital goods. Despite American pressure, France and

Germany continued to insist on short-term credits. France demanded dollar payments for fertilizer purchases from French North Africa and Germany charged interest on the swing debit beyond the interest paid to German suppliers of machinery.[18] Only the United Kingdom increased the amount of the swing from $4.2 million in 1953 to $7 million in 1954.[19] Clearly, US assistance in obtaining Spanish credits did not yield much fruit. The global amount of credit provided by bilateral agreements with the OEEC countries could hardly compensate for Spain's lack of EPU membership. Spain's payments difficulties continued to be the major obstacle to the expansion of trade; bilateral trade credits continued to shape the flow of trade more intensively than any other factor, including the price and quality of the products to be purchased (most particularly during the period of low agricultural exports). Reciprocal credits were isolated actions and altogether a very limited and unstable solution. In April 1951, overall swap facilities amounted to $31.781 million. That year, with a surplus of $35.2 million in trade balance, Spain had to make payments in gold to a total value of $13 million to settle debts with individual countries.[20] From this perspective, EPU credit facilities were far from inconvenient. Two years later, commercial credits and overdraft facilities had increased to $61.6 million, but they decreased again in October 1954 to approximately $50 million.[21]

By its exclusion from the EPU, Spain remained in the straitjacket of bilateral clearings, which meant that as the bilateral credit lines were exhausted and the creditor was not willing to extend further credit, import license applications were turned down and trade stagnated. Very rarely was Spain willing to pay gold in order to continue importing from a country whose credit facilities had already been drained. Trade with that specific country was put on hold and purchases were transferred to a different country – which did not necessarily offer the same commodities at better prices or at better terms – whose trade credit was still unconsumed. Spanish exporters were forced to accept disadvantageous trade terms in order to obtain the imports required, when better terms could have been obtained from third countries. Conversely, when importing, the country was forced to accept in payment goods of limited usefulness to its economy in order to balance the bilateral account. With Spain outside the EPU, the granting of import licenses to individual countries continued to be influenced largely by the availability of a specific currency at any given time.

*   *   *

The purpose of the third section of this book was to show how Spanish bilateralism survived and behaved within a context moving progressively toward free trade and multilateral payments. Against a background of increasing economic interdependence, the expected collapse of Spain's bilateral trade was avoided because of the determination of Spain's main trading partners in Western Europe, especially the United Kingdom, to sustain their trade with Spain.

Britain's non-discriminatory treatment of Spain was essential because the latter was able to use its sterling earnings to make payments to a large number of countries. British governments (both Labour and Conservative, despite the former's ideological aversion to the Franco regime) refused to discriminate against Spanish exports. As part of their general commercial policy, the British were determined to maintain trade under any circumstances. This was stated right after the war, when international pressure was at its greatest; it was maintained despite the severe difficulties encountered in running bilateral agreements. It was preserved when the OEEC liberalization applied; confirmed when import restrictions were imposed due to balance-of-payments difficulties; and finally reaffirmed after 1953, when the Spanish import authorities failed to comply with licensing British less essentials at the levels agreed upon.

The arguments in favor of adopting a firm attitude toward Spain to force the fulfilment of formal undertakings under the bilateral agreements were persuasive, but never firm enough to impose the adoption of measures such as removing Spain from the transferable account area or refusing to grant OGLs to Spanish export products. With one temporary exception, sanctions against Spain only met with objections in the different departments of the British Cabinet. In October 1953, when the British authorities excluded Spain from OGLs for grapes and nuts, the bilateral quotas were sufficient to allow all feasible trade. The British gave Spain complete OEEC treatment from June 1954.

The early trade liberalization measures among OEEC countries had a rather limited effect on bilateral trade between Spain and its main trade partners within the OEEC area. The effects of exclusion from the general pattern of trade liberalization in the early 1950s were far from homogenous in all three sectors – agricultural products, raw materials, and manufactured goods – simply because trade liberalization had a different impact on different groups of goods. Spain's main exports faced a situation broadly similar to that of the OEEC countries because the OEEC liberalization program either remained ineffective in agricultural trade or was extended to non-member countries in the case of raw materials. The British, French, and German governments applied to Spain the first article of the Code of Liberalization of Trade which stated that any member state was free to determine the nature and degree of freedom in its economic and financial relations with the outside world in the light of its individual situation and, thus, if it so desired, could take trade liberalization measures with respect to a non-member country. That Spain escaped severe discrimination in the process of trade liberalization, particularly in agricultural trade, was significant because its largest consumers of agricultural produce were the OEEC countries (61 per cent of Spain's total agricultural exports in the period from 1949 to 1953), providing the Spanish economy with 24 per cent of total foreign currency receipts registered in current and capital accounts during that period. It is this background which enables us to understand Madrid's immediate reaction when the idea of organizing European agricultural markets, following integrationist schemes, was launched.[22]

Considering the narrow margins within which the policy was applied, Franco's foreign economic administration was masterful in adjusting to new political and economic variables during the first postwar decade. It was quick to benefit from any favorable circumstance created by the clash of particular interests within and among the nations involved in economic cooperation. Spain benefited from the fact that bilateralism could not be eliminated completely because non-discrimination was never fully extended. Spanish literature on the period concentrates on placing Spain against a uniform bloc of countries propelled by the experiences of the 1930s and the disasters of the war to solve their problems together in the seamless continuum that was 1945 to 1957. Certain elements seem never to have existed: the predominance of bilateral trade in Western Europe up to 1953; the failure of the United States to push Western Europeans from the shopping-list approach to common standpoints at the time of the CEEC; the limits of trade liberalization among OEEC countries and their balance-of-payments set-backs in the early 1950s; the permanence of tariffs as effective means for domestic protection once non-tariff protection was removed; the late implementation of a multilateral payments mechanism; and the various guillotined initiatives to move more quickly in the removal of all forms of trade discrimination. Yet these elements all undermine the idea that Spanish bilateralism in trade was an indisputable and permanent breach with Europe's free trade system.

Nevertheless, Spain's non-participation in the OEEC and EPU schemes had serious economic disadvantages. The settlement of inconvertible balances remained Spain's main trade obstacle. Spain's financial resources, apart from export earnings, a few loans, and reduced American aid, were governed by the reciprocal swings and overdraft facilities provided by payments agreements with trading partners to finance short-term deficits in bilateral trade. As a debtor, Spain could accumulate inconvertible debit balances only up to the limits of the agreed swings; the remainder of the balance was payable to the creditor in gold and dollars. The inability or unwillingness to take more Spanish goods, and thus supply the Spanish authorities with additional currency with which to buy more from the given partner, led automatically to the contraction of bilateral trade. On the other hand, the Ministry of Commerce had to limit the total amount of imports from each and every monetary area to the exchange resources available at any given time; it had to allocate foreign exchange resources to those areas it deemed most essential. The fact that Spain needed to seek a structural balance in its individual payments, without EPU credit facilities, did not facilitate the relaxation of trade and foreign exchange controls. The extent to which licenses and quantitative restrictions protected national industries was determined by the distortion of trade practices imposed by the permanent lack of gold reserves and convertible currencies. The obsession with saving foreign exchange shifted the emphasis of trade regulations away from promoting traditional exports and toward providing import supply to develop subsequent exports. Altogether, this tended to reduce the total volume of trade. The Spanish administration created a vicious circle whereby imports were restricted due to the lack of foreign currency while the exchange rate handicapped exports, thus diminishing foreign currency earnings. In 1947, Madrid pleaded for foreign assistance in order to break this vicious circle. By the end of the period covered by this book, the circle had grown even more vicious. The basic needs of the Spanish economy had not changed, while the set of economic interests favoring protectionism became even more entrenched. Only a gradual expansion of production would have permitted the Spanish government to progress toward the implementation of freer trading practices.

The extension of liberalization to Spain was neither complete nor automatic, and it was, more often than not, used as a bargaining counter in bilateral trade discussions. Spain frequently suffered from breaches of declared undertakings. Thus, by the time Spain suceeded in obtaining one set of liberalization measures, it was already too late because a fresh set would already have been implemented among the OEEC countries. Spain was, consequently, always running behind schedule. Such a situation could never provide the basis for long-term growth strategies.

Bilateral trade worked relatively well as an emergency short-run measure while intra-European trade was distorted by controls. At that time, Spain's bilateralism proved to be expansive rather than restrictive, like the intra-European bilateral agreements of the immediate postwar period. It made possible exchanges of goods that would not otherwise have taken place. But it could not be a long-term solution once intra-European trade was liberated from the constraints of bilateralism. As trade liberalization and multilateral payments extended, Spain's trade was severely affected because of the relatively small proportion of essential commodities among Spain's exportable surpluses and because of its dependence upon imports for basic industries. Import trade, apart from the years from 1952 to 1954, was in almost permanent stagnation, whereas exports expanded in 1951 and then decreased. Spain's export performance was already bad in 1950, the year when the OEEC liberalization program and the EPU were effectively working before the full effects of the Korean War had major disturbing effects. However, when protectionism and import restrictions returned, the Spanish authorities effectively maintained what was a crisis and emergency device.

Concluding Remarks

For generations to come, it should not be forgotten that the bloody origins and the undemocratic nature of the Franco regime caused Spain's exclusion from all the initiatives at international cooperation after World War II. The institutions which resulted from these initiatives embodied the sort of welfare capitalism responsible for one of the fastest and most solid patterns of economic growth, social consensus, and democratic political stability which Western Europe has ever enjoyed. The main consequences of exclusion from this institutional set was thus to condemn the Spanish population to a lower standard of living than would have been the case had Spain not become a political *rara avis* among its peers.

The first question that needs careful consideration therefore is the survival of the Franco regime itself. The fact that the Second World War broke five months after the end of the Spanish Civil War, favored the continuance of General Franco in power. Domestic political repression and the fear of involvement in another armed conflict pushed aside any major revolt against the dictatorship ruling the country. Internationally, for both Allies and Axis powers, the main goal was to avoid Spain becoming a liability and try to use available Spanish assets in the largest possible measure. Explaining the Franco regime's survival however becomes particularly intriguing after 1945, when it was unanimously praised as a last vestige of the Fascism against which the Allies had fought and won the war.

That *Generalissimo* Franco was a dictator was not the major problem, nor that the coalition of forces he headed had destroyed Spain's democracy, but that his position of power had derived from the intervention by nazi and fascist armed forces, now defeated. Salazar's authoritarian regime posed a lesser problem to the Allies because it was considered to be a result of the development of internal forces in Portugal. The Franco regime was considered by democratic public and parliamentary opinion as unfinished business at the end of the war, an anomaly in the new order which was about to be implemented by the victorious Allies. How did the Francoist vessel manage thus to steer in the turbulent waters of an ocean of international political animosity?

Two traditional positions have been suggested to explain this apparent paradox; first, the poor performance of opposition forces within Spain and, second, the safehaven to Franco's regime provided by the Cold War. Fragmentation and controversy among the different forces opposing the Franco

189

regime weakened any active Allied policy to expel Franco from power. No political group was in a position to take over. The Allies were unwilling to provoke major unrest anywhere in Western Europe, particularly if the outcome was uncertain. Even if the groups opposed to Franco had come together, the question remained whether the Spanish army and the bulk of the conservative elements within Spain, including the monarchists, could be sufficiently convinced that the advantage of getting rid of Franco and his regime balanced the obvious risks involved. If there had been a unified political force to replace Franco, would the Allies have been willing to undertake the necessary measures to assure the replacement?

In no circumstance were the Allies willing to place a change of the Spanish political regime highly on their political agenda for immediate action. The western nations found in the Spanish economy a valuable resource in a world scourged by the war's destruction, general starvation, and economic dislocation. The maintenance of political stability in Spain was deemed essential in the first months after the war so the Spanish economy could continue contributing at the maximum of its capability to European recovery. Franco's unwillingness to step down meant, in their view, that any serious attempt to force a change would have awakened the possibility of renewed bloodshed in the Iberian Peninsula, a chaos which the Communists could exploit.

Although there was never any attempt to show political clemency toward the Franco regime, political ostracism was toned down significantly by the economic interest in maintaining a trouble-free source of supply which provided necessary and scarce food and raw materials for economic recovery and reconstruction. In a period when issues such as immediate relief of distressed populations, long-term reconstruction of national economies, creation of a new international economic and political order, and re-foundation of the Nation State's social and political support, the Spanish question merited no more attention than what was strictly necessary for public opinion purposes. The predicament of the European economies in the aftermath of World War II led to political appeasement which, in turn, favored the survival of the Franco regime. The European governments' opposition to decisive action against Franco and his regime was part of a straightforward defense of their own national interest.

Although Spain's foreign commerce was relatively small, it played a fairly important role when relief and reconstruction had to be undertaken mainly on the basis of depleted national resources. The generally low level of dollar earnings with which to face the extremely large import needs from the dollar area was such a fundamental constraint everywhere in Europe that any imports from non-dollar suppliers was highly appreciated by any government. Importation from Spain reduced the pressure on imports from the dollar area and saved hard currency for more important or scarce imports which could only come from hard-currency areas.

Spanish commercial authorities, fully aware that the economic circumstances of postwar Europe rated high all possible sources of non-dollar supply, decided to provide credit to major European powers so that they could buy from Spain immediately after the end of the war. This was done despite the fact that Spain was in great need of financial assistance itself. The clear political intent was that Spanish exports eclipsed the political antipathy. Actually, trade intensification pushed aside any impulse for political retaliation. To be sure, most of the countries trading with Spain could have substituted other sources for Spanish imports, but they continued trading with Spain because acting otherwise would have required sacrificing a certain degree of diet improvement and a higher import bill for denominated-in-dollar raw materials when the speedy success of rapid national reconstruction policies was the single most important objective of all west European governments. Once the Franco regime survived the immediate postwar period, it was there to stay.

International resolutions on Spain effectively emphasized the regime's political ostracism but the immediate short-term effect was advantageous to Franco in the sense of closing the ranks of the Civil War victors. The nationalistic cry in the face of foreign hostility caused by the different Allied resolutions, the guerilla war carried on by commandos from bases beyond the Pyrenees, the French decision to close the frontier with Spain, and the decision adopted by the United Nations to withdraw ambassadors from Madrid, all acted unfavorably upon those working for internal political evolution. If these actions attempted to undermine Franco so that he could be overthrown or leave power, they had in fact the reverse effect. Franco's tight control of the country was substantially strengthened; his situation of *dictator* holding a temporary and extraordinary office was finally transformed into permanent power. As a reaction to the condemnatory resolutions of December 1946, a new five-peseta coin carried Franco's effigy bordered with the inscription 'Francisco Franco, Caudillo of Spain by the Grace of God'. Vacuous political declarations against Franco contented public opinion in western democracies and fulfilled the necessary political objective of maintaining Franco Spain at arm's length, while less visible means were used to avoid the collapse of the Spanish economy.

Application of economic sanctions against Spain was always possible but this would have been effective only if taking place with full cooperation among the Allies and other major suppliers, and with any countries from which goods could be re-exported. Apart from the outright position for non-discrimination adopted by countries like Argentina and Portugal from the onset of the debate, the British government remained firmly opposed to economic sanctions. London always opposed the use of their navicert control for political purposes and felt strongly that a stoppage of even one product, such as petroleum, would result in serious hardship among the mass of the Spanish people without producing any guarantee that in the short term a stable moderate government would replace the Franco regime. International political verbiage confronted effective economic assistance carried out on a bilateral trade basis.

Commercial policy became the most important element in Spanish foreign policy and bilateral trade the most important factor in the survival of the Franco regime immediately after 1945. Bilateral trade agreements suited everyone's purpose. Presented by the western democracies as technical accommodations which would yield improved standards of living in their own countries, they tended to arouse far less domestic hostility to the fragile democratic governments of the postwar period. For its part, Spanish economic authorities were happy to keep the only source of foreign exchange earnings they had, while at the same time providing for the international recognition of the Franco regime. If Spain did not take full advantage of the opportunities offered by European reconstruction to expand its trade, it was certainly not due to any political or economic ostracism operating between the end of 1944 and the spring of 1947; it was due, rather, to the slow rate of its own domestic recovery and to the economic policy deployed by the Spanish authorities. At that time, Spain's poor trade performance was not directly attributable to external discriminatory measures.

Providing relief and avoiding the collapse of the Spanish economy are not sufficient reasons for the survival of the Franco regime in the long run; national economic reconstruction was necessary. Reconstruction required, first, to complete rehabilitation from Civil War dislocation and World War II disruption, and second, the accomplishment of a program of economic modernization able to prepare the national economy for the open international economic system agreed at Bretton Woods in 1944. The Spanish program of imports to be financed by the Marshall Plan was drafted within a clear reconstruction perspective. It was no surprise that the Franco regime's economic authorities expected to participate in Marshall Plan arrangements. In the absence of major foreign obstacles to trade from 1945 to 1947, the Spanish economic authorities believed that they had reached a basic measure of compatibility between their economic policy and external events, and to be able to continue mutually beneficial trade relations with Spain's main commercial partners in their effort to achieve full recovery and sustained industrial growth. Spain's response to the Marshall Plan was the result of the country's favorable experience during the period of relief and first phase of reconstruction efforts in Western Europe.

The Spanish government expected that Marshall aid would finance the supply of raw materials and machinery needed to break bottlenecks and provide for the modernization of industrial structures and to initiate a long-term economic adjustment process in order to achieve a higher standard of living. The official Spanish reasoning was that the attainment of 1935 levels would not spell adequate economic conditions in Spain, since the Civil War was in part a result of the economic misery that prevailed prior to its outbreak. The poor state of the Spanish economy, the Spanish officials argued, did not permit any sizeable expansion of exports, particularly to the principal source of capital goods for reconstruction. Wherever the responsibility should go, the reality was that Spain could not compete in the American markets to obtain dollars which in turn were needed to service imports. It was a situation replicated in most European countries: having to face a modernization effort well beyond the gold and hard-currency reserves available.

More important than Spain's application to Marshall Plan assistance, however, was that, fully aware of the importance of the Marshall Plan as well as the strong political turmoil which Spanish membership would have implied, the Spanish government offered to Washington the possibility of assisting Spain outside the Marshall Plan structure in exchange for greater concessions in economic policy and trade liberalization than membership into the ERP would have entailed, though no political liberalization should be requested. The ideological content of the Marshall Plan, however, rendered totally unacceptable this compromise. The Marshall Plan was conceived to give stability to the weak democratic coalitions that formed most of the governments of Western Europe. It was not the purpose of the Marshall Plan to help out an authoritarian political regime which disrupted the democratic social and political consensus which constituted the very basis of the new European order which the Americans were eager to shape. The Marshall Plan embodied the American belief that economic growth and free trade were inextricably linked with democratic governance.

The ERP was by its own nature incompatible with the Franco regime. Bringing Franco Spain along would have distorted the ideological basis of the Marshall Plan in unparalleled ways to the distress produced by Salazar's Portugal. Yet isolation helps no one. It helps neither the marginalized country nor the international community in its effort to obtain changes within that country. By excluding Spain from this initiative, the western powers lost all leverage over policy trends, and provided the most inward-looking groups among the coalition of forces which formed the Franco regime the perfect excuse to follow even more nationalistic and interventionist policies. In general, insisting on Franco leaving power as a *sine qua non* of aid simply delayed economic development without even offering the hope of political evolution.

Access to Marshall aid or direct American aid outside the ERP and conditioned upon specific terms, would have forced the Spanish economic authorities to undertake necessary economic reforms. Some scholars have argued that the small relative proportion of Marshall aid to total resources gave the United States little bargaining power to impose specific economic policy decisions.[1] Yet this argument would have not applied to Spain if aid had been given outside the ERP. But the Truman administration did not consider stepping outside the collective approach until 1951 when it finally decided to open bilateral negotiations with the Spanish government and offered financial assistance in return for military facilities.

Spain's exclusion from what has been recently labelled 'history's most successful structural adjustment program' meant to confide domestic economic recovery to domestic resources and thus significantly diminished the prospect of any radical change.[2] The short-term problems posed by lack of foreign exchange not only discouraged any sudden change in economic policy; it also retarded recovery and led to unstable economic growth. Indeed, compensation and combined accounts were only introduced in August 1947 and the system of multiple exchange rates in December 1948, after the failure to obtain Marshall aid to complement domestically-produced earnings. From then onwards the situation fluctuated along the profile of both the national foreign currency holdings and the international investment ratings for Spain. The actual balance of payments position kept economic authorities on the verge of a permanent nervous breakdown. Having no access to foreign aid programs when the country's own financial resources were incommensurably inferior to the task of economic reconstruction, and, particularly, when all its regional partners were placed in a more advantageous position, meant the adoption of policies leading to the worst nightmares of public intervention.

While not ignoring the obstacles to healthy recovery for which the economic policy of the Franco regime alone must bear full responsibility, the aim of this work has been to examine those external factors which rendered interventionist policies more likely. The position I defend is intermediate between those who exclusively stressed external constraints on economic recovery, and the views of those who point to the inefficiency and corruptness of Spanish foreign economic policy. This book, limited to foreign economic policy toward Western Europe, suggests that the extreme forms of trade controls and intervention, not intervention itself, but its paralysing forms, were closely linked to the availability of resources in the form of gold and foreign currency holdings, particularly US dollars. Because of the foreign exchange difficulties, trade dislocation evolved like a gangrene, the treatment of which became more complex every year until a drastic decision finally came in 1959 along with a foreign assistance package as a sort of anaesthesia.

The inclusion of Spain on the list of ERP countries for financial assistance granted outside the Marshall Plan would certainly have spared the Spanish population a decade of retardation and low standards of living. The almost mythical Stabilization Plan of 1959 might have become totally unnecessary if Spain had been able to move toward economic liberalization earlier. However, linking inexorably financial assistance to a change of the political regime frustrated an earlier evolution of the Spanish economy toward any greater degree of economic liberalization. Foreign exchange scarcity and abundance of interventionist bureaucrats were directly proportional to Spain's isolation. In a historical perspective, the Allied attitude was total failure: excluding Spain from the Marshall Plan produced neither democratic evolution nor economic growth. On the contrary, it strengthened the authoritarian lines of the Francoist political system, and led to temporary economic stagnation.

One of the first means conceived to avoid a further deterioration of the Spanish economy, although not the most successful one in the long run, was direct access to American assistance through military dealings. The failure to be included in the ERP may explain why Spain entered into bilateral military negotiations with the US authorities to trade the right to use military bases in exchange for dollar aid. The granting of military bases on Spanish territory was the most accessible route to obtain quickly substantial foreign economic assistance without the threat of having to deal with demands for political democratization. Concerning assistance from the United States, we have come to face the main argument traditionally used to explain the survival of the Franco regime after World War II: the Cold War.

Spain did not properly benefit from its anti-Communist stance until the signature of the Pact of Madrid in September 1953. Before then, all financial assistance from the United States was of little benefit. While it is true that the US Congress twisted the Truman administration's arm and authorized a $62.5 million loan to Spain as early as August 1950, barely weeks after the outbreak of war in Korea, it is also true that the President, the Department of State, the Economic Cooperation Administration and the Export-Import Bank all tried their hardest to block the authorization. In fact, it took five years to make the 1950 congressional loan fully available. All subsequent congressional authorizations to Spain were subject to the final conclusion of the bilateral agreement for the use of bases in the Spanish territory during peacetime as well as wartime. Once the agreement had been concluded, Spanish officials doubtlessly hoped that the United States would provide assistance for general economic rehabilitation. After Korea, however, the only aid authorized by the US Congress was to support the military build-up, that is NATO and foreign military bases. The so-called *defense support* was never intended to have a multiplying effect on Spain's overall level of production. If the Pact of Madrid was the first real and direct benefit of the Cold War that Spain could effectively reap, it is hard to believe that the Cold War rescued the Franco regime.

The Cold War argument assumes that the US government was willing to cooperate with any country as long as it was anti-Communist. This was certainly not the case for the greatest part of the Truman administration years. Had it been so, the US government would have sought a rapprochement with the Spanish regime as early as the autumn of 1947 when the Policy Planning Staff of the State Department requested a policy U-turn on Spain; or when the United States lost the atomic monopoly two years later; or immediately after the outbreak of the Korean war, seen as the Soviet rehearsal for direct military confrontation with the West. Certainly, the military establishment in Washington, as in London and Paris, valued the contribution Spain could make to defend Western Europe against a soon-expected Soviet advance. The job of the military is to present solutions to the worst possible war scenario, the job of governments is to check them out against major foreign and domestic goals. In the harsh social and economic circumstances reigning in Western Europe in the aftermath of the war, when national Communist parties aimed at power through the electoral ballot, the strategy of containment was based on speedy economic recovery which would improve living standards and deprive Communists of electoral support. European security was not a purely military matter.

A free, politically stable, socially cohesive, economically dynamic, and possibly unified, Western Europe was the Marshall Plan's main goal. While these goals existed, there was no question of any understanding with the Franco regime; Spain weakened rather than strengthened western defense against Communism. Bringing Spain in for reasons of military expedience would have risked major dissension within European cabinets and among the Allies, and aroused severe controversy in public opinion. Spain was judged an asset unworthy of such controversy. It was Washington's frustration with the weak European efforts to reach military integration which finally imposed a change in the policy toward Spain. The latter's anti-Communist position, which hitherto had been meaningless, became the ideal justification for unilateral action, which definitively ended concerted Allied policy over Spain. After 1951, the US general strategy for the defense of Western Europe was based on a collective system as well as on more flexible arrangements negotiated with individual countries on a bilateral basis according to the specific difficulties of any given area.

Since defense support was not intended to do for Spain what the Marshall Plan had earlier done for OEEC countries, the Spanish economic authorities were forced to divert their attention from foreign financial assistance to exports and from short-term to long-term transformation of their economy. Bilateral trade relations provided a path toward the recovery of prewar levels of output everywhere in Europe, but could not allow for the kind of effort that would assure a proper performance of any national economy in the future world context of free trade and convertibility. This perspective serves to reveal the true relevance of the Spanish–Argentine trade.

Although Argentina was the major source of foreign relief to the Spanish population between 1939 and 1955, it could not provide a lasting basis for economic growth and development. Commercial relations between the two countries were not founded on economic complementarity but on short-lived political circumstances. It is undeniable that Argentinean supplies contributed to improving the living conditions of the Spanish population and political regime. Imports of cereals averted the danger of famine and, consequently, social unrest. Yet while Argentina accounted for almost a quarter of overall Spanish imports in 1947–8, the potential for growth provided was nil.

It was, rather, the maintenance of active trade relations with Western Europe which allowed Spain to undergo a smooth and cumulative process of productivity improvement, which, in turn, may in part explain the rate of growth attained during the 1950s (Figure 1). The case of Spain does not confirm the opinion that without the Marshall Plan, Western Europe would have descended into desperation and chaos because there was no alternative course of action. In reality, the Spanish experience shows that the alternative was not chaos but retarded recovery and unstable growth.

Europeans realized that once the ERP and the exclusion of Spain were matters of fact, it was necessary to maintain – and increase whenever it was possible to do so – trade with Spain. They remained self-confident that an excessive deterioration of the economic conditions in Spain would create a conflict which could well become a source of distress and uncertainty for the continent. Moreover, there was no reason to dismiss a source of soft-currency supplies; the Spanish market was also useful for less-competitive manufacture producers. Eventually, bilateral trade relations provided inputs for a long-term process of economic transformation allowing a modest rate of growth which early assistance from the United States did not.

Economists properly argue that the rate of growth achieved by Spain was far below its potential. Notwithstanding this, if a model of growth based on productivity improvement on the basis of importation of capital goods from Western Europe – a model which no doubt requires future quantification – is a sensible working hypothesis, researchers should pay attention to the way in which bilateral relations survived within a multilateral context, rather than on the *fait accompli* of Spanish exclusion. While Spain stood outside the

198

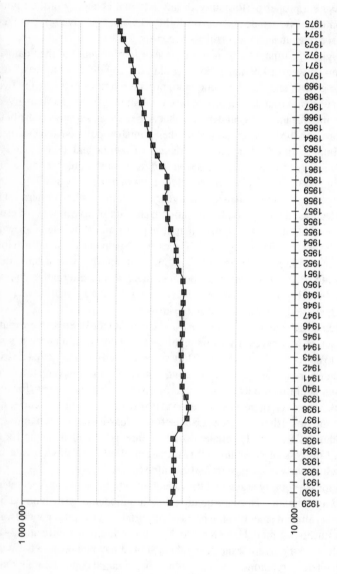

FIGURE 1   SPAIN'S REAL GDP AT MARKET PRICES, 1929–75 (Billions of pesetas 1980, Logarithmic Scale)

Source: L. Prados de la Escosura, 'Spain's Gross Domestic Product, 1850–1993: Quantitative Conjectures. Appendix', Universidad Carlos III Working Paper 95–06, Economic Series, Madrid, February 1995, tables D4 and E2, pp. 179 ff and 192 ff.

institutions of economic cooperation, European governments found ways and means of reducing the most dramatic consequences of exclusion. With the cooperation of the European nations, mainly on the basis of bilateral dealings and frequently on the basis of unilateral concessions unrequited by Madrid, the Spanish economy remained open to the influence of the leading economies and connected to the dynamic forces for growth unleashed in Europe during what might be termed the golden age of Western capitalism.[3]

Excluding Spain from the benefits of OEEC/EPU membership represented a larger handicap to the Spanish economy in the long run than the lack of any ERP dollar aid. Both OEEC and EPU constituted successful milestones in the path toward economic growth and interdependence in Western Europe precisely for the help they provided in reducing the levels of intervention within the economies and the levels of discrimination among countries, and in allowing for an expansion of intra-European trade, particularly trade with Germany, which acted as an important transmitter of productivity throughout Europe.[4] Spain could not benefit from this environment propitious to growth which others exploited to the extent of their own capacity and willingness.

The early expansion of intra-European trade was linked to EPU's automatic credit and offsetting mechanism of bilateral monthly surpluses and deficits, which substantially reduced gold payments. With the benefit of EPU's system of currency transferability, Spain could have reduced intervention in trade and payments and, with US financial assistance, could have encountered a foreseeable chronic debtor position within EPU. However, when the possibility of Spain's EPU membership was considered, on a non-official basis, Spain found it difficult to finance the necessary average percentage of import liberalization without financial collaboration from the United States or the Union itself. In turn, Spain's access to the EPU, if it was to be beneficial to the Spanish economy, would have meant concessions that might have proved incompatible with the Union's philosophy, especially if granted to a later entrant.

Spain's lack of OEEC/EPU membership, however, had less of a negative effect on trade than might have been expected. This is particularly true for the OEEC trade liberalization program. The balance-of-payments difficulties encountered in various countries restricted the overall efficiency of this program in the early 1950s. When fully active, though, the program failed, especially in agricultural trade, and trade liberalization in raw materials was extended to non-OEEC members. This way, Spain's main export commodities, which as the principal source of foreign currency were essential to the development of the whole economy, faced no distinctive discrimination. Furthermore, some countries extended trade liberalization to Spain on a nonreciprocal and unilateral basis. Perhaps most significant of all was that a palliative credit mechanism partly tackled the prejudices of lack of EPU membership: Spain's European commercial partners granted bilateral credits whose value actually outweighed the amount of credit Spain would have been entitled to had it been an EPU member.

In general, OEEC/EPU discrimination against Spain could only be applicable to exports of manufactured goods. One could reasonably argue that given Spain's overall level of industrial output and total factor productivity rates, excluding it from those mechanisms that allowed the rapid growth in the exchange of manufactured goods between high-income economies was irrelevant. The low proportion of manufactured goods in Spain's exports saved this country from having to face effective OEEC discrimination. In the short-run, Spain suffered more from the consequences of its economic and commercial practices than from the discriminatory devices raised by multilateral institutions.

Although this book has put the emphasis on what could be labelled as the foreign constraints on the expansion of Spain's trade, by pointing at a somewhat non-discriminatory treatment, it cannot be left aside that strong domestic constraints for the promotion of trade existed in Spain. Devaluation, followed by a relaxation of export controls, unification of exchange rates, and the elimination of the extreme features of state intervention were always presented as long-term strategies, which failed to materialize until the 1960s. Before then, the full extension of the liberalization measures to Spain would have not necessarily led to an automatic increase in exports to the OEEC markets if it was not accompanied by drastic changes in the domestic economic policy. The case of Spain presents the limits of economic cohabitation between an inward-looking economy and a worldwide system of progressive interdependence.

Bilateral concessions by various OEEC countries at one time or another (in a few cases for several years) constituted a temporary situation intended to avoid the collapse of the Spanish trade which was subject to changing situations on which Madrid had almost no influence. The most talented personnel within the Spanish foreign economic authorities were always conscious that any favorable situation was easily reversible. The sort of workable cohabitation skilfully constructed by Spain within the surrounding multilateral world did not provide the long-term prospects for stability that the postwar international settlement provided to other countries in Europe.

When the Franco regime was installed bilateral agreements were the only means of channelling trade. After 1945, there was no real choice between bilateralism and multilateralism. All throughout Western Europe the choices were dictated by the availability of reserves and credits, as much as by the public will to protect those economic sectors considered, for one or another reason, strategic in either economic, political, social, or military terms. Although bilateralism was somewhat strangled when the first moves toward multilateralism were conceived and implemented, it was not eradicated. By October 1954, there were approximately 90 bilateral and similar agreements in force between EPU members, and, in general, there were about 235 agreements between pairs of European countries.[5] In the sphere of defense, as mentioned before, there was little specifically Francoist in the bilateral agreement with the United States. What made Spain a special case was that it conducted its foreign and trade relations exclusively on the basis of bilaterally negotiated agreements.

Was bilateralism the preferred course of action for the Spanish economic authorities? After 1947 bilateralism was not Spain's choice, but a dictate of its resources. Multilateral organizations rejected Spanish membership and the granting to Spain of the same financial back-up that induced European countries to adopt, support and finally accept – with numerous exceptions and safe-guard clauses – multilateral trade liberalization and payments. The distaste the Franco regime produced in the western democracies made Spain's isolation inevitable and undisputable while the whole of Western Europe moved toward multilateralism. Spain's bilateral agreements with members of the OEEC and EPU were not the result of autarkic thinking, but the evidence of the need to carry on trade that would not have taken place otherwise. In other words, in the case of Spain, bilateralism was a trade creation device rather than the contrary.

Initiatives based on supranational institutions appeared as new threats to the Spanish trading performance in Western Europe. Fortunately for Madrid, the Schuman Plan did not have the effect of isolating Spain even further. Central European coal and steel were of scant interest given the inward-looking nature of Spanish industries in the sector. The European Coal and Steel Community's lack of a commercial policy impeded the immediate distortions of the very limited but essential trade flows between Spain and each of the Six, which would have been the case otherwise. The prospect which lay before the Spanish authorities changed dramatically when integration expanded to high priority areas such as agriculture. The attempt to set up a European Agricultural Community following the line of the Schuman Plan, however, did not have negative impact on the Spanish economy. The supranational aspects of this initiatives were deserted almost immediately and thus Spanish officials were invited to defend the interests of their government. The Spanish administration was thus largely able to overcome the negative implications of the early integration attempts.

By the mid-1950s, the Spanish administration had come to the wrong conclusion that progressive economic interdependence in Western Europe was a serious, but not insurmountable obstacle to its trade performance. The creation of the European Economic Community (EEC) by the Six and the further creation of the European Free Trade Association by seven non-EEC OEEC countries, proved that Franco Spain could never be confident. More than before, Spain's external policy aimed at obtaining from the international community a credible commitment in favor of the country's stable economic development and peaceful political evolution. The request to open negotiations with the EEC in 1962 could be seen in this light. The increasing anxiety that the Spanish authorities felt about the EEC was proportional to the awareness of the inevitable collapse of the comfortable status quo that Madrid had been progressively able to reach within the Western European multilateral system.

The degree of success of those policies implemented while the exclusion from international organizations persisted, remains of problematic measurement. Compared to most European countries, the lack of participation itself would imply total failure. But if compared to the actual set of options at hand for the Spanish foreign economic authorities at the time, this book suggests that they acted as effectively as possible in dealing with the challenge of European economic cooperation. This book points at the Spanish foreign economic administration being able to maintain the institutional dealings that may have allowed a constant technological up-dating on the basis of bilateral trade with countries fully involved both in a strong catching-up process with the world's technological leader and in rapid convergence among themselves.[6] All of this occurred from the weak position granted to the representatives of a political regime which had been the object of formal condemnation and denunciation by international organizations. This implies a highly efficient team of officials acting within political and economic structures poorly fitted for the sort of economic relations developed in Western Europe after 1948. In this sense, a story of frustration exists underneath this book – the frustration felt by a handful of men who attempted, while reducing the degree of discrimination then threatening Spain, to induce the convergence toward European-like modes of policy action.

It is completely legitimate to doubt whether any declared intentions on liberalization signified any true commitment to economic amendment before 1959. The real value of any such commitment is hard to measure, simply because there was no opportunity to test it. The fear of lending international legitimacy to the Spanish power structure was widespread in influential circles throughout the West and Spain's official early promises of economic stabilization and liberalization, if genuine economic assistance was granted, looked like an effort to get help for consolidating the existing economic system, rather than for altering it fundamentally to conform to western norms.

Those who argued that bringing Spain into the western family was the best way of reforming the system carried little weight until the late 1950s. Some may argue that only by devaluing the national currency, lifting most direct controls, sharply reducing subsidies, and offering a stabilization program meeting IMF criteria, would official statements by Spaniards about aspiration for liberalized international trade and payments have come credible, as in 1959. This argument gives little weight to the deep distrust as to the real intentions of the western powers felt by the higher echelons of the Francoist regime.

Officials high in the Spanish administration felt there was no guarantee that after having adopted economic stabilization and liberalization measures, the international community, particularly the United States, would provide the financial assistance necessary to avoid the anticipated deterioration. Their fear was that the United States would then request Franco to adopt political reforms. At this point came the blockade, not necessarily because no political evolution could be conceived, but because no political reform of the Franco regime, no matter how important, short of Franco himself leaving office, would appease western desires for political democratization in Spain. It has been one of the arguments of this book that assistance could have been granted in a way to assure effective overall liberalization, but that the main obstacle which the Spanish administration faced at the time was the widely-shared and strongly-held ideological conviction that political authoritarianism and economic liberalism were natural foes. Spanish personnel could not accept the link between economic and political liberalization nor could their foreign colleagues accept to disassociate the two processes. The result was that neither economic liberalization nor political democratization occurred in Spain. It was only when the two elements were separated in the late 1950s that the international community considered it appropriate to grant financial assistance to Franco's Spain.

Economic historians have dealt almost exclusively with the forces inimical to Spanish growth during the period covered in this book. To be sure, Spain consistently performed short of the rates of growth that it could have attained if it had adopted the kind of policies elaborated in other countries, particularly Italy. The most recent quantitative evidence on Spain's real GDP shows that continuous growth after 1950, with the stop-and-go interregnum of the late 1950s, is notwithstanding all less surprising than the fact that, during a period of exceptional growth and strong convergence of European economies, Spain did not diverge from the set of countries shown in Figure 2, the only exception being Germany.

If there were no clear exogenous obstacles to growth, historians of domestic economic policies under the Franco regime should face the painstaking

FIGURE 2   SPAIN'S REAL GDP PER HEAD: AN INTERNATIONAL COMPARISON (1990 Geary-Khamis US$, in percentages)

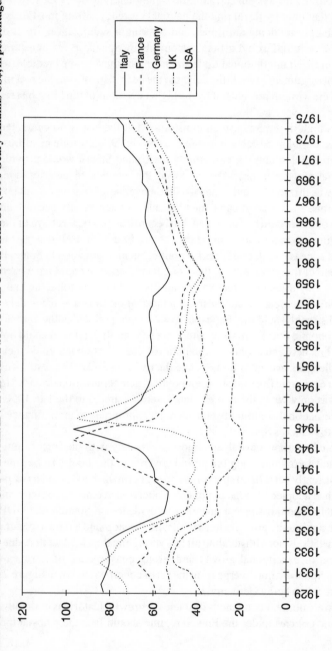

Source: L. Prados de la Escosura, 'Spain's Gross Domestic Product, 1850–1993: Quantitative Conjectures. Appendix', Universidad Carlos
III Working Paper 95–06, Economic Series, Madrid, February 1995, tables D4 and E2, pp. 179 ff and 192 ff.

evidence that, despite an obtuse domestic economic policy, Spain was a golden-age partner in Europe. Scholars thus should be looking for those elements that could explain this evidence rather than limiting themselves to hammer again and again at the mass of the obstructionist measures then in place. In other words, if existing accounts were to be taking to the letter, Spain's economic performance in the 1950s should not be qualified as poor and disappointing but as little short of miraculous because the matching quantitative evidence should have been stagnation and rapid divergence. When quantitative evidence and explanations differ, there appear a whole range of questions to be properly readdressed.

It is an erroneous though commonly held view among scholars that Spanish efforts toward integration in the international economy began only in 1959. By the same token, that Spain was excluded from almost all forms of cooperation among the nations of the West has led to the equally mistaken view that the Spanish government disregarded the early efforts toward western economic cooperation. I have attempted to show that the Spanish authorities were keenly aware of the significance and danger of the various initiatives for intra-European and Atlantic economic cooperation. They watched closely, even anxiously, as Western European countries edged toward economic interdependence. Not only did they observe, they reacted accordingly. Even more important in view of future developments, a growing awareness of the dangers of economic isolation developed during the 1950s.

The perceptions, successful reactions and disappointments of the Spanish authorities in their effort to bring Spain back into the realm of European economic cooperation formed a cumulative *learning process* which allowed future Cabinets to react promptly and decisively when new initiatives at cooperation and integration were launched. The Spanish administration had learned that a national economy cannot remain isolated from the world economic system and that delayed access to major international organizations only meant more rigid conditions and less initial assistance. The sectors of the Spanish administration dealing with foreign economic policy considered cooperation with Western Europe to be the correct strategy for economic growth, the only way to resist the attacks from true believers of introversion. By the mid-1950s, the *Europeanization* of the Spanish economy had already become the official policy. It only remained to be seen how this was to be accomplished.

By the mid-1950s the Spanish government adopted economic development as a major ideological device. The government was to deliver not only national security against real and invented threats (a Communist take-over, first, and then foreign hostility) but an improved living standard for a larger proportion of Spaniards. The Franco regime's stability could no longer rely on the memories of Civil War horrors, or continue to derive legitimacy from a coercive maintenance of order. Future legitimacy was to be derived from the creation and preservation of economic prosperity.

It was unfortunate that economic deterioration coincided with the first tentative steps toward trade liberalization after 1955. This conjunction gave rise within the Spanish Cabinet to even greater opposition to the argument that economic liberalization could be monitored in such a way as to avoid social or political fractures. Yet it was clear to everyone that drastic measures were necessary. Policy-makers were perfectly aware that the all-interventionist approach was prejudicial to good economic performance because it engendered widespread inefficiency and corruption. In the long run, the major threat to the stability of the Franco regime came from popular unrest over living conditions.

The Cabinet which took office in 1957 inherited the progressive approach adopted by previous cabinets toward economic stabilization and trade liberalization, as well as the idea that foreign financial assistance was prior to any drastic alteration of economic practices. In foreign economic policy the new Cabinet represented no significant change. Its European policy was no more than the traditional policy of adopting the best possible courses of action to preserve what policy-makers considered the national interest to be and to reduce as far as possible the negative effects of exclusion from the most effective cooperation schemes. The new Cabinet should properly be seen less as a revolutionary rupture with the past, and the vaunted stabilization program of 1959 more the conclusion of long-standing efforts to find an economic viability to Francoism.

Notes

NOTES TO THE INTRODUCTION

1. A challenging utilization of the concept of interdependence in historical research is A.S. Milward *et al.*, *The Frontier of National Sovereignty. History and Theory 1945–1992* (London, 1992).
2. For a comprehensive study of Franco's regime, S.G. Payne, *The Franco Regime 1936–1975* (Madison, 1987); for surveys on economic performance under Franco within a long-run perspective, G. Tortella, *El desarrollo de la España contemporánea. Historia económica de los siglos XIX y XX* (Madrid, 1994) and contributions to P. Martín Aceña and J. Simpson (eds), *The Economic Development of Spain since 1870* (Aldershot, 1995); for survey of relevant scholarship specifically referred to the Franco regime's economic policies and performance, J. Harrison, *The Spanish Economy. From the Civil War to the European Community* (London, 1993). A. Viñas *et al.*, *Política comercial exterior en España (1931–1975)* (Madrid, 1979) remains the best published study on Spain's post-1945 commercial policy. For a survey of Spanish foreign policy at the time, M. Espadas Burgos, *Franquismo y política exterior* (Madrid, 1988).
3. For a brilliant biography of Franco, P. Preston, *Franco. A Biography* (London, 1993).
4. The literature is mainly concerned with the post-1957 period when a major economic turning point in the Franco period occurred, with the exception of Viñas, 'La conexión entre autarquía y política exterior en el primer franquismo (1939–1959)' and 'La política exterior española durante el franquismo y el Ministerio de Asuntos Exteriores', both in his *Guerra, dinero, dictadura. Ayuda fascista y autarquía en la España de Franco* (Barcelona, 1984) 205–37 and 288–308, respectively; and, 'La administración de la política económica exterior en España, 1936–1979', *Cuadernos Económicos de ICE*, 13 (1980) 157–272.
5. An excellent example is J.A. Suanzes, 'Franco y la economía', in his *Ocho discursos de Suanzes* (Madrid, 1963) 123–63.
6. H. Paris Eguilaz, *El desarrollo económico español, 1906–1964* (Madrid, 1965), and J. Velarde Fuertes, 'Política de desarrollo', in E. Fuentes Quintana (ed.), *El desarrollo económico de España. Juicio crítico del Informe del Banco Mundial* (Madrid, 1963).
7. J. Esteban, 'The Economic Policy of Francoism: An Interpretation', in Preston (ed.), *Spain in Crisis. The Evolution and Decline of the Franco Régime* (Hassocks, 1976) 82–100.
8. For a very early view of this aspect, although set in a much wider context, Ch. S. Maier, 'The Two Postwar Eras and the Conditions for Stability in Western Europe', *American Historical Review*, vol. 86/2 (1981) 327–62. For a fresh and interesting approach, B. Eichengreen, 'Institutions and Economic Growth: Europe after World War II', in N. Crafts and G. Toniolo (eds),

Economic Growth in Europe since 1945 (Cambridge, 1996) 38–72. For the 'rescue' concept, Milward, *The European Rescue of the Nation State* (London, 1992).

NOTES TO CHAPTER 1

1. For the extensive use of 'reconstruction', Milward, *The Reconstruction of Western Europe 1945–51* (London, 1984), which constitutes the best published analysis on the institutional aspects of economic cooperation in Western Europe after 1945 and has provided the broad framework for the present book.
2. They were, together with the Law of National Referendum of October 1945, Fundamental Laws of the Kingdom, of which the principles were defined as permanent and immutable. The legal texts in E. Tierno Galván (ed.), *Leyes políticas españolas fundamentales (1808–1978)* (Madrid, 1968).
3. HSTL, NAF, Berlin Conference File, box 4: 'Spain. Soviet Proposal Presented to Foreign Ministers', 19 July 1945.
4. Unless otherwise stated, all international declarations can be found in Department of State, *A Decade of American Foreign Policy. Basic Documents 1941–1949* (Washington DC, 1985).
5. See documents reproduced in L. López Rodó, *La larga marcha hacia la Monarquía* (Barcelona, 1977) 58 and 60.
6. For a complete list of Spain's bilateral treaties, Ministerio de Asuntos Exteriores, Secretaría General Técnica, *Censo de Tratados Internacionales suscritos por España desde 16 de Septiembre de 1125 a 21 de Octubre de 1975, Vol. I Bilaterales* (Madrid, 1976).
7. Paragraph based on AD, Z/E vol. 65, Telegram from Jacques Truelle, Delegate of the French Provisional Government, Madrid, 24 February 1945; and HSTL, NAF, box 20: State Department brief, 11 May. Navicert derives from a code word: navis + cert(ificate). It was originally a consular certificate granted to a neutral ship testifying that its cargo was correctly described in the manifest and not contraband destined for the enemy. It became one of the chief instruments in the prevention of enemy trade during World War II.
8. MAE, Leg. 1374, exp. 10: Artajo to Spanish Ambassador in London, 30 July 1945.
9. J.-P. Rioux, *The Fourth Republic, 1944–1958* (Cambridge, 1987) 23 ff.
10. AD, Z/E vol. 92: 'Note pour le Ministre' by the Director General of Economic Affairs at the Quai d'Orsay, 23 November 1945.
11. Paragraph based on PRO, BOT 11/3067: Minute of a meeting held at the FO on 28 February 1946 to consider the possible consequences of a rupture of relations with Spain; ibid. 11/3068: Minute of the same meeting; BOT to Overseas General Division, Ministry of Information, 7 March; 'British Imports from Spain', which relates to the year ending 31 March 1947, annex to Intel 27, Bevin to Douglas F. Howard, Chargé d'Affaires in Madrid, 21 January.
12. A.E. Eckes, Jr., *The United States and the Global Struggle for Minerals* (Austin, 1979).

13. Economic Commission for Europe of the United Nations (ECE), *Economic Survey of Europe in 1950* (Geneva, 1951) 5.
14. ECE, *A Survey of the Economic Situation and Prospects of Europe* (Geneva, 1948) 11; henceforth referred to as *A Survey*.
15. UN, *Statistical Yearbook 1948* (New York, 1949) 216; henceforth, *SY 1948*.
16. PRO, BOT 11/3068: 'Raw Materials Suplies from Spain', 2 March 1946.
17. *SY 1948*, p. 167.
18. PRO, BOT 11/3068: BOT to FO, 'Estimate of Alternative Sources of Supply for UK Raw Materials Needs from Spain', 19 November 1946. It considers the year ending 30 June 1946, and the following fertilizer season for the 1946/47 harvest.
19. The percentage refers only to iron pyrites, while for Europe it refers to output of iron and cupreous pyrites plus pyrite concentrates obtained as a by-product from copper, lead and zinc ore operations. Own elaboration from *SY 1948*, pp. 164–5.
20. AD, Z/E vol. 92: Head of the Economic Affairs Division at the Quai d'Orsay, 'Note pour le Ministre. Négociations commerciales avec l'Espagne', 8 February 1945.
21. AN, 80AJ/15: 'Résumé du Plan de Modernisation de la Production Végétale', June 1946.
22. *A Survey*, p. 47.
23. *SY 1948*, p. 139. Data referring to iron content of ores mines, excluding pyrites.
24. *Ibid.*, pp. 136–46 and 153.
25. ECE, *Economic Survey of Europe in 1953. Study of Economic Development in Southern Europe* (Geneva, 1954).

NOTES TO CHAPTER 2

1. A. Cowan, 'The Guerrilla War Against Franco', *European History Quarterly*, vol. 20 (1990) 227–53.
2. AD, Z/E vol. 3: Truelle to Bidault, Madrid, 22 September 1944.
3. Ibid., vol. 92: 'Note du Conseiller Commercial résumant la situation économique de l'Espagne', Truelle to Bidault, 3 November 1944, annex; and, 'Note pour le Ministre. Negociations commerciales avec l'Espagne', 8 February 1945.
4. Ibid., vol. 3: 'Sécurité des Consulats d'Espagne en France', Bidault to his colleague of Interior, 9 March 1945.
5. Press Conference of 12 October 1945; Gaulle, *Discours et Messages vol. I Pendant la guerre Juin 1940–Janvier 1946* (Paris, 1946) 640–1.
6. AD, Z/E vol. 92: Truelle to Bidault, Madrid, 7 April 1945.
7. R. Frank, 'France – Grande-Bretagne: la mésentente commerciale (1945–1958)', *Relations internationales*, 55 (1988) 333.
8. AD, Z/E vol. 66: Direction d'Europe, Sous-Direction de l'Europe Méridionale, 'Note Relations franco-espagnoles', 28 January 1946.
9. Blum, *L'oeuvre de Léon Blum, 1945–1947* (Paris, 1958) 184.
10. F. Portero, *Franco aislado. La cuestión española (1945–1950)* (Madrid, 1989) 133–4.

11.   Note to London and Washington; AD, Z/E vol. 67; PRO, FO 371/49614; and
       FRUS 1945 V, US Ambassador in France to Secretary of State, pp. 698–9.

12.   Paragraph based on PRO, FO 371/49614: Under-Secretary of Foreign Af-
       fairs, Orme Sargent, to Prime Minister, 17 December 1945; Ambassador
       Victor Mallet to Bevin, Madrid, 24 December; ibid. 371/60349: British Em-
       bassy to Quai d'Orsay, 24 December; *FRUS* 1945 V, Acting Secretary of
       State to US Ambassador in France, 22 December; PRO, BOT 11/3068: Tele-
       gram 8547, Washington to FO, 23 December; and AD, Z/E vol. 66: 'Note
       pour le Général de Gaulle sur le problème espagnol', 20 December; dis-
       patches in December 1945 and January 1946 by the French Chargé d'Af-
       faires Bernard Hardion.

13.   AD, Z/E vol. 67: 'Espagne', record of a conversation at the FO, 1 February
       1946; and PRO, FO 371/60350: 'Extract from the Secretary of State's
       Record of Conversation with Monsieur Bidault on 1st February'.

14.   PRO, FO 371/60350: Record of the Bevin-Bidault meeting of 18 February
       1946.

15.   AD, Z/E vol. 66: Direction d'Europe, Sous-Direction de l'Europe Méridion-
       ale, 'Note France–Espagne', 2 January 1946.

16.   Ibid. vol. 84: 'Réunion interministérielle du 26 Février 1946'. In his auto-
       biography Bidault recalls the Spanish problem as 'a train of unpleasant and
       rather absurd developments', *D'une Résistance à l'autre* (Paris, 1965) 132.

17.   PRO, FO 371/49612: 'Extract of minutes of the Third Plenary Meeting, Pots-
       dam Conference', 19 July 1945.

18.   A. Bullock, *Ernest Bevin: Foreign Secretary (1945–1951)* (London, 1983)
       163.

19.   M.R. Gordon, *Conflict and Consensus in Labor's Foreign Policy 1914–1965*
       (Stanford, 1969) 131.

20.   W.N. Medlicott, *The Economic Blockade* vol. 2 (London, 1978) 627–9.

21.   Paragraph based on NARA, RG 59, 852.50/3–2946, State Department Mem-
       orandum, 'Views on the Imposition of Economic Sanctions Against Spain',
       29 March 1946; and PRO, BOT 11/3067 and 3068: Minutes of an interde-
       partmental meeting, 28 February 1946.

22.   *FRUS* 1947 III, US Ambassador in London to Marshall, 10 May, pp. 1077–
       8.

23.   By 31 October 1945 British net gold and dollar reserves were about £450
       million and the United Kingdom's external debts £3500 million; the Chan-
       cellor of the Exchequer to the House of Commons, 12 December 1945, 417
       HC DEB, 226.

24.   M. Liniger, *L'orange d'Espagne sur les marchés européens* (Geneva, 1962) 165.

25.   HSTL, NAF, Alphabetical File, box 16: Intelligence Review, 10, 18 April
       1946, p. 16.

26.   Minutes of the interdepartmental meeting of 28 February 1946 cit.

27.   For details on *Safehaven* negotiations from the French viewpoint see J.-M.
       Delaunay, 'La liquidation des avoirs allemands en Espagne (1945–1961)', in
       J.-P. Etienvre and J.R. Urquijo, *España, Francia y la Comunidad Europea*
       (Madrid, 1989) 219–45.

28.   PRO, BOT 11/3067: CM(47) 2nd, Conclusions, Minute 4, 3 January 1947.

29.   Ibid. 11/3068: Minutes of a meeting of Board of Trade, Treasury and Foreign
       Office officials, 4 January 1946.

30. The credit margin – established on the basis of the volume and timing of reciprocal trade expected – was the limit to which each partner was prepared to sell its currency for the other's currency without demanding cover in convertible currencies or gold. For more details on this essential feature of postwar payments agreements, J.H.C. de Looper, 'Current Usage of Payments Agreements and Trade Agreements', *International Monetary Fund Staff Papers*, 4 (1955) 345.
31. PRO, FO 371/67895: Notes for a parliamentary question, 3 April 1947.
32. Gordon, *Conflict and Consensus*, p. 105.
*Safehaven corresponds to an operational code to block German assets in either occupied or neutral countries which could be used by pre-eminent Nazis to escape judgement at the end of the war.

NOTES TO CHAPTER 3

1. R. Rubottom and J.C. Murphy, *Spain and the United States Since World War II* (New York, 1984) and P. Brundu Olla, *L'anello mancante. Il problema della Spagna franchista e l'organizzazione della difesa occidentale (1947–1950)* (Sassari, 1990).
2. *FRUS* 1946 V, US Ambassador in France to the Secretary of State, 27 February, pp. 1043–4.
3. Brundu Olla, 'L'Espagne franquiste et la politique étrangère de la France au landemain de la Deuxième Guerre Mondiale', *Relations Internationales*, 50 (1987) 165–81.
4. Paragraph based on HSTL, NAF, Alphabetical File, boxes 15–16: Military Intelligence Division, War Department, Intelligence Reviews from March to June 1946; PRO, FO 371/60355: FO to British Delegation at the UN, 13 April; *FRUS* 1946 V, Secretary of State to the US Delegation at the UN, 12 April, p. 1067; and HSTL, NAF, box 20: State Department brief, 15 April. For a full story of Spain's early postwar relations with the UN, R.E. Sanders, *Spain and the United Nations 1945–1950* (New York, 1966).
5. E. Luard, *A History of the United Nations. Vol. 1 The Years of Western Domination, 1945–1955* (London, 1982) 363.
6. P.H. De Garmo, 'Beyond the Pyrenees; Spain and Europe Since World War II', PhD thesis, University of California, 1971, p. 67.
7. Harrison, *The Spanish Economy in the Twentieth Century* (London, 1985) 125 and 131. The idea that Spain suffered from economic boycott or embargo in the 1940s is common place in the literature; Sima Lieberman, *Growth and Crisis in the Spanish Economy 1940–93* (London, 1995) 2; and K.G. Salmon, *The Modern Spanish Economy. Transformation and Integration into Europe* (London, 1991) 2.
8. AHBE, IEME, box 3: C/P, 19 May 1947.
9. AD, Z/E vol. 92: 'Note du Conseiller Commercial résumant la situation économique de l'Espagne', Truelle to Bidault, annex, 3 November 1944.
10. BOT, Department of Overseas Trade, *Spain. Review of Commercial Conditions* (London, 1945), and PRO, BOT 11/3067: CM(47) 2nd, Conclusions, Minute 4, 3 January 1947.

11. Respectively: AD, Z/E vol. 3: European Division, 'Note pour le Cabinet du Ministre', 17 March 1945; vol. 92: Director General of Economic Affairs, 'Note pour le Ministre', 23 November; and vol. 86: 'La fermeture de la frontière Franco-Espagnole. Ses conséquences économiques. La reprise des relations commerciales entre la France et l'Espagne. Perspectives actuelles' by the Commercial Counselor at the Embassy, Madrid, 15 June.
12. Figures in ibid. vol. 66: Direction des Affaires Économiques, 'Note pour le Ministre a.s. des intérêts économiques français en Espagne', 10 January 1946; and vol. 48: Direction Politique, 'Note', 1 June 1945.
13. Respectively: ibid. vol. 66: French Chamber of Commerce and Industry to the President of the Government, Madrid, 28 January 1946; and vol. 84: The Director of the Chamber to the Quai d'Orsay, 18 February.
14. Ibid. vol. 84: Embassy to Quai d'Orsay, 15 February 1946.
15. Ibid. vol. 84: 'Réunion interministerielle du 26 Février 1946', and Hardion to Quai d'Orsay, 8 March; and vol. 86: 'La fermeture de la frontière Franco-Espagnole. Ses conséquences économiques', 15 June, and 'Etude en vue d'une réouverture éventuelle de la frontière franco-espagnole', 27 August 1947.
16. PRO, BOT 11/3068.
17. For the ideological reasons of this attitude see Suanzes, *Instituto Nacional de Industria: notas en relación con la creación y desenvolvimiento de este Instituto* (Madrid, 1941).
18. NARA, RG 59, 852.51/9–1446, Acting Secretary of State to US Embassy in Madrid, 23 September 1946.
19. *FRUS* 1945 V, Roosevelt to the Ambassador in Madrid, 10 March, pp. 667–8; and ibid. 1947 III, Acheson to the Ambassador in London, 7 April, p. 1066.
20. 'Participation in UNRRA, March 28, 1944. Joint Resolution to Enable the United States To Participate in the Work of the United Nations Relief and Rehabilitation Organization', *American Foreign Policy. Basic Documents, 1941–1949* (New York, 1971) 21–2.
21. 'Agreement for United Nations Relief and Rehabilitation Administration, November 9, 1943', ibid., pp. 14–21.
22. W.A. Brown and R. Opie, *American Foreign Assistance* (Washington, 1953) 110.
23. For Spain's economic performance during World War II, J. Catalán, *La economía española y la segunda guerra mundial* (Barcelona, 1995). Catalán's research is complementary to my own research for the post-1945 period – with inevitable occasional disagreement; for a full list of his research output, 'Sector exterior y crecimiento industrial. España y Europa, 1939–59', *Revista de Historia Industrial*, 8 (1995) 99–145.
24. Paragraph based on AHBE, IEME, box. 7: IEME *Memoria de 1945*; box 2: C/A, 21 November 1945 (quotation), 28 May 1946, and 24 July.
25. The purchase of State bonds in foreign hands and the nationalization of the National Telephone Company from the American ITT involved £11 millions out of a total exchange expenditure of £68.6 million in 1945.
26. Negotiation of trade agreements in the second half of 1945 took place with Switzerland, France, Italy, Portugal, Denmark, Sweden, Belgium, the Netherlands, and Argentina. This prosperous vision was reflected in the IEME annual report for 1945.

27. Bank of Spain, 'Informe sobre el Fondo Monetario Anglo-Norteamericano', n/d, probably June 1944, cit. in J. Muns, *Historia de las relaciones entre España y el Fondo Monetario Internacional, 1958–1982. Veinticinco años de economía española* (Madrid, 1986) 20.
28. Paragraphs based on AHBE, IEME, box 2: C/A, 11 December 1945, 15 January and 28 March 1946.
29. Franco's public address in Segovia, 9 February 1946, quoted from AD, Z/E vol. 68: French Ambassador to Bidault, London, 15 April.

*This refers exclusively to commodities paid off in foreign currency. Import of wheat from Argentina, for instance, took place on credit basis involving no foreign currency expenditure.

NOTES TO CHAPTER 4

1. Viñas, 'El Plan Marshall y Franco', in Viñas, *Guerra, dinero, dictadura*, pp. 265–87.
2. Finland was the other West European country that, although invited, did not participate in the Marshall Plan; M. Majander explains the reasons in 'The Limits of Sovereignty. Finland and the Question of the Marshall Plan in 1947', *Scandinavian Journal of History*, vol. 19/4 (1994) 309–26.
3. Ch.P. Kindleberger makes the strongest pledge for the sincerity of the offer, *Marshall Plan Days* (London, 1987) 92.
4. MAE, Leg. 2309, exp. 2: 'Discurso General Marshall sobre política exterior norteamericana', 10 June 1947.
5. HSTL, Papers of Joseph M. Jones, Special Assistant to the Secretary of State: Jones to Walter Lippmann, 7 May 1947. See also the reactions of Marshall, and former Secretary of State James F. Byrnes in R.M. Freeland, *The Truman Doctrine and the Origins of McCarthyism* (New York, 1985) 100.
6. *FRUS* 1947 III, Acheson to the US Embassy in London, 7 and 25 April, pp. 1066 and 1074.
7. PRO, FO 371/67868: Bevin to Sargent, 25 April 1947.
8. Account based on documentation in *FRUS* 1947 III, pp. 1066–85, and PRO, FO 371/67897: Report by the Economic Intelligence Department at the Foreign Office, 'Vulnerability to Import Embargo', 23 April.
9. MAE, Leg. 2309, exp. 2: Commercial Counsellor to Under-Secretary for Foreign Economy and Commerce, 'Sobre la propuesta norteamericana de auxilio financiero para la reconstrucción europea', Paris, 18 June 1947.
10. For Salazar's position on cooperation with Western Europe, J.C. Magalhães, *Portugal na Europa: o caminho certo* (Lisbon, 1997).
11. ASMAE, Amb. Parigi, b. 413: 'Spagna e Conferenza di Parigi', Italian Embassy in London to Rome, 30 July 1947. There is also reference to an Anglo-Saxon *entente* on the question of excluding Spain in *FRUS* 1948 III, Memorandum by the Assistant Chief of the Division of Western European Affairs at the Department of State, Outerbridge Horsey, of conversation with the Second Secretary of the British Embassy in Washington, 16 February, p. 1026.
12. Documentation in Ministère des Affaires Etrangères, *Documents de la Conférence des Ministres des Affaires Etrangères de la France, du Royaume-Uni,*

de l'U.R.S.S. tenue à Paris du 27 Juin au 3 Juillet 1947 et pièces relatives aux négociations diplomatiques engagées à la suite du discours prononcé par le Général Marshall Secrétaire d'Etat des Etats-Unis, le 5 Juin 1947 (Paris, 1947). The most up-to-date guide to the Marshall Plan is Ch.S. Maier and G. Bischof (eds), *The Marshall Plan and Germany: West German Development within the Framework of the European Recovery Plan* (New York, 1991).

13.   MAE, Leg. 2309, exp. 2: Memorandum No. 422 by the Ministry of Foreign Affairs, 15 November 1947, and the propaganda leaflet distributed by the Spanish Embassy in Washington entitled 'Spain Must Cooperate. How Spain can help the American tax-payer', attached to the Director General of Economic Policy to the Director General of Foreign Policy, 2 December.

14.   S. Chamorro *et al.*, *Las balanzas de pagos de España del período de autarquía* (Madrid, 1976).

15.   In very ambiguous terms, A. Whitaker refered to the amounts of $451 and $676 million for a Spanish ERP request; *Spain and the Defence of the West: Ally and Liability* (New York, 1962) 34. Only the largest amount was retained by J.B. Donges, *La industrialización en España. Políticas, logros y perspectivas* (Barcelona, 1976) 39, from which it was taken into L. Prados de la Escosura and J.C. Sanz, 'Growth and macroeconomic performance in Spain, 1939–93', in N.F.R. Crafts and G. Toniolo, *Economic Growth in Europe since 1945* (Cambridge, 1996) 363. Viñas *et al.*, *Política comercial*, p. 479, made a quick reference to this document's second draft to show the existence of a request to implement an 'ambitious import-substitution plan'. None of these authors went beyond stating the amounts; all assumed a request for a one-year aid package. A leading Spanish industrial bank estimated special imports required up to 1952 to place the Spanish economy on a sound footing at over $1475 million, $777 million of which corresponded to capital goods and raw materials for basic industries and $438 million for foodstuffs and feeding stuffs; *Informe presentado a la Junta general del Banco Urquijo celebrada el 16 de marzo de 1948, por el Presidente del Consejo, Excmo. Sr. Marqués de Urquijo, sobre el ejercicio del año 1947* (Madrid, 1948) 72. H. Paris Eguilaz, *Diez años de política económica en España 1939–1949* (Madrid, 1949) 235–40, put the annual amount of minimal aid required for urgent reconstruction investment at $200 million.

16.   For a history of INI, P. Martín Aceña and F. Comín, *INI 50 años de industrialización en España* (Madrid, 1991).

17.   The best study of the energy sector is C. Sudrià, 'Un factor determinante: la energía', in J. Nadal *et al.* (eds), *La economía española en el siglo XX. Una perspectiva histórica* (Barcelona, 1987) 313–63.

18.   J. Walker, *Economic and Commercial Conditions in Spain* (London, 1949) 45.

19.   AD, Z/E vol. 95: French Delegation to Quai d'Orsay, 'Eléctrification des chemins de fer espagnols', Madrid, 11 March 1947.

20.   'Plan para la fabricación nacional de combustibles líquidos, lubricantes e industrias conexas', Law of 26 May 1944, BOE of 27.

21.   S. Coll and Sudrià, *El carbón en España, 1770–1961. Una historia económica* (Madrid, 1987) 577.

22.   ECE, *Economic Survey of Europe in 1953*, p. 143.

23. Information about the different railways plans in RENFE, *Los ferrocarriles en España 1848–1958* (Madrid, 1958) and C. de Inza y Tudela, 'Transportes' in *Estudios sobre la unidad económica de Europa* vol. 7 (Madrid, 1957) 799–812.
24. MAE, Leg. 2185, exp. 9: 'Nota sobre las necesidades de importación de la RENFE', 11 April 1947.
25. Figure for passengers, A. Gómez Mendoza, 'Transporte y comunicaciones', in A. Carreras (ed.), *Estadísticas Históricas de España. Siglos XIX y XX* (Madrid, 1989) 289; for passenger cars, Table 4.2.
26. 'Post-war Import Licensing Policy in Spain', *The Board of Trade Journal* (28 August 1948) 412.
27. With only a local firm, EUCORT, producing some prototypes based on the German D.K.W. at no significant scale, this output target makes evident the desire of the Ministry of Industry and Commerce to conclude previous negotiations with FIAT; E. San Román, 'El nacimiento de la SEAT: autarquía e intervención del INI', *Revista de Historia Industrial*, 7 (1995) 141–65.
28. HSTL, NAF, box 17: War Department, Intelligence Review 26, 8 August 1946, p. 43.
29. E. Fuentes Quintana and J. Plaza, 'Perspectivas de la economía española (1940–1953)', *Revista de Economía Política*, vol. 4/1–2 (1952) 72.
30. Prados de la Escosura, 'Spain's Gross Domestic Product'.
31. Data concerning 1934 from Grupo de Estudios de Historia Rural, 'El sector agrario hasta 1935'; post-1936 data from C. Barciela, 'El sector agrario desde 1936', both in *Estadísticas históricas*, pp. 108 and 145, respectively.
32. Figures from M.J. González, *La economía política del franquismo (1940–1970). Dirigismo, mercado y planificación* (Madrid, 1979) 374–7.
33. Barciela, 'El mercado negro de productos agrarios en la posguerra', in J. Fontana (ed.), *España bajo el franquismo* (Barcelona, 1986) 195.
34. NARA, RG 59, 852.5018, telegrams from the US Chargé d'Affaires in Madrid to the Secretary of State, 4 June and 23 September 1947.
35. C. Velasco, 'El pensamiento agrario y la apuesta industrializadora en la España de los cuarenta', *Agricultura y Sociedad*, 23 (1982) 223–72.
36. M. Buesa, 'Industrialización y agricultura: una nota sobre la construcción de maquinaria agrícola y la producción de fertilizantes en la política industrial española (1939–1963)', *Agricultura y Sociedad*, 28 (1983) 223–48.
37. F. Bustelo, 'La industria del nitrógeno en España', in *Problemas técnicos de importancia económica en la nueva organización de España* (Barcelona, 1940) 247–52.
38. AHBE, IEME, box 2: C/A, 8 July 1947.
39. Carreras, 'La producció industrial espanyola i italiana des de mitjans del secle XIX fins a l'actualitat', Ph.D. thesis, Universitat Autònoma, Barcelona, 1983, p. 345.
40. AHBE, IEME, box 2: The Director General of Agriculture at C/A, 13 September 1949.
41. Ibid. box 117 bis: Note on Argentine Supply, 31 January 1948. The different credit facilities granted by Argentina at the end of 1947 amounted to 33 per cent of the foreign currency earned in 1946 (as registered by the IEME), to 23 per cent in 1947, and to 75 per cent of the increase between 1946 and 1947.
42. For information on prices, MAE, Leg. 1453, exp. 1.
43. ECE, *Economic Survey of Europe in 1948* (Geneva, 1949) 95.
44. AHBE, IEME, box 7: IEME's annual reports for 1946 and 1947.

45. Fontana and Nadal, 'Spain, 1914–1970', in C.M. Cipolla (ed.), *The Fontana Economic History of Europe. Contemporary Economies. Part Two* vol. 6/2 (London, 1975) 506–7.
* One of the aims of the IEFC was to match supply and demand of nitrogen fertilizers; it was transferred to the UN Food and Agricultural Organization in January 1948

NOTES TO CHAPTER 5

1. AHBE, IEME, box 2: C/A, 8 July 1947.
2. Ibid. box 7, IEME's annual report for 1947, and Table 3.7.
3. Paragraph based on ibid. box 3: C/P, 14 July and 16 October 1947.
4. Explicitly recognized by Antonio de Miguel, Councillor of National Economy and former Director General of Commerce and Tariff Policy; ibid. box 66: 'Nota sobre la balanza de pagos en relación con la situación económica en general', n/d, probably May 1946.
5. Ibid. box 3: C/P, 30 October 1947. Rest of the paragraph based on box 2: C/A, 7 September and 17 October 1945; and box 3: C/P, 6 October 1947.
6. G. Fodor, 'Perché nel 1947 l'Europa ebbe bisogno del Piano Marshall?', *Rivista di Storia Economica*, n.s., vol. 2/1 (1985) 89–123.
7. ECE, *Economic Survey of Europe in 1948*, p. 95.
8. Paragraph based on AHBE, IEME, box 2: C/A, 17 October 1945; and box 117 bis: 'Informe relativo a las cuentas combinadas de importación y exportación' by the National Import-Export Federation, Barcelona, 31 October 1947.
9. PRO, FO 371/67895: Treasury to Foreign Office, 18 June 1947.
10. Paragraph based upon AHBE, IEME, box 3: C/P, 3 and 16 October 1947.
11. Ibid. box 2: C/A, 21 November and 11 December 1945.
12. Data mentioned in the previous two paragraphs based on ibid. box 7: IEME's annual reports for the corresponding years; box 3: C/P, 29 May and 16 October 1947.
13. E.K. Keefe *et al.*, *Area Handbook for Spain* (Washington DC, 1976) 275; and AHBE, box 3: C/P, 1 June 1948.
14. MAE, Leg. 4618, exp. 2: 'Nota relativa a los problemas que se plantean en la Subsecretaría llamada de Comercio, Política Arancelaria y Moneda', Saint Sebastian, 29 July 1946.
15. AHBE, IEME, box 3: C/P, 16 October 1947.
16. NARA, RG 59, 852.51/7–546, 'Reported Negotiations in Lisbon looking toward a Portuguese Loan to Spain' by the First Secretary of the US Embassy in Lisbon, 5 July 1946.
17. AHBE, IEME, box 2: C/A, 8 July 1947, and box 3: C/P, 16 October.
18. Note dated Saint Sebastian, 29 July 1946, cit.
19. AHBE, IEME, box 2: C/A, 8 July 1947. See also box 3: C/P, 16 October. Currency earnings data from box 7, IEME's annual reports for 1945 and 1946.
20. Paragraph based on ibid. box 2: C/A, 28 March and 24 July 1946; box 7: IEME's annual report for 1946; box 66: de Miguel's 'Nota sobre la balanza de pagos' cit.; and box 117 bis: 'Disminución de exportaciones' by the Chief

of the Export Service at the Ministry of Industry and Commerce to the General Director of Trade, 10 May.

21. Previous two paragraphs based on ibid. box 7: IEME's annual report for 1947 (quotation); box 2: C/A, 8 July; and box 3: C/P, 19 May and 16 October.
22. Based on ibid. box 117 bis: 'Informe relativo a las cuentas combinadas de importación y exportación' by the National Import-Export Federation, Barcelona, 31 October 1947; and box 3: C/P, 11 November.
23. MAE, Leg. 2309, exp. 2: 'Memorandum' cit., 15 November 1947.
24. Paragraphs based on the source of Table 5.5.
25. MAE, Leg. 2185, exp. 9: 'Su nota 22.5.47. Importaciones de carbón y chatarra', Under-Secretary of Foreign Economy and Commerce to the Under-Secretary of Industry, 26 May 1947.
26. AHBE, IEME, box 117 bis: Consejo Regulador del Comercio Exterior, 25th and 26th sessions, 'Anejo al memorandum confidencial relativo al plan de distribución del contingente de divisas. Primer semestre de 1948', 30 January 1948.

*It is important to bear in mind that not all exports earned foriegn exchange. Part of Spain's export trade took place on the basis of a barter system of exchange or diverted exchange earnings to the black market. This percentage of trade is unimportant here because it could not be channelled to finance the Import Program. The IEME recorded only trade involving foreign exchange operations. Those commodities imported on the basis of credits (the total imports of cereals from Argentina in 1946) or through a barter system of exchange (Chilean nitrate) were, therefore, excluded.

NOTES TO CHAPTER 6

1. MAE, Leg. 3159, exp. 26: Artajo's cifra 836, 18 July 1947. Protests went first to Paris and London; ibid., Artajo's cifra 340, 8 July; and PRO 371/ 67869: 'Memorandum' by the Spanish Embassy in London to FO, 4 July.
2. MAE, Leg. 2418, exp. 33: Note resumé (uncompleted) of an interview between the US Chargé d'Affaires in Madrid and Artajo, 23 February 1948.
3. Franco to United Press, 27 June 1947; ASMAE, Amb. Paris, b. 413: 'Dichiarazioni ufficiali'.
4. Paragraph based on MAE, Leg. 2309, exp. 2: Artajo to Logos News Agency, 4 January 1948, cit. in 'A.r. Despacho 178 y remite recortes de prensa s/ Plan Marshall', 16 January; and exp. 4: 'Condiciones generales del Plan Marshall y del Plan Bevin', n/s, n/d, which was presented to the Council of Ministers on 12 March.
5. Since the CEEC's first meeting Spain had concluded commercial agreements with Sweden (July 1947, prolonging the 1946 trade and payments agreement), Ireland (September), Turkey (September, comercial operations through compensation), the Netherlands (December), and Switzerland (December, an additional protocol to the 1935 agreement, preceded by an exchange of notes in March). The trade agreement signed with Belgium in February 1946 still remained operative; Denmark did not extend that year its 1941 bilateral agreement, but it was under negotiation; the United Kingdom

signed a trade agreement in March 1947, obtaining £10 million as credit from Spain; Italy renewed the January 1946 agreement in June 1947; Norway never suspended its commercial operations through compensation; and Portugal continued to maintain its agreement revised half-yearly.

6. MAE, Leg. 2309, exp. 3: Artajo to the Chargé d'Affaires in Washington, 21 January 1948.
7. HSTL, PSF, IF, ORE 52 'The Current Situation in the Mediterranean and the Near East', 17 October 1947; ORE 53 'The Current Situation in Spain', 5 November; and ORE 56 'The Political Future of Spain', 5 December.
8. Franco to International News Service, 18 August 1947; ASMAE, Amb. Parigi, b. 413: 'Dichiarazioni ufficiali'.
9. *FRUS* 1947 I, 'US Assistance to Other Countries from the Standpoint of National Security. Report by the Joint Strategic Survey Committee', 29 April, pp. 734–50. There has been too much eagerness to grasp any reference to strategic values in the attempt to create a comfortable continuum from 1947 to the US–Spanish agreement for military bases in 1953; Viñas, *Los pactos secretos de Franco con Estados Unidos. Bases, ayuda económica, recortes de soberanía* (Barcelona, 1981); and Brundu Olla, *Ostracismo e Realpolitik. Gli Alleati e la Spagna franchista negli anni del dopoguerra* (Cagliari, 1984).
10. *FRUS* 1947 III, Culbertson to Marshall, Madrid, 23 October, p. 1089.
11. Congressional Record, Proceedings and Debates of the 80th Congress, 2nd Series, Washington, vol. 94/56, 24 March 1948, p. 3522.
12. MAE, Leg. 2309, exp. 2: Artajo's cifra 1335, 24 December 1947.
13. Declarations to be found, respectively, in ibid. exp. 3: 'Extract from Testimony of Secretary Marshall before House Foreign Affairs Committee', 12 January 1948; and *FRUS* 1948 III, Memorandum of Conversation by Horsey, 16 February, p. 1026.
14. 447 HC DEB 5 s., Oral Answers, 9 February 1948, p. 25.
15. MAE, Leg. 2309, exp. 4: Dispatch 278, Spanish Embassy, London, 28 February 1948.
16. *FRUS* 1948 III, Bevin to the Ambassador to Washington, 1 April, p. 411.
17. A most unrealistic view of the different national positions was presented to Cabinet on 12 March; MAE, Leg. 2309, exp. 4: 'Actitud de los países participantes en el Plan Marshall ante la posible inclusión de España en dicho plan', n/d.
18. MNE-SE, RNP 2° P, A 60, M 381(B): Telegram 119, Caeiro de Matta to Salazar, Paris, 16 March 1948.
19. Ibid., telegrams 1040 and 1068 from Portugal's legations in London and Paris, 13 and 14 March 1948, respectively.
20. MAE, Leg. 2309, exp. 4: Artajo to the Ambassador in Lisbon, 19 March 1948, and MNE-SE, RNP 2° P, A 60, M 381(B): 'Resumo de conversa com Ambaixador de Espanha' by the Secretary General of the Portuguese Ministry of Foreign Affairs, 23 March. For a general view on Portugal and the Marshall Plan see F. Rollo, *Portugal e o Plano Marshall. Da rejeição à solicitação da ajuda financeira norte-americana (1947–1952)* (Lisbon, 1994).
21. *Present at the Creation: My Years in the State Department* (New York, 1969) 169.

22. Marshall's reply to Bevin's aide-memoire of 1 April, in *FRUS* 1948 III, the Acting Secretary of State to the Embassy in Spain, 6 April, p. 412.
23. This time records and memoirs coincide: MAE, Leg. 2309, exp. 8: Artajo to Areilza, 2 April 1948, and Areilza, *Memorias Exteriores, 1947–1964* (Barcelona, 1984) 52. For the most complete study on Argentina–Spain relations, Raanan Rein, *Franco-Peron Alliance: Relations Between Spain and Argentina, 1946–1955* (Pittsburgh, 1993).
24. A. Ballestero, *Juan Antonio Suanzes, 1891–1977. 'La política industrial de la posguerra'* (Leon, 1993) 214.
25. MAE, Leg. 2418, exp. 1: Areilza to Artajo, 'Conversaciones con el General Perón en esta Embajada', Buenos Aires, 30 September 1947.
26. R. Carr, *Spain 1808–1975* 2nd ed. (Oxford, 1982) 715 and 740.
27. *FRUS* 1947 III, 'US Policy Towards Spain', 24 October, pp. 1092–5. The PPS was established in May 1947 in the office of the Under-Secretary of State to assure the development of long-range policy and to draw together the views of the geographical and functional offices of the Department of State and other non-departmental sources.
28. See documentation in HSTL, PSF, NSC Meetings, box 203, and ibid., NSC, Chronological File 1947–8, box 9.
29. All quotations from NARA, RG 59, 840.50 Recovery/11–2547, Culbertson to the Secretary of State, 'Comments on Memorandum Received from the Director General of Economic Policy in the Spanish Ministry of Foreign Affairs [Mariano de Yturralde y Orbegoso] Regarding Spain's Relation to the Marshall Plan', Madrid, 25 November 1947.
30. *FRUS* 1947 III, Under-Secretary in the State Department Robert A. Lovett to the US Embassy in Spain, 18 December, p. 1096.
31. Ibid. 1948 III, Memorandum of Conversation with Artajo and attached 'Notes' by Culbertson, Madrid, 2 February, pp. 1020–4; and, MAE, Leg. 2418, exp. 33: Note resumé (uncompleted) of an interview between Culbertson and Artajo, n/s, n/d.
32. Paragraph based on Table 7.1; APG, JE, records from the Ministry of Foreign Affairs, Leg. 13, 1.5: 'Acuerdo entre un grupo de bancos españoles y otro de bancos americanos que facilite a los primeros un crédito de 300 a 500 millones de dólares a un plazo de cinco años', attached to Memorandum of conversation with the US commercial counsellor Mr Randall, 29 January 1948; MAE, Leg. 10077, exp. 26: The Under-Secretary of Foreign Economy and Commerce to Ministers of Foreign Affairs and of Industry and Commerce, 12 February; and ibid. 2418, exp. 33: 'Informe reservado a petición del señor Martín Artajo. Impresiones de un viaje a Norteamérica, 9 de Marzo-1 de Abril', n/s, n/d.
33. *FRUS* 1948 III, Chief of the Division of Western European Affairs at the Department of State to Culbertson, 5 January, p. 1018.
34. APG, JE, records from the Ministry of Foreign Affairs, Leg. 13, 1.5: Memorandum of conversation with Randall, 29 January 1948.
35. MAE, Leg. 10077, exp. 26: 'Short reference of the interview [Culbertson/Artajo] of Monday March the 8th'.
36. As the Italian Embassy in Madrid reported to Rome on 3 April 1948, AS-MAE, Amb. Parigi, b. 413: 'Spagna: Piano Marshall', 4 May. In the memorandum of his conversation with Franco that Taylor sent to Truman on

220   *Notes*

1 April, this aspect was not mentioned; E. Di Nolfo, *Vaticano e Stati Uniti 1939–1952. Dalle carte di Myron C. Taylor* (Milan, 1978) 557–8.

37. MAE, Leg. 2309, exp. 4: 'Condiciones generales del Plan Marshall y del Plan Bevin', 12 March 1948.
38. *FRUS* 1948 III, Memorandum by Culbertson of conversation with Artajo, 2 February, pp. 1021–2.
39. MAE, Leg. 10077, exp. 26: 'Short reference of the interview of Monday March the 8th', and, *FRUS* 1948 III, Culbertson to Marshall, Madrid, 24 March, p. 1029.
40. *FRUS* 1948 III, Memorandum by Horsey, 16 February, p. 1026.
41. Ibid., 'Policy Statement by the Department of State on Spain', 26 July, p. 1043.
42. Paragraph based on *FRUS* 1947 III, Culbertson to Marshall, Madrid, 30 December, p. 1101; ibid. 1948 III, Culbertson to Marshall, 29 March, p. 1032; APG, JE, Records from the Ministry of Foreign Affairs, Leg. 13, 9.4: The President of Westinghouse to Franco, 5 November; ASMAE, Amb. Parigi, b. 413: Piero Quaroni, Italian Ambassador in Paris, 19 February; and PRO, FO 371/73338: Confidential dispatch, Roy Makins, British Under-Secretary of State for Foreign Affairs, to Edmund Hall-Patch, Permanent Representative to the OEEC, 1 November. Negrín expressed his ideas in a three-part article in the *New York Herald Tribune* (European Edition), 'Spain and the Marshall Plan', 'Franco Spain and ERP' and 'Spain and the Sixteen', 1–3 April.
43. Artajo to Logos News Agency, 4 January 1948, quoted in ASMAE, Amb. Paris, b. no. 413: 'Dichiarazioni ufficiali'.
44. *FRUS* 1948 III, Culbertson to Marshall, Madrid, 9 March.
45. José Sebastián de Erice y O'Shea, Director General of Foreign Policy at the Ministry of Foreign Affairs, as recorded in ibid., Culbertson to Marshall, 17 November, p. 1063.
46. MAE, Leg. 3159, exp. 26: 'Nota para su Excelencia', n/d, n/s, probably 14 July 1947.
47. *FRUS* 1948 III, Madrid, 29 March, p. 1034.
48. 'Brouillon d'une note de synthèse' by Jean Monnet, n/d, cit. by Ph. Mioche, 'The Origins of the Monnet Plan', EUI Working Paper 79, January 1984, p. 7.
49. MAE, Leg. 4618, exp. 2: 'Nota relativa a los problemas que se plantean en la Subsecretaría llamada de Comercio, Política Arancelaria y Moneda', San Sebastian, 29 July 1946.
50. B. Pollack, *The Paradox of Spanish Foreign Policy. Spain's International Relations from Franco to Democracy* (London, 1987) 131.
51. J.M. Maravall, *El desarrollo económico y la clase obrera* (Barcelona, 1985) 154.

NOTES TO CHAPTER 7

1. So far, this chapter is based on Guirao, '«¡Bienvenido Míster Marshall!» or the Limits of Foreign Financial Assistance', chapter 4 of 'Spain and European Economic Cooperation, 1945–1955. A Case Study in Spanish Foreign

Economic Policy', PhD thesis, European University Institute, Florence, March 1993.

2. PRO, FO 371/73337: Extract from 'Record of Meeting at the Quai d'Orsay on 4th October 1948'.

3. Bevin and Schuman were joined in this opinion by the Ministers of Foreign Affairs of the Benelux countries, Messrs. Paul-Henri Spaak, Dirk U. Stikker, and Joseph Bech; PRO, FO 371/73338: Extract from the 'Record of a meeting of the Consultative Council [of the Brussels Treaty countries] held at the Quai d'Orsay at 10 a.m. and 4 p.m. on October 26th, 1948'. Marshall's memorandum of this conversation in *FRUS* 1948 III, p. 1054. When the Scandinavian foreign ministers agreed to normalize trade relations with Spain, they clarified that it did not imply any change in diplomatic relations with the Franco government; ibid., the US Ambassador in Norway to Marshall, Oslo, 25 February, pp. 31–2.

4. ECE, *A Survey* and OEEC, *Dix ans de coopération. Réalisations et Perspectives. 9ème Rapport* (Paris, April 1958).

5. PRO, FO 371/73350: 'Spain' by Sir Hugh Ellis-Rees, member of the delegation to the OEEC, 22 April 1948; and ibid. 371/79710: Sir Edmund Hall-Patch, leader of the delegation and Chairman of OEEC's Executive Committee, to Makins, Paris, 21 October.

6. Vincent Auriol (President of the French Republic between January 1947 and January 1954), *Journal du Septennant 1947–1954* vol. 2 (Paris, 1974) 73; 165; 620; 635.

7. For a detailed explanation see John Walker (British commercial counsellor at the Embassy in Madrid), *Economic and Commercial Conditions in Spain* (London, 1949).

8. PRO, FO 371/73353: 'Note by Treasury: Spain', n/d, n/s.

9. Ibid. 371/89547: Minutes of a meeting of Treasury, Bank of England, and FO officials, 17 May 1950.

10. Ibid. 371/89548: 'Note on Trade with Spain', 17 June 1950.

11. Ibid. 371/89547: 'Record of discussions between representatives of the Government of Spain and of the Government of the United Kingdom in Madrid from 30 November to 3 December 1949'.

12. Membership of the different areas at the end of 1949 in International Monetary Fund, *First Annual Report on Exchange Restrictions March 1, 1950*, pp. 48–51. For the operation of the sterling area after 1945, C. R. Schenk, *Britain and the Sterling Area: From Devaluation to Convertibility in the 1950s* (London, 1994).

13. Clinton G. Pelham, *Economic and Commercial Conditions in Spain* (London, 1951) 109.

14. A.M. Leyshon, 'Import Restrictions in Post-War Britain', *Scottish Journal of Political Economy*, vol. 4 (1957) 181; a useful guide to British import licensing techniques.

15. PRO, FO 371/73350: Amended instructions to Delegation, BOT to Cabinet, 24 April 1948.

16. V. Sørensen, 'Defense without Tears: US Embargo Policy and Economic Security in Western Europe, 1947–1951', in F.H. Heller and J.R. Gillingham (eds), *NATO: The Founding of the Atlantic Alliance and the Integration of Europe* (New York, 1992) 257 and 276.

17. 'Post-war Import Licensing Policy', art. cit., pp. 411–12.
18. The British list of essential imports from Spain referred to raw materials (iron ore, potash, pyrites, cork, zinc concentrates, rosin, salt, mercury, and wolfram) and foodstuffs (citrus fruit, tomatoes, bananas, sherry, onions, potatoes, olives, nuts, and fish). The Spanish list of essentials from the United Kingdom referred, basically, to raw materials and semi-manufactured goods for Spanish coal, iron, and steel industries, plus cotton, petroleum products, chemical and pharmaceutical components, heavy electrical plant, and transport equipment.
19. PRO, FO 371/79710: British Embassy in Madrid to the Treasury, 4 May 1949.
20. Ibid., Howard to FO, Madrid, 10 May 1949.
21. PRO, FO 371/89547: BOT to FO, 27 January 1950.
22. Paragraph based on and quotations corresponding to ibid., 'Minutes on Anglo-Spanish Trade Negotiations', meeting of officials representing the BOT, the Bank of England, the Treasury, and the FO, 8 May 1950.
23. Paragraph based on MAE, Leg. 6285, exp. 2, carp 3: Yturralde to Súñer, 'Informe solicitando normas de tipo general en materia de negociación para los próximos acuerdos comerciales', 9 March 1950; PRO, FO 371/89547: Pelham to BOT's Export Department, 3 April; and ibid. 371/89548; British Embassy to BOT, Madrid, 30 October.
24. The OEEC members were Austria, Belgium, Denmark, France, the western zones of Germany (the Federal Republic after 1949), Greece, Iceland, Ireland, Italy, Luxembourg, the Netherlands, Norway, Portugal, Sweden, Switzerland, Turkey, and the United Kingdom. Trieste was a member until the absorption of its territory by Italy and Yugoslavia.
25. The European Customs Union Study Group was set up in September 1947 by the national delegates to the Paris Conference. For a detailed consideration of American expectations of the Study Group, W. Diebold, *Trade and Payments in Western Europe. A Study in Economic Cooperation 1947–51* (New York, 1952); for the Europeans' own interests and goals, Milward, 'The Committee of European Economic Cooperation and the advent of the Customs Union', in W. Lipgens, *A History of European Integration 1945–1947. The Formation of the European Unity Movements* (Oxford, 1982); and 'L'integrazione dell'Europa occidentale negli anni dell'ERP: l'esperienza del Grupo di Studio Europeo per l'Unione Doganale', in E. Agga Rossi (ed.), *Il Piano Marshall e l'Europa* (Rome, 1983).
26. The concept of liberalization used by the OEEC meant the absence of import controls, either because licensing did not exist or because the granting of import licenses was automatic and it was accompanied by the allocation of the foreign exchange provisions required for importation. The year 1948 was chosen as the datum year for calculating the liberalization percentages, except for Germany and Austria for which the base years were 1949 and 1952, respectively. For a detailed account of the OEEC trade liberalization mechanisms until November 1954, F. Boyer and J.P. Sallé, 'The Liberalization of Intra-European Trade in the Framework of OEEC', *International Monetary Fund Staff Papers*, vol. 4/2 (1955) 179–216.
27. Data from AHBE, IEME, box 163: IEME's general balance of payments for 1949.
28. MAE, Leg. 6285, exp. 2, carp. 3: 'Informe solicitando normas...' cit., 9 March 1950.

29. Ibid., Yturralde to Súñer, Madrid, 15 April 1950.
30. PRO, FO 371/89547: 'Minutes on Anglo-Spanish Trade Negotiations' cit., 8 May 1950; PRO, FO 371/89548: 'Agreed Minutes of Discussions between the United Kingdom and Spanish Delegations held in Madrid in June 1950', and joint press statement of June 23th.
31. 'Relaciones Comerciales de España con el Reino Unido', *Información Comercial Española (ICE)*, 209 (1951) 35–8.
32. AD, Z/EE vol. 96: Note by the Directorate of Economic and Financial Affairs, 'Commission mixte franco-espagnole', 13 October 1949.
33. MAE, Leg. 4228, exp. 10: Report to Súñer, 'Comisión Mixta hispano-francesa celebrada en París del 15 al 23 de Marzo de 1950', 15 April 1950.
34. Griffiths and Guirao, 'The First Proposals for a European Agricultural Community: The Pflimlin and Mansholt Plans', in Griffiths and Girvin (eds), *The Green Pool and the Origins of the Common Agricultural Policy* (London, 1995) 1–19.
35. MAE, Leg. 6285, exp. 2, carp. 1: 'Informe para el Señor Ministro sobre negociaciones comerciales', by the Director-General of Economic Policy, annex 2, 9 November 1950.
36. It contained agricultural machinery, medical instruments, automobiles, trucks, trolley-buses, railway wagons, equipment for railway trucks and other material for railways, and, finally, books; AD, Z/EE, vol. 96: Direction des Affaires économiques et financières, 'S. Relations économiques franco-espagnoles', 18 February 1952.
37. Paragraph based on and quotation from 'Commercial Post-War Relations between Spain and Germany' by the Spanish Commercial Attaché in Bonn, *ICE*, 209 (1951) 85–6.
38. M. Trued and R. Mikesell, *Postwar Bilateral Payments Agreements* (Princeton, 1955) 40.
39. Ludwig Erhard (Minister for Economics in the Federal Republic), *Germany's comeback in the world market* (New York, 1954) 132.
40. Germany had completely liberalized the following Spanish agricultural export commodities: dried fruits, saffron, olives, apricot pips, dried salted sausages, lemons, grapefruits, hazelnuts, almonds and other dried fruits, bananas, oranges and mandarins, cacao, semi-prepared rice. Germany had only partially liberalized the following commodities: citrus fruit peels, fruit pulp, mashed potatoes, canned tomatoes, ground pepper and canned capsicum, capers, canned fish, olive oil, canned artichokes, green beans, mushrooms, and truffles; MAE, Leg. 3238, exp. 6: Yturralde, acting as president of the trade delegation, to Minister of Commerce Manuel Arburúa de la Miyar, 'Propuesta de instrucción para las negociaciones comerciales hispano-alemanas, al objeto de renovar el acuerdo comercial', 20 September 1952.
41. APG, JE, sources from the Ministry of Foreign Affairs, Leg. 14, 8.5 (519): Director-General of Economic Policy, Ministry of Foreign Affairs, 'Nota sobre los convenios comercial y de pagos entre España y Alemania firmados en la mañana de hoy', 14 October 1952.
42. Spanish Minister of Agriculture Rafael Cavestany y Anduaga, to his German partner, cit. in MAE, Leg. 4613, exp. 1: Under-Secretary of Foreign Economy and Commerce Jaime Argüelles Armada to Artajo, 31 July 1954.
43. Ibid. 3238, exp. 4: President of Delegation to Arburúa, Instructions to the mixed Spanish–German Commission, March 1953.

224   *Notes*

44. Ibid., 'Réplica enviada por la Cámara Oficial de España en Alemania a la Handelsstadt de Dusseldorf', Bonn, 7 October 1953.
45. A. Marquina, 'La primera aproximación a las comunidades europeas', in Étienvre and Urquijo, op. cit., p. 138.
46. MAE, Leg. 5915, exp. 1: Carlos Gamir, Attaché of Foreign Economy at the Embassy, to Argüelles, 'Aumento de la liberalización para importar productos de los países de la OECE. Comparación de ella con la concedida a España', Bonn, 26 February 1954; and 'Liberalización para importar ciertos productos de los países del área del dólar. Comparación de ella con la concedida a España', Bonn, 10 March.
47. Data elaborated from *Der Aussenhandel des Vereinigten Wirtschaftsgebietes im Jahre 1949. Der Spezialhandel nach Waren (Statistische Nummern)* and *Foreign Trade of the Federal Republic of Germany and Berlin (West)*. Part 5, *Special Trade according to the Standard International Trade Classification and by Countries of Production and Consumption, December and Year 1956*.
48. Speech to Cortes on 18 December 1951, in Arburúa, *Cinco años al frente del Ministerio de Comercio (Discursos y Declaraciones, 1951–1956)* (Madrid, 1956) 55.
49. PRO, FO 371/102036: Agreed minutes of discussions between Spanish and the United Kingdom delegations held in Madrid in December 1952.
50. Ibid. 371/101997: 'Spain: Annual Report for 1951', and MAE, Leg. 4612, exp. 16: Note by the Under-Secretariat of Foreign Economy and Commerce to Arburúa, 'Negociaciones en curso', 20 March 1952.
51. PRO, FO 371/102036: British Embassy to Sir Anthony Eden, Foreign Secretary after October 1951, Madrid, 17 December 1952.
52. The UN agricultural agency provides one of the rare examples of price information which includes Spain in comparative terms; Food and Agriculture Organization, *Yearbook of Food and Agricultural Statistics, Production*, vol. X (1956) 278; 280. It refers to average wholesale prices to producers of *bionda, Jaffa, Florida* and *blanca común* orange types, and of common red wine, calculated in local currencies.
53. 'Accord commercial franco-espagnol du 30 octobre 1953, valable du 1er novembre 1953 au 31 octobre 1954', in Chambre du Commerce Franco-Espagnole, *Guide du Commerce avec l'Espagne* (Paris, 1953).
54. MAE, Leg. 4613, exp. 1: Argüelles to Artajo, 6 July 1954; and AD, Z/EE vol. 97: Directorate-General of Economic and Financial Affairs, Quai d'Orsay, 'Accord commercial franco-espagnol paraphé le 19–11–1954', 8 December.
55. Paragraph based, in general, on MAE, Leg. 5919, exp. 1: 'Claúsulas de los acuerdos bilaterales en vigor entre España y países miembros de la OECE concediendo la liberalización de ciertos productos españoles cuando son importados en dichos países', n/s, n/d; ibid. 5915, exp. 1: Argüelles to the Spanish Ambassador in Bonn, 'Información sobre trato que España recibe de los países de la OECE en lo que respecta a la liberalización de sus importaciones', 30 July 1954; and AGA, C/36622, folder 2: OECE, C/WP11/W(56)26, 'Association de l'Espagne aux Travaux de l'Organisation. Difficultés rencontrées par les exportations espagnoles sur les marchés européens', Paris, 23 June 1956. For Norway, Trued and Mikesell, op. cit., p. 92; for Sweden, 'Protocolo anual sobre el intercambio comercial y de

pagos entre España y Suecia de 13 de Agosto de 1954', *ICE. Boletín Mensual*. 387 (2 September 1954) 1467; for the Netherlands, the Federal Republic, and Italy, the text of the bilateral agreements of June 1953, April 1955, and April 1956, respectively. Austria, Portugal, and Turkey are excluded, because Spain had no commercial agreement with Austria, obtained special treatment from Portugal, and traded on a compensation basis with Turkey.

56. See contributions to B. Martin and Milward (eds), *Agriculture and Food Supply in the Second World War* (Ostfildern, 1985).

57. M.F.W. Hemming, C.M. Miles, and G.F. Ray, 'A Statistical Summary of the Extent of Import Control in the United Kingdom since the War', *The Review of Economic Studies*, vol. 26/69–71 (1958–59) 83.

58. W. Asbeek Brusse; 'West European Tariff Plans, 1947–1957', PhD dissertation, European University Institute, Florence, 1991.

59. AD, DE-CE, 1945–61, vol. 353: France's Minister of Finance to Minister of Industry and Energy, 'Suspension de la liberalisation des échanges', 16 February 1952.

60. AD, Z/EE vol. 97: Directorate-General of Economic and Financial Affairs at the Quai d'Orsay, 'Note pour Monsieur [Georges] De la Tournelle [Ambassador to Spain]. Relations économiques franco-espagnoles', n/d.

61. MAE, Leg. 3445, exp. 16: Memorandum of the French Government to the Spanish Government, 20 November 1952.

62. AN, F/10/5553: Press cutting without reference to source or date.

63. PRO, FO 371/107718: Commercial Counsellor at the British Embassy to FO, Madrid, 14 August 1953; and BOT 11/5011: Press note, n/d.

64. Boyer and Sallé, 'The Liberalization of Intra-European Trade', p. 204.

65. Milward, 'Una comparación del comercio de exportación español, italiano y portugués, 1950–1959', in L. Prados de la Escosura and V. Zamagni (eds), *El desarrollo económico de la Europa del sur. España e Italia en perspectiva histórica* (Madrid, 1992).

NOTES TO CHAPTER 8

1. For a detailed discussion on the nature and limitations of intra-European payments agreements before the establishment of the EPU, R.W. Bean, 'European Multilateral Clearing', *The Journal of Political Economy*, vol. 56/5 (1948) 403–15; R. Triffin, *Europe and the Money Muddle. From Bilateralism to Near-Convertibility, 1947–1956* (New Haven, 1957); and G.L. Rees, *Britain and the Postwar European Payments Systems* (Cardiff, 1963).

2. *Agreement for the Establishment of a European Payments Union (with Annexes and Protocol of Provisional Application)* (London, 1950). For the most complete study of EPU, J.J. Kaplan and G. Schleiminger, *The European Payments Union. Financial Diplomacy in the 1950s* (Oxford, 1989). A didactic presentation is B.J. Eichengreen, *Reconstructing Europe's Trade and Payments. The European Payments Union* (Oxford, 1993).

3. MAE, Leg. 5915, exp. 1: Jaime Alba, Economic Counsellor at the Embassy in London, to Súñer, 'La Unión Europea de Pagos y España', 17 & 19 January 1951, respectively.

4. Ibid. 5915, exp. 1: Alba to Súñer, London, 17 January 1951. Calculations were based on the official exchange rate of Pts 10.95 to $1, which might have proved unacceptable to the Union.
5. Ibid. 5332, exp. 1: 'Informe sobre la eventual entrada de España en la Organización Europea de Cooperación Económica', Paris, June 1955.
6. Ibid. 10077, exp. 42: 'Anteproyecto. Apunte relativo a los diferentes aspectos de una eventual accesión de España a la EPU o para la negociación de un posible 'working arrangement' entre la EPU y España', n/d, most probably 11 April 1951.
7. AHBE, IEME, box 3: C/P, 1 December 1950.
8. MAE, Leg. 5919, exp. 1: 'Informe para el Sr. Director. Sobre la Unión Europea y España', 22 February 1951.
9. Speech before the American Chamber of Commerce in Madrid, 12 November 1951; Arburúa, op. cit., p. 32.
10. MAE, Leg. 10077, exp. 42: Alba to Súñer, 11 April 1951.
11. PRO, FO 371/96195: Top secret 'Possible entry of Spain into OEEC', 10 March 1951.
12. *FRUS* 1951 IV, part 1, US Chargé in Madrid to Acheson, 13 September, and Acting Secretary of State to US Embassy, 18 September, pp. 851 and 853, respectively.
13. Handwritten note dated 8 May 1951 in MAE, Leg. 5915, exp. 1: Under-Secretariat of Foreign Economy and Commerce, Directorate General of Economic Policy, 'Nota para el Señor Director. Incorporación de España a la Unión Europea de Pagos', 5 May 1951.
14. Ibid. 3446, exp. 57: 'Nota de la Dirección de Organismos Internacionales. La Unión Europea de Pagos', 14 February 1953.
15. Ibid. 5915, exp. 1: Gamir to Argüelles, Bonn, 9 February 1953.
16. Ibid. 3238, exp. 5: Gamir to Argüelles, 'Propuesta alemana de acercamiento de España a la Unión Europea de Pagos', Bonn, 18 February 1953.
17. Ibid. 5915, exp. 2: 'Informe sobre la Unión Europea de Pagos (U.E.P.)', 25 April 1953.
18. *FRUS* 1952–54 VI, part 2, Records of meetings of the Director of the Foreign Operations Administration, Harold E. Stassen, and other officials with Arburúa, 20 April 1954; Stassen's memoranda to the Secretary of State and of conversation with Arburúa [on 28 and 29 October], 1 and 12 November, pp. 1974–7, 1994 and 1998, respectively.
19. AGA, C/36622: OEEC, C/WP11/W(56) 15, 'Association of Spain in the work of the Organization. Balance of Payments with Member Countries', Paris, 6 June 1956.
20. Ibid., A/6815: National Institute for Agricultural Research, 'Aspectos económicos de la Conferencia Europea sobre la Organización de Mercados Agrícolas', s/f.
21. MAE, Leg. 10078, exp. 21: Report entitled 'Posibilidad de ingreso de España en la Unión Europea de Pagos' for Argüelles, 11 October 1954.
22. Guirao, 'Spain and the 'Green Pool': Challenge and Response, 1950 to 1955', in Griffiths and Girvin (eds), *The Green Pool*, pp. 261–87.

NOTES TO THE CONCLUDING REMARKS

1. Ch. Esposito, 'Influencing Aid Recipients: Marshall Plan Lessons for Contemporary Aid Donors', in B. Eichengreen (ed.), *Europe's Post-War Recovery* (Cambridge, 1995) 68–90.

2. J.B. De Long and Eichengreen, 'The Marshall Plan: History's Most Successful Structural Adjustment Program', in R. Dornbusch, W. Nolling, and R. Layard (eds), *Postwar Economic Reconstruction and Lessons for the East Today* (Cambridge, MA, 1993).

3. For the debate on the causes of growth in most West European countries during the golden age, contributions to N. Crafts and G. Toniolo (eds), *Economic Growth in Europe since 1945* (Cambridge, 1996); Crafts, 'The Golden Age of Economic Growth in Western Europe, 1950–1973', *Economic History Review*, vol. 48/3 (1995) 429–47; and S.N. Broadberry and Crafts, 'British Economic Policy and Industrial Performance in the Early Post-War Period', *Business History*, vol. 38/4 (1996) 65–91.

4. Milward, 'The Marshall Plan and German Foreign Trade', in Maier and Bischof (eds), *The Marshall Plan*, 452–87.

5. Looper, 'Current Usage', p. 340.

6. For the meaning and implications of these concepts, M. Abramovitz, 'Catching Up, Forging Ahead, and Falling Behind', *Journal of Economic History*, vol. 46/2 (1986) 385–406 and 'The Catch-Up Factor in Postwar Economic Growth', *Economic Inquiry*, vol. 28/1 (1990) 1–18.

Bibliography

Abramovitz, M. 'Catching Up, Forging Ahead, and Falling Behind', *Journal of Economic History*, vol. 46/2 (1986) 385–406.

—, 'The Catch-Up Factor in Postwar Economic Growth', *Economic Inquiry*, vol. 28/1 (1990) 1–18.

Acheson, D. *Present at the Creation: My Years in the State Department* (New York, 1969).

Arburúa de la Miyar, M. *Cinco años al frente del Ministerio de Comercio (Discursos y Declaraciones, 1951–1956)* (Madrid, 1956).

Areilza, J.M. *Memorias Exteriores, 1947–1964* (Barcelona, 1984).

Asbeek Brusse, W. 'West European Tariff Plans, 1947–1957', PhD thesis, EUI, Florence, 1991.

Auriol, V. *Journal du Septennant 1947–1954* vol. 2 (Paris, 1974).

Ballestero, A. *Juan Antonio Suanzes, 1891–1977. 'La política industrial de la posguerra'* (Leon, 1993).

Banco Urquijo *Informe presentado a la Junta general del Banco Urquijo celebrada el 16 de marzo de 1948, por el Presidente del Consejo, Excmo. Sr. Marqués de Urquijo, sobre el ejercicio del año 1947* (Madrid, 1948).

Barciela, C. 'El mercado negro de productos agrarios en la posguerra', in J. Fontana (ed.) *España bajo el franquismo* (Barcelona, 1986) 192–205.

—, 'El sector agrario desde 1936', in A. Carreras (ed.) *Estadísticas Históricas de España. Siglos XIX y XX* (Madrid, 1989) 131–67.

Bean, R.W. 'European Multilateral Clearing', *The Journal of Political Economy*, vol. 56/5 (1948) 403–15.

Bidault, G. *D'une Résistance à l'autre* (Paris, 1965).

Blum, L. *L'oeuvre de Léon Blum, 1945–1947* (Paris, 1958).

Board of Trade, Department of Overseas Trade *Spain. Review of Commercial Conditions* (London, 1945).

Boyer, F. and J.P. Sallé 'The Liberalization of Intra-European Trade in the Framework of OEEC', *International Monetary Fund Staff Papers*, vol. 4/2 (1955) 179–216.

Broadberry, S.N. and N.F.R. Crafts 'British Economic Policy and Industrial Performance in the Early Post-war Period', *Business History*, vol. 38/4 (1996) 65–91.

Brown, W.A. and R. Opie *American Foreign Assistance* (Washington, 1953).

Brundu Olla, P. *Ostracismo e Realpolitik. Gli Alleati e la Spagna franchista negli anni del dopoguerra* (Cagliari, 1984).

—, 'L'Espagne franquiste et la politique étrangère de la France au landemain de la Deuxième Guerre Mondiale', *Relations Internationales*, 50 (1987) 165–81.

—, *L'anello mancante. Il problema della Spagna franchista e l'organizzazione della difesa occidentale (1947–1950)* (Sassari, 1990).

Buesa, M. 'Industrialización y agricultura: una nota sobre la construcción de maquinaria agrícola y la produción de fertilizantes en la política industrial española (1939–1963)', *Agricultura y Sociedad*, 28 (1983) 223–48.

Bullock, A. *Ernest Bevin: Foreign Secretary (1945–1951)* (London, 1983).

Bustelo, F. 'La industria del nitrógeno en España', in *Problemas técnicos de importancia económica en la nueva organización de España* (Barcelona, 1940) 247–52.

Carr, R. *Spain 1808–1975* 2nd edition (Oxford, 1982).

Carreras, A. 'La producció industrial espanyola i italiana des de mitjans del secle XIX fins a l'actualitat', PhD thesis, Universitat Autònoma, Barcelona, 1983.

Carreras, A. (ed.) *Estadísticas Históricas de España. Siglos XIX y XX* (Madrid, 1989).

Catalán, J. *La economía española y la segunda guerra mundial* (Barcelona, 1995).

— 'Sector exterior y crecimiento industrial. España y Europa, 1939–59', *Revista de Historia Industrial*, 8 (1995) 99–145.

Chambre du Commerce Franco-Espagnole *Guide du Commerce avec l'Espagne* (Paris, 1953).

Chamorro, S. *et al. Las balanzas de pagos de España del período de autarquía* (Madrid, 1976).

Coll, S. and C. Sudrià *El carbón en España, 1770–1961. Una historia económica* (Madrid, 1987).

Corden, W.M. 'The control of imports: A Case Study. The United Kingdom Import Restrictions of 1951–2', *Journal of the Manchester School*, vol. 26/3 (1958).

Cowan, A. 'The Guerrilla War Against Franco', *European History Quarterly*, vol. 20 (1990) 227–53.

Crafts, N.F.R. 'The Golden Age of Economic Growth in Western Europe, 1950–1973', *Economic History Review*, vol. 48/3 (1995) 429–47.

Crafts, N.F.R. and G. Toniolo (eds) *Economic Growth in Europe since 1945* (Cambridge, 1996).

Curzon, G. *Multilateral Commercial Diplomacy* (New York, 1966).

Delaunay, J.-M. 'La liquidation des avoirs allemands en Espagne (1945–1961)', in J.-P. Etienvre and J.R. Urquijo *España, Francia y la Comunidad Europea* (Madrid, 1989) 219–45.

Department of State *A Decade of American Foreign Policy. Basic Documents 1941–1949* (Washington DC, 1985).

Diebold, W. *Trade and Payments in Western Europe. A Study in Economic Cooperation 1947–51* (New York, 1952).

—, *The Schuman Plan. A Study in Economic Cooperation 1950–1959* (New York, 1959).

Donges, J.B. *La industrialización en España. Políticas, logros y perspectivas* (Barcelona, 1976).

Dornbusch, R., W. Nolling and R. Layard (eds) *Postwar Economic Reconstruction and Lessons for the East Today* (Cambridge, MA, 1993).

Eckes, A.E. *The United States and the Global Struggle for Minerals* (Austin, 1979).

Economic Commission for Europe of the United Nations *Economic Survey of Europe in 1948* (Geneva, 1949).

—, *A Survey of the Economic Situation and Prospects of Europe* (Geneva, 1948).

—, *Economic Survey of Europe in 1948* (Geneva, 1949).

—, *Economic Survey of Europe in 1950* (Geneva, 1951).

—, *Economic Survey of Europe in 1953. Study of Economic Development in Southern Europe* (Geneva, 1954).

Eichengreen, B.J. *Reconstructing Europe's Trade and Payments. The European Payments Union* (Oxford, 1993).

230   *Bibliography*

Eichengreen B.J. 'Institutions and Economic Growth: Europe after World War II', in N.F.R. Crafts and G. Toniolo (eds) *Economic Growth in Europe since 1945* (Cambridge, 1996) 38–72.

—, (ed.) *Europe's Post-War Recovery* (Cambridge, 1995).

Erhard, L. *Germany's comeback in the world market* (New York, 1954).

Espadas Burgos, M. *Franquismo y política exterior* (Madrid, 1988).

Esposito, Ch. 'Influencing Aid Recipients: Marshall Plan Lessons for Contemporary Aid Donors', in B.J. Eichengreen (ed.) *Europe's Post-War Recovery* (Cambridge, 1995) 68–90.

Esteban, J. 'The Economic Policy of Francoism: An Interpretation', in P. Preston (ed.) *Spain in Crisis. The Evolution and Decline of the Franco Régime* (Hassocks, 1976) 82–100.

Fodor, G. 'Perché nel 1947 l'Europa ebbe bisogno del Piano Marshall?', *Rivista di Storia Economica*, ns vol. 2/1 (1985) 89–123.

Fontana, J. and J. Nadal 'Spain, 1914–1970', in C.M. Cipolla (ed.) *The Fontana Economic History of Europe. Contemporary Economies. Part Two* vol. 6/2 (London, 1975) 460–529.

Frank, R. 'France – Grande-Bretagne: la mésentente commerciale (1945–1958)', *Relations internationales*, 55 (1988) 323–39.

Freeland, R.M. *The Truman Doctrine and the Origins of McCarthyism* (New York, 1985).

Fuentes Quintana, E. and J. Plaza 'Perspectivas de la economía española (1940–1953)', *Revista de Economía Política*, vol. 4/1–2 (1952) 1–117.

Gardner, R.N. *Sterling-Dollar Diplomacy: The Origins and the Prospects of Our International Economic Order* (Oxford, 1956).

Garmo, P.H. de 'Beyond the Pyrenees; Spain and Europe Since World War II', PhD thesis, University of California, 1971.

Gaulle, Ch. de *Discours et Messages vol. I Pendant la guerre Juin 1940-Janvier 1946* (Paris, 1946).

Gómez Mendoza, A. 'Transporte y comunicaciones', in A. Carreras (ed.) *Estadísticas Históricas de España. Siglos XIX y XX* (Madrid, 1989) 269–325.

González, M.J. *La economía política del franquismo (1940–1970). Dirigismo, mercado y planificación* (Madrid, 1979).

Gordon, M.R. *Conflict and Consensus in Labor's Foreign Policy 1914–1965* (Stanford, 1969).

Griffiths, R.T. and F. Guirao 'The First Proposals for a European Agricultural Community: The Pflimlin and Mansholt Plans', in R.T. Griffiths and B. Girvin (eds) *The Green Pool and the Origins of the Common Agricultural Policy* (London, 1995) 1–19.

Grupo de Estudios de Historia Rural 'El sector agrario hasta 1935', in A. Carreras (ed.) *Estadísticas Históricas de España. Siglos XIX y XX* (Madrid, 1989) 91–129.

Guirao, F. 'Spain and European Economic Cooperation, 1945–1955. A Case Study in Spanish Foreign Economic Policy', PhD thesis, EUI, Florence, March 1993.

—, 'Spain and the 'Green Pool': Challenge and Response, 1950 to 1955', in R.T. Griffiths and B. Girvin (eds) *The Green Pool and the Origins of the Common Agricultural Policy* (London, 1995) 261–87.

—, 'Spain's Role in Western European Economic Relief and Reconstruction, 1945 – Spring of 1947', in M. Dumoulin (ed.) *Wartime Plans for Postwar Europe (1940–1947)* (Paris 1995) 563–88.

Guirao, F. 'The United States, Franco, and the Integration of Europe', in F.H. Heller and J.R. Gillingham (eds) *The United States and the Integration of Europe. Legacies of the Postwar Era* (New York, 1996) 79–101.

—, 'Association or Trade Agreement? Spain and the EEC, 1957–64', *Journal of European Integration History*, vol. 3/1 (1997) 103–20.

Harrison, J. *The Spanish Economy in the Twentieth Century* (London, 1985).

—, *The Spanish Economy. From the Civil War to the European Community* (London, 1993).

Hemming, M.F.W., C.M. Miles and G.F. Ray 'A Statistical Summary of the Extent of Import Control in the United Kingdom since the War', *The Review of Economic Studies*, vol. 26/69–71 (1958–59) 75–109.

International Monetary Fund *First Annual Report on Exchange Restrictions March 1, 1950*.

Inza y Tudela, C. de 'Transportes', in *Estudios sobre la unidad económica de Europa* vol. 7 (Madrid, 1957) 799–812.

Kaplan, J.J. and G. Schleiminger *The European Payments Union. Financial Diplomacy in the 1950s* (Oxford, 1989).

Keefe, E.K. *et al. Area Handbook for Spain* (Washington DC, 1976).

Kindleberger, Ch.P. *Marshall Plan Days* (London, 1987).

Leyshon, A.M. 'Import Restrictions in Post-War Britain', *Scottish Journal of Political Economy*, vol. 4 (1957) 177–93.

Lieberman, S. *Growth and Crisis in the Spanish Economy 1940–93* (London, 1995).

Liniger, M. *L'orange d'Espagne sur les marchés européens* (Geneva, 1962).

Long, J.B. de and B. Eichengreen 'The Marshall Plan: History's Most Successful Structural Adjustment Program', in R. Dornbusch, W. Nolling and R. Layard (eds) *Postwar Economic Reconstruction and Lessons for the East Today* (Cambridge, MA, 1993) 189–230.

López Rodó, L. *La larga marcha hacia la Monarquía* (Barcelona, 1977).

Looper, J.H.C. de 'Current Usage of Payments Agreements and Trade Agreements', *International Monetary Fund Staff Papers*, 4 (1955) 339–95.

Luard, E. *A History of the United Nations. Vol. 1 The Years of Western Domination, 1945–1955* (London, 1982).

Magalhães, J.C. *Portugal na Europa: o caminho certo* (Lisbon, 1997).

Maier, Ch.S. 'The Two Postwar Eras and the Conditions for Stability in Western Europe', *American Historical Review*, vol. 86/2 (1981) 327–62.

Maier, Ch.S. and G. Bischof (eds) *The Marshall Plan and Germany: West German Development within the Framework of the European Recovery Program* (New York, 1991).

Majander, M. 'The Limits of Sovereignty. Finland and the Question of the Marshall Plan in 1947', *Scandinavian Journal of History*, vol. 19/4 (1994) 309–26.

Maravall, J.M. *El desarrollo económico y la clase obrera* (Barcelona, 1985).

Marquina, A. 'La primera aproximación a las comunidades europeas', in Etienvre and Urquijo *España, Francia y la Comunidad Europea* (Madrid, 1989) 135–43.

Martin, B. and Milward, A.S. (eds) *Agriculture and Food Supply in the Second World War* (Ostfildern, 1985).

Martín Aceña, P. and F. Comín *INI 50 años de industrialización en España* (Madrid, 1991).

Martín Aceña, P. and J. Simpson (eds) *The Economic Development of Spain since 1870* (Aldershot, 1995).

Medlicott, W.N. *The Economic Blockade* vol. 2 (London, 1978).

Milward, A.S. 'The Committee of European Economic Cooperation and the advent of the Customs Union', in W. Lipgens (ed.) *A History of European Integration 1945–1947. The Formation of the European Unity Movements* (Oxford, 1982) 507–68.

—, 'L'integrazione dell'Europa occidentale negli anni dell'ERP: l'esperienza del Grupo di Studio Europeo per l'Unione Doganale', in E. Agga Rossi (ed.) *Il Piano Marshall e l'Europa* (Rome, 1983) 109–18.

—, *The Reconstruction of Western Europe 1945–51* (London, 1984).

—, 'The Marshall Plan and German Foreign Trade', in Maier and Bischof (eds) *The Marshall Plan and Germany. West European Development within the Framework of the European Recovery Program* (New York, 1991) 452–87.

—, 'Una comparación del comercio de exportación español, italiano y portugués, 1950–1959', in L. Prados de la Escosura and V. Zamagni (eds) *El desarrollo económico de la Europa del sur. España e Italia en perspectiva histórica* (Madrid, 1992) 444–61.

—, *The European Rescue of the Nation State* (London, 1992).

Milward, A.S. *et al. The Frontier of National Sovereignty. History and Theory 1945–1992* (London, 1992).

Ministère des Affaires Etrangères *Documents de la Conférence des Ministres des Affaires Etrangères de la France, du Royaume-Uni, de l'U.R.S.S. tenue à Paris du 27 Juin au 3 Juillet 1947 et pièces relatives aux négociations diplomatiques engagées à la suite du discours prononcé par le Général Marshall Secrétaire d'Etat des Etats-Unis, le 5 Juin 1947* (Paris, 1947).

Ministerio de Asuntos Exteriores, Secretaría General Técnica *Censo de Tratados Internacionales suscritos por España desde 16 de Septiembre de 1125 a 21 de Octubre de 1975, Vol. I Bilaterales* (Madrid, 1976).

Mioche, Ph. 'The Origins of the Monnet Plan', EUI Working Paper 79, January 1984.

Muns, J. *Historia de las relaciones entre España y el Fondo Monetario Internacional, 1958–1982. Veinticinco años de economía española* (Madrid, 1986).

Nolfo, E. di *Vaticano e Stati Uniti 1939–1952. Dalle carte di Myron C. Taylor* (Milan, 1978).

Organisation for European Economic Cooperation *Dix ans de coopération. Réalisations et Perspectives. 9ème Rapport* (Paris, 1958).

Paris Eguilaz, H. *Diez años de política económica en España 1939–1949* (Madrid, 1949).

—, *El desarrollo económico español, 1906–1964* (Madrid, 1965).

Payne, S.G. *The Franco Regime 1936–1975* (Madison, 1987).

Pelham, C.G. *Economic and Commercial Conditions in Spain* (London, 1951).

Pollack, B. *The Paradox of Spanish Foreign Policy. Spain's International Relations from Franco to Democracy* (London, 1987).

Portero, F. *Franco aislado. La cuestión española (1945–1950)* (Madrid, 1989).

Prados de la Escosura, L. 'Spain's Gross Domestic Product, 1850–1993: Quantitative Conjectures. Appendix', Universidad Carlos III Working Paper 95–06, Madrid, February 1995.

Prados de la Escosura, L. and J.C. Sanz 'Growth and macroeconomic performance in Spain, 1939–93', in N.F.R. Crafts and G. Toniolo, *Economic Growth in Europe since 1945* (Cambridge, 1996) 355–87.

Bibliography   233

Preston, P. *Franco. A Biography* (London, 1993).
Rees, G.L. *Britain and the Postwar European Payments Systems* (Cardiff, 1963).
Rein, R. *Franco-Peron Alliance: Relations Between Spain and Argentina, 1946–1955* (Pittsburgh, 1993).
RENFE *Los ferrocarriles en España 1848–1958* (Madrid, 1958).
Rioux, J.-P. *The Fourth Republic, 1944–1958* (Cambridge, 1987).
Rollo, F. *Portugal e o Plano Marshall. Da rejeição à solicitação da ajuda financeira norte-americana (1947–1952)* (Lisbon, 1994).
Rubottom, R. and J.C. Murphy *Spain and the United States Since World War II* (New York, 1984).
Salmon, K.G. *The Modern Spanish Economy. Transformation and Integration into Europe* (London, 1991).
San Román, E. 'El nacimiento de la SEAT: autarquía e intervención del INI', *Revista de Historia Industrial*, 7 (1995) 141–65.
Sanders, R.E. *Spain and the United Nations 1945–1950* (New York, 1966).
Schenk, C.R. *Britain and the Sterling Area: From Devaluation to Convertibility in the 1950s* (London, 1994).
Sørensen, V. 'Defense without Tears: US Embargo Policy and Economic Security in Western Europe, 1947–1951', in F.H. Heller and J.R. Gillingham (eds) *NATO: The Founding of the Atlantic Alliance and the Integration of Europe* (New York, 1992) 253–81.
Suanzes, J.A. *Instituto Nacional de Industria: notas en relación con la creación y desenvolvimiento de este Instituto* (Madrid, 1941).
—, 'Franco y la economía', in J.A. Suanzes *Ocho discursos de Suanzes* (Madrid, 1963) 123–63.
Sudrià, C. 'Un factor determinante: la energía', in J. Nadal *et al.* (eds) *La economía española en el Siglo XX. Una perspectiva histórica* (Barcelona, 1987) 313–63.
Tierno Galván, E. (ed.) *Leyes políticas españolas fundamentales (1808–1978)* (Madrid, 1968).
Tortella, G. *El desarrollo de la España contemporánea. Historia económica de los siglos XIX y XX* (Madrid, 1994).
Triffin, R. *Europe and the Money Muddle. From Bilateralism to Near-Convertibility, 1947–1956* (New Haven, 1957).
Trued, M. and R. Mikesell *Postwar Bilateral Payments Agreements* (Princeton, 1955).
US Overseas Loans and Grants and Assistance from International Organizations. Obligations and Loans Authorizaions July 1, 1945 – September 30, 1982.
Velarde Fuertes, J. 'Política de desarrollo', in E. Fuentes Quintana (ed.) *El desarrollo económico de España. Juicio crítico del Informe del banco Mundial* (Madrid, 1963).
Velasco, C. 'El pensamiento agrario y la apuesta industrializadora en la España de los cuarenta', *Agricultura y Sociedad*, 23 (1982) 223–72.
Viñas, A. 'La conexión entre autarquía y política exterior en el primer franquismo (1939–1959)', in Viñas *Guerra, dinero, dictadura. Ayuda fascista y autarquía en la España de Franco* (Barcelona, 1984) 205–37.
—, 'El Plan Marshall y Franco', in ibid., pp. 265–87.
—, 'La política exterior española durante el franquismo y el Ministerio de Asuntos Exteriores', in ibid., pp. 288–308.

234   *Bibliography*

Viñas, A. 'La administración de la política económica exterior en España, 1936–1979', *Cuadernos Económicos de Información Comercial Española*, 13 (1980) 157–272.

—, *Los pactos secretos de Franco con Estados Unidos. Bases, ayuda económica, recortes de soberanía* (Barcelona, 1981).

Viñas, A. *et al. Política comercial exterior en España (1931–1975)* (Madrid, 1979).

Walker, J. *Economic and Commercial Conditions in Spain* (London, 1949).

Whitaker, A. *Spain and the Defence of the West: Ally and Liability* (New York, 1962).

Index